THE
PRACTICAL
GARDENER

THE PRACTICAL GARDENER

AN A-TO-Z GUIDE
TO TECHNIQUES AND TIPS

Ann Reilly Dines
Photography by Derek Fell

ILLUSTRATIONS BY ANNE MESKEY

FRIEDMAN/FAIRFAX
PUBLISHERS

A FRIEDMAN/FAIRFAX BOOK

Library of Congress Cataloging-in-Publication Data

Reilly Dines, Ann
    The practical gardener : an A-Z guide to techniques and
tips / Ann Reilly Dines ; photographs by Derek Fell ; illustrations
by Anne Meskey.
        p.   cm.
    Originally published: American Garden Associated illustrated
encyclopedia of gardening / Ann Reilly Dines.
    Includes bibliographical references and index.
    ISBN 1-56799-157-2
    1.Gardening—Encyclopedias.   2. Gardening—Pictorial works.
I. Reilly Dines, Ann. American Garden Association illustrated
encyclopedia of gardening. II. Title.
SB450.95.R45 1995   94-27977
635.9′03—dc20   CIP

Editor: Elizabeth Viscott Sullivan
Art Director: Jeff Batzli
Designer: Devorah Levinrad
Photography Editors: Christopher C. Bain and Emilya Naymark

Originally published as *American Garden Association Illustrated Encyclopedia of Gardening*

Typeset by The Interface Group, Inc.
Color separations by Excel Graphic Arts, Inc.
Printed in China by Leefung-Asco Printers Ltd.

DEDICATION

This reprint is dedicated to Ann Reilly Dines, who died tragically in 1994 in Belize, where she made her home, and to her children, Pat and Lynn, who brightened her life the way flowers brighten a garden and to whom this volume was originally dedicated.

Table of Contents

INTRODUCTION

Gardening is both an art and a science. It is a science in that knowing a plant's light, moisture, and fertilizer requirements, and its preferred climates, will help you garden successfully. Art comes into play when you combine the plants that best meet your garden's environmental conditions to create a beautiful garden, one that you will be proud of, and one that friends will strive to emulate.

While there are certain rules and guidelines that you should follow if you are going to achieve gardening success, you can bend those rules and guidelines somewhat to achieve equally good, and sometimes better, results. There is an old adage that says something like, "If it works for you, don't change it." That couldn't be truer with gardening. This book intends to give you the best general information possible, but don't be afraid to experiment as it can open many new doors.

Landscape design, including choice of plants, textures, and colors, is a matter of personal taste, so there are few rights and wrongs. Garden design follows certain loose guidelines, but is a creative act that results in a living expression of your personality.

Creating a comprehensive book like this required a number of different things, the first of which was my desire to share my gardening knowledge and experiences so that you will be more rewarded in your gardening efforts. Although I gardened as a child under the watchful eye of my aunt in her small New York City backyard, and grew houseplants in my college dorm room long before interiors were filled with green, I didn't seriously garden until twenty years ago, when my family and I moved into our first house. There were then, as there are now, many excellent books on gardening, but none seemed to answer all of my questions. My dream of sharing information came true when my first gardening book was published in 1977, and I have published many books since that time.

Desire to share your gardening experience is not enough, however; knowledge is that sometimes evil necessity that enables you to see your desire through to the end. I, like you, search for knowledge in many places. I studied horticulture at a local university. I took many courses offered by local clubs, societies, and botanical gardens, which is an excellent method of learning from experts in their particular fields. I read books like the one you are reading now. But most of all, I gardened, and that experience is the best teacher of all.

You, too, will find that as you create and maintain your garden, as you learn from experience, there are certain techniques that work for you which may not work for others (and vice versa), and you can stretch the limits of some plants' tolerances to environmental factors with a little TLC. This book, therefore, is the culmination of desire, knowledge, and experience. Hopefully, your garden will be the culmination of these same things.

HOW TO USE THIS BOOK

This book is straightforward in its approach, and is laid out in such a way that it will be easy for you to find out how to grow any garden plant. Categories are listed in alphabetical order, so you can refer to the book as you would any dictionary or encyclopedia. There is also a detailed key to help you when you are referring to the book's many charts.

Broad headings, such as annuals, bulbs, perennials, roses, trees, or shrubs, group together similar plants and discuss their characteristics and care. These sections are also cross-referenced to other sections that pertain to all types of plants, such as fertilizing, mulching, and watering, to provide greater detail. Other topics, such as cutting flowers, drying plants, and container gardens, are discussed to help you enjoy your garden even more, and to expand its potential.

If you want to grow a garden of annual flowers for cutting, for example, you'll want to read the section on annuals first. The section helps you select flower colors and sizes, and discusses their growth requirements as well. The section on annuals refers you to other pertinent sections you may need to turn to for help, such as fragrance, planting, propagation, soil, and weeds. You'll also want to read the section on cutting flowers.

The book contains a number of definitions, also in alphabetical order, which not only define new terms, but refer you to the sections where more detail is given on the subject.

Gardening can be a challenge, but most of all, it is a relaxing and rewarding pastime. Enjoy your garden, and enjoy this book as it helps you to gain the knowledge and experience that will make you the best gardener on the block.

METRIC CONVERSIONS

1 teaspoon = 5 milliliters
1 tablespoon = 15 milliliters
1 cup = 250 milliliters
1 pint = 500 milliliters
1 quart = .95 liters
1 gallon = 3.8 liters

1 square inch = 6.5 square centimeters
1 square foot = .09 square meters
1 square yard = .8 square meters
1 inch = 2.5 centimeters
1 foot = 30 centimeters
1 yard - .9 meters

1 ounce = 28 grams
1 pound = .45 kilograms

PLANT CHART KEY

AI		Autumn interest
	B	berries
	C	color (foliage)
	S	colored stems
	BK	bark
	N	nuts
	SP	seedpods
BC		Berry color
BT		Bloom time
	VESp	very early spring
	ESp	early spring
	MSp	mid-spring
	LSp	late spring
	ESu	early summer
	MSu	midsummer
	LSu	late summer
	Su	summer
	ASu	all summer
	A	autumn
	EB	everblooming
D		Direct seeding
	Y	yes, direct seed only
	N	no, start seeds indoors
	E	either, start seeds indoors or direct seed
	L	direct seed outdoors, but only where the growing season is 8 months or more
DH		Days to harvest
DR		Distance between rows
F		Amount of nitrogen fertilizer (in lbs.) to use per 1,000 square feet per year
FC		Flower color
GT		Grass type
	C	cool season
	W	warm season
H		Hardiness
	VH	very hardy, will withstand heavy frost
	H	hardy, will withstand light frost
	HH	half-hardy, will withstand cool weather, but not frost
HU		Humidity
	L	low
	M	moderate
	H	high
HZ		Hardiness zone

L		Light requirement
	S	full sun
	LSh	light shade
	PSh	partial shade
	Sh	shade
	D	direct
	B	bright
	I	indirect
M		Maintenance level
	H	high
	M	medium
	L	low
MA		Method of attachment
	H	holdfasts
	Te	tendrils
	Tie	must be tied
	Tw	twining
MH		Mowing height
MO		Moisture requirement
	D	dry
	A	average
	M	moist
P		Propagation method
	A	air layering
	C	cuttings
	Cl	clove
	Co	corm
	D	division
	G	grafting
	L	layering
	LC	leaf cuttings
	O	offsets
	P	plugs
	RC	root cuttings
	S	seeds
	SC	stem cuttings
	So	sod
PD		Planting distance
	AF	after frost (where plants are not hardy)
	A	autumn
PDe		Planting depth (from water surface to top of container)
PH		Plant height
PL		Planting time
PO		Time to plant plants outdoors
	ESp	early spring
	ESu	early summer
	LSp	late spring
	LSu	late summer

	LW	late winter
	MSp	mid-spring
	MSu	midsummer
PP		Planting depth
PPH		Plant parts harvested
	L	leaves
	F	flowers
	S	seeds
	R	roots
	St	stem
PT		Plant type
	A	annual
	B/A	biennial grown as an annual
	Bi	biennial
	P/A	perennial grown as an annual
	P	perennial
	B	bulb
	C	corm
	D	deciduous
	DV	deciduous vine
	E	evergreen
	EP	evergreen perennial
	ES	evergreen shrub
	EV	evergreen vine
	Fo	foliage
	Fl	flowering
	HA	hardy annual
	HP	herbaceous perennial
	R	rhizome
	T	tuber
	TA	tender annual
	TR	tuberous root
S		Soil requirement
	D	dry
	A	average
	M	moist
	P	poor (no organic matter added)
	R	rich (abundant organic matter added)
	I	infertile
SI		Time to start seeds indoors
	ESp	early spring
	ESu	early summer
	LSp	late spring
	LSu	late summer
	LW	late winter
	MSp	mid-spring
	MSu	midsummer
SO		Time to start seeds outdoors

	ESp	early spring
	ESu	early summer
	LSp	late spring
	LSu	late summer
	LW	late winter
	MSp	mid-spring
	MSu	midsummer
SP		Seasonal preference
	C	cool
	W	warm
SZ		Size (height × spread)
T		Temperature
		for annuals/biennials/herbs
	C	cool (below 70°F or 21°C)
	A	average (70° to 85°F or 21° to 29°C)
	H	hot (above 85°F or 29°C)
		for houseplants
	C	cool (below 68°F or 20°C)
	A	average (68° to 72°F or 20° to 22°C)
		for perennials
	C	cool (summer temperature below 75°F or 24°C)
	A	average (summer temperature 75° to 90°F or 24° to 32°C)
	H	hot (summer temperature above 90°F or 32°C)
		for vines
	C	cool (below 75°F or 24°C)
	A	average
	H	hot (above 90°F or 32°C)
U		Uses
	C	culinary
	Co	cosmetic
	D	drinks, hot or cold
	F	dried flower
	G	garnish
	H	hedge
	I	insect repellent
	M	medicinal
	P	potpourri
WT		Wear tolerance
	L	low
	A	average
	H	high

AERATION

Aeration is the process by which air and other gasses are maintained in the soil in the correct proportions. For more information, read about **Soil.**

ANNUALS

An annual is a plant that grows, flowers, sets seed, and dies in the same year. The term "annual" is also applied to some tender perennials that survive in frost-free climates, but flower during the summer in areas that have cold winters. Some biennials, when started early enough, can also be treated as annuals.

Annuals add the finishing touch to a garden. They can create a mood, add dimension, and enhance the beauty of any home for many months—longer than almost any other flowering plants. Annuals are available in all colors, sizes, and shapes. Because they are temporary plants, one can create new designs and color schemes every year to achieve ultimate diversity in the landscape at a minimal cost.

SELECTING ANNUALS

When selecting annuals, you should choose plants that are appropriate for the climate and growing conditions of your garden, as well as for their visual impact.

Annuals have definite climatic preferences. Cool-season annuals prefer growing temperatures under 70° F (21°C), and many will tolerate frost. They are used in the spring and autumn in warmer areas, and in the summer where temperatures are cool, such as in the north, along a cool coastline, or at high altitudes. Warm-season annuals need warm to hot temperatures to grow, and should not be added to the garden until the spring, after all danger of frost has passed.

Annuals also have specific preferences for either sun or shade, and either wet or dry soil. The **Annual Chart** outlines the environmental needs for the most popular annuals. Study this chart carefully before selecting annuals for your garden.

Once you have matched plants to your garden's growing conditions, select annuals that are the size, shape, and flower color you like. If your gardening time is limited, select annuals that require little maintenance.

DESIGNING WITH ANNUALS

With few exceptions, annuals can be used almost everywhere in the garden. Flower beds can be situated in the lawn. Borders can be planted along fences and walls. Edgings of annuals can line walkways and the driveway. Plants can be tucked into the foundation planting, or under shrubs and trees. Why not frame the front door with color, or hide a storage area with an annual vine? Annual vines can also be used to highlight arbors or create screens.

Low-growing annuals can be used as ground covers to unite different parts of the garden. Any annual can be combined with perennials, bulbs, and roses to create a mixed-flower border. Many varieties of annuals grow well in containers and hanging baskets, and many are beautiful in indoor arrangements, either fresh or dried. Some varieties add delicious fragrance to the garden.

Annuals can be mass-planted with one variety, or grown in mixed beds and borders. The decision is personal, but try to avoid too much clutter when planting different plants near each other.

Annuals can be planted almost anywhere in the garden. **Top:** *These marigolds and zinnias were planted as a mixed border.* **Above:** *This summer-flowering border of annuals was planted so that the short plants occupy the front and the tall plants take up the rear. The short edging plants include blue ageratum, red wax begonias, and purple and pink verbenas; the medium-height plants include rose-pink nicotianas and yellow African marigolds; the tall plants include tuberous dahlias, pink cosmos, and spire-like delphiniums.* **Far right:** *This flowering tobacco, mixed with other varieties, was planted as a mixed border lining a walkway.*

For more information, see **Cutting Flowers, Container Gardening, Drying Plants, Fragrance,** and **Landscape Design.** Refer to **Drought Resistance** when designing an annual flower garden in areas where water supplies are short, and to **Shade Gardening** where mature trees or tall buildings block the sun.

GROWING AND MAINTAINING ANNUALS

PLANTING ANNUALS

Almost without exception, annuals are grown from seeds. For techniques on starting your own plants from seed, consult the **Propagation** section. Some annual seeds can be sown directly into the garden, while others must have a head start indoors. Specifics are included in the **Annual Chart.**

If you do not wish to start your own annuals from seed, you can buy transplants (bedding plants) at the garden center in spring. Select plants that are healthy in appearance and preferably not in bloom, and water them regularly until planting time.

Planting time for annuals depends on each variety's hardiness; see the **Annual Chart.** Very hardy annuals can be planted as soon as the soil can be worked in early spring. Wait to plant hardy annuals until mid-spring, or about four weeks before the last frost. Annuals that are tender or half-hardy can not be planted until the spring, when all danger of frost has passed. Half-hardy annuals can be planted if it is still cool, provided there is no further danger of frost. Wait to plant tender annuals until the soil is warm. (The **Annual Chart** outlines planting distances, but you can also check the seed packet or plant label.)

Before planting, read the sections on **Soil** and **Planting.**

FERTILIZING ANNUALS

Keeping your annual garden in the best condition will require a certain amount of care. With the exception of amaranthus, cosmos, treasure flower, nasturtium, moss rose, bearded tongue, and spider flower, which like poor, infertile soil, annuals need nutrients. Incorporate a balanced fertilizer such as 5-10-5 into the soil before planting, and fertilize your plants once or twice more during the growing season. As an alternative, soluble fertilizer can be applied about every four weeks. See **Fertilizing.**

WATERING ANNUALS

Annuals have varying water requirements (see the **Annual Chart**). Plants with average moisture requirements need 1 inch (25 mm) of water per week; of course, others may need either more or less water. Water deeply and as infrequently as possible to encourage deep roots. Do not water annuals prone to diseases or to be used for cutting overhead. See **Watering.**

PRUNING ANNUALS

Some annuals, mainly wax begonias, impatiens, coleus, sweet alyssum, ageratum, lobelia, and vinca require little care. Their flowers fall off cleanly as they fade and do not need to be cut off. Other varieties need to have their flowers removed as soon as they fade (referred to as deadheading), which enables the plants to continue to grow and produce new flowers.

To be kept compact, petunias, snapdragons, and pansies may need to be pinched back after planting, or after the first flush of bloom. If sweet alyssum, candytuft, phlox, or lobelia sprawl out of bounds, they may be headed back with hedge clippers.

Some annuals will reseed from one year to the next, including impatiens, moss rose, scarlet sage, and flowering tobacco in particular. Remove these seedlings as they appear because they are usually less vigorous than their parents.

In autumn, after they are killed by frost, annuals should be removed from your garden beds to remove breeding sites for insects and diseases, and for better visual appearance.

See also **Diseases and Disease Control, Insects and Insect Control, Mulching, Staking and Tying,** and **Weeds.**

ANNUALS

	PD	M	PH	FC	L	MO	T	H	D
Ageratum Houstonianum Ageratum, Floss Flower	5–7″	L	4–8″	BLUE PINK WHITE	S, PSh	A–M	A	HH	N
Amaranthus species Amaranthus	15–18″	M	18–36″	RED (Foliage)	S	D	A–H	HH	N
Anchusa capensis Summer Forget-me-not	8–10″	M	9–18″	BLUE	S	D–A	A–H	HH	L
Antirrhinum majus Snapdragon	6–8″	M	6–15″	MIX	S	A	C–A	VH	E
Arctotis stoechadifolia Blue-eyed African daisy	8–10″	M	10–12″	MIX	S	D	C	H	E
Begonia Semperflorens-Cultorum Hybrids Wax begonia	7–9″	L	6–8″	WHITE PINK RED	PSh,Sh	A	A	HH	N
Brassica oleracea Flowering cabbage, Kale	15–18″	L	15–18″	PINK WHITE (Foliage)	S	M	C	VH	N
Browallia speciosa Browallia	8–10″	L	10–15″	BLUE WHITE	PSh,Sh	M	C	HH	N
Calendula officinalis Pot marigold	8–10″	H	10–20″	YELLOW ORANGE	S,LSh	M	C–A	H	E
Callistephus chinensis China aster, Annual aster	6–18″	H	6–30″	MIX	S,PSh	M	A	HH	E
Capsicum annuum Ornamental pepper	5–7″	L	4–8″	RED ORANGE (Fruit)	S,PSh	M	A–H	HH	N
Catharanthus roseus Vinca, Periwinkle	6–8″	L	4–12″	WHITE PINK	S,PSh	D–M	A–H	HH	L
Celosia cristata Cockscomb	6–10″	L	6–20″	MIX	S	D	A–H	HH	E
Centaurea cyanus Bachelor's button	6–12″	M	12–36″	BLUE PINK	S	D–A	A	VH	E
Cleome Hasslerana Spider flower	12–15″	L	30–48″	PINK WHITE	S	D	A–H	HH	E

ANNUALS cont.

	PD	M	PH	FC	L	MO	T	H	D
Coleus × *hybridus* Coleus	8–10"	L	10–24"	MIX (Foliage)	PSh,Sh	A–M	A–H	T	N
Cosmos species Cosmos	9–18"	M	18–30"	MIX	S	D–A	A	HH	E
Dianthus chinensis China pink	7–10"	L	6–18"	PINK RED WHITE	S,PSh	A	C–A	HH	N
Dyssodia tenuiloba Dahlberg daisy	4–6"	L	4–8"	YELLOW	S	D–A	A–H	HH	N
Fuchsia × *hybrida* Fuchsia	8–10"	H	12–24"	MIX	PSh,Sh	M	A	T	N
Gaillardia pulchella Blanketflower	8–15"	M	10–18"	RED ORANGE	S,LSh	D–A	A–H	HH	E
Gazania rigens Treasure flower	8–10"	H	6–10"	GOLD YELLOW ORANGE	S	D–A	A–H	HH	E
Gerbera Jamesonii Transvaal daisy	12–15"	M	12–18"	MIX	S	M	A	HH	N.
Gomphrena globosa Globe amaranth	10–15"	M	9–30"	MIX	S	D	A–H	HH	N
Helianthus annuus Sunflower	12–24"	M	15–144"	YELLOW	S	D	H	T	E
Helichrysum bracteatum Strawflower	7–9"	M	12–30"	MIX	S	D	A–H	HH	E
Hibiscus moscheutos Rose mallow	24–30"	M	48–60"	WHITE PINK RED	S,LSh	M	A	H	E
Iberis species Candytuft	7–9"	L	8–10"	WHITE PINK LAVENDER	S	D–A	C–H	HH	E
Impatiens balsamina Balsam	10–15"	L	12–36"	MIX	S,PSh	M	H	T	E
Impatiens New Guinea New Guinea impatiens	10–12"	L	10–12"	MIX (Foliage)	S,LSh	M	A	T	N
Impatiens Wallerana Impatiens	8–10"	L	6–18"	MIX	PSh,Sh	M	A	T	N
Ipomoea species Morning glory	12–18"	M	5–10"	MIX	S	M	A	T	E

ANNUALS cont.

	PD	M	PH	FC	L	MO	T	H	D
Kochia scoparia trichophylla Red summer cypress, Burning bush	18–24″	L	24–36″	RED (Foliage)	S	D	A–H	HH	E
Lantana camara Lantana	8–10″	M	10–24″	YELLOW ORANGE PINK	S	A	A	T	N
Lathyrus odoratus Sweet pea	6–15″	M	24–60″	MIX	S	M	C–A	H	Y
Lavatera trimestris Lavatera	12–15″	M	18–30″	PINK RED WHITE	S	D–A	A	H	E
Limonium sinuatum Statice	12–24″	M	12–36″	MIX	S	D	A–H	HH	E
Lobelia Erinus Edging lobelia	8–10″	L	3–5″	BLUE PURPLE	S,PSh	M	C–A	HH	N
Lobularia maritima Sweet alyssum	10–12″	L	3–6″	WHITE PINK LAVENDER	S,PSh	A–M	A	H	E
Matthiola incana Stock	10–12″	H	12–24″	MIX	S	M	C	H	N
Mimulus × hybridus Monkey flower	5–7″	L	6–8″	YELLOW RED GOLD	PSh,Sh	M	C	HH	N
Mirabilis Jalapa Four-o'clock	12–18″	L	18–36″	MIX	S	D–A	C–H	T	E
Myosotis sylvatica Forget-me-not	8–12″	L	6–12″	BLUE PINK	PSh	M	C	H	E
Nemophila Menziesii Baby blue-eyes	8–12″	L	6–8″	BLUE	S,LSh	D–M	C	VH	E
Nicotiana alata Flowering tobacco	8–10″	L	12–15″	MIX	S,PSh	M	A–H	HH	E
Nierembergia hippomanica Cup flower	6–9″	L	6–15″	BLUE PURPLE	S,LSh	M	A–H	HH	N
Pelargonium peltatum Ivy geranium	10–12″	M	24–36″	MIX	S	A	A	T	N
Pelargonium × hortorum Geranium, Zonal geranium, Bedding geranium	10–12″	H	10–15″	MIX	S	A–M	A	T	N

ANNUALS cont.

	PD	M	PH	FC	L	MO	T	H	D
Petunia × hybrida Petunia	10–12″	M	6–12″	MIX	S	D	A—H	HH	N
Phlox Drummondi Annual phlox	7–9″	L	6–10″	MIX	S	M	C–A	H	E
Portulaca grandiflora Moss rose	6–8″	L	4–6″	MIX	S	D	H	T	E
Rudbeckia hirta Gloriosa daisy	12–24″	L	18–36″	GOLD YELLOW	S,LSh	A	A–H	HH	E
Salpiglossis sinuata Painted tongue	10–12″	M	18–24″	MIX	S	M	C	HH	N
Salvia splendens Scarlet sage	6–8″	L	12–24″	RED WHITE PURPLE	S,PSh	A–M	A–H	HH	N
Sanvitalia procumbens Creeping zinnia	5–7″	M	4–8″	YELLOW ORANGE	S	D–A	A–H	HH	E
Tagetes erecta African marigold	12–15″	H	18–30″	GOLD YELLOW ORANGE	S	A	A	HH	N
Tagetes patula French marigold	3–6″	H	5–10″	GOLD YELLOW	S	A	A	HH	E
Thunbergia alata Black-eyed Susan vine	12–15″	M	3–6′	WHITE YELLOW ORANGE	S,PSh	M	A	HH	L
Tithonia rotundifolia Mexican sunflower	24–36″	M	48–60″	ORANGE	S	D	A–H	T	E
Torenia fournieri Wishbone flower	6–8″	L	8–12″	PURPLE	PSh,Sh	M	C	HH	N
Tropaeolum majus Nasturtium	8–12″	L	12–24″	YELLOW ORANGE RED	S,LSh	D	C–A	T	Y
Verbena × hybrida Verbena	5–7″	M	6–8″	MIX	S	D–A	H	T	N
Viola × Wittrockiana Pansy	6–8″	M	4–8″	MIX	S,PSh	M	C	VH	N
Zinnia elegans Zinnia	4–24″	H	4–36″	MIX	S	D–A	A–H	T	E
Various genera Dusty miller	6–8″	L	8–10″	MIX (Foliage)	S,PSh	D–A	A–H	HH	N

ANTIDESICCANTS

Antidesiccants are sprays applied to foliage to prevent the leaves from transpiring water. These sprays are particularly useful in protecting evergreen trees and shrubs during the winter. See also **Winter Protection.**

BARE ROOT

Bare-root plants are plants that are dormant. They have no soil or growing medium around their roots.

BIENNIALS

A biennial is a plant that takes two growing seasons to flower and set fruit or seed, and then dies. Plant growth occurs during the first season; flowers and seeds are produced during the second season. While they are unlike annuals, which flower, set seed, and die in one growing season, some biennials can be treated as garden annuals because they will flower the first year if seeds are started indoors in late winter or early spring.

Although most biennials are garden flowers, some herbs are also biennials. If grown for foliage only, as in the case of parsley, the fact that the herb plants will never flower does not matter to most gardeners. Other biennials, such as foxglove, reseed so freely once they are established that there will be plants in bloom every year, and therefore they can be treated as perennials.

SELECTING BIENNIALS

Selecting the right biennials for your garden depends on several factors. You need to consider your garden's climate and growing conditions; choose only those plants that will grow and flower in that environment. The **Biennial Chart** outlines the light, moisture and temperature requirements for the most common biennials. Read about **Hardiness,** too.

A second factor to consider is visual appeal. Of course, you'll choose plants you like, but consider flower color, plant shape, and height in relationship to the overall design of your garden. Finally, think about blooming time. Most biennials bloom for only four to six weeks, so choose those plants that will give color to the garden when it is most needed and coordinate with the rest of the flower bed or border.

DESIGNING WITH BIENNIALS

Because biennials have a short blooming period, they are best used as seasonal accents, or incorporated with other biennials, bulbs, annuals, or perennials in mixed flower beds and borders. Read the sections on designing in the listings under **Annuals, Bulbs,** and **Perennials** for more ideas on flower bed and border locations and uses.

Biennials can also be thought of as temporary plants. A planting of forget-me-not with wallflower provides a magnificent display of color from mid- to late spring. When their blooming period is finished, biennials can be removed and replaced with annuals.

For more information, see **Cutting Flowers, Container Gardening, Drying Plants, Fragrance,** and **Landscape Design.**

GROWING AND MAINTAINING BIENNIALS

☐
PLANTING BIENNIALS
Almost without exception, biennials are grown from seeds. For techniques on starting your own plants from seed, read the appropriate parts of **Propagation.** Many biennial seeds can be started indoors in late winter or early spring if you desire blooms the first year. If you are going to treat the plants as two-year plants, you can start them either indoors, or directly in the garden from early summer to about two months before the first autumn frost.

If you do not wish to start your own biennials from seed, you can buy transplants (bedding plants) at the garden center in spring. Select plants that are healthy in appearance and preferably not in bloom, and water them regularly until

A popular biennial, English foxgloves (TOP) *produce tall spires of tubular flowers. Like most biennials, they readily reseed themselves and reliably come back every year. Because biennials such as wallflower* (ABOVE) *and Sweet William* (RIGHT) *have a short blooming period, they are best used as seasonal accents, or incorporated with other biennials, bulbs, annuals, or perennials in mixed flower beds and borders.*

BIENNIALS

	PD	BT	PH	FC	L	MO	T	HZ
Alcea rosea Hollyhock	18"	ES	4–10'	MIX	S	M	A–H	3–8
Bellis perennis English daisy	6"	LSp,ES	6"	WHITE, PINK, RED	S,PSh	M	C	3–7
Campanula Medium Canterbury bells	12–15"	LSp,ES	2–3'	MIX	S,PSh	A	A	5–7
Cheiranthus Cheiri Wallflower	12–15"	MSp,LSp	1–1½'	YELLOW, ORANGE	S	A–M	C	5–7
Dianthus barbatus Sweet William	6–9"	LSp,ES	6–24"	MIX	S	A–M	C–A	3–7
Digitalis purpurea Foxglove	15–24"	LSp,ES	3–6'	MIX	P,PSh	A–M	A	4–7
Lunaria annua Honesty, Money plant	12–15"	LSp,ES	3'	PINK	S,PSh	A	A	3–8
Myosotis sylvatica Forget-me-not	6–8"	MSp,LSp	6"	BLUE	LSh	M	C	3–8

planting time. Many biennial transplants will be ready to bloom and therefore will be one-season plants.

Planting time for biennials depends on their specific hardiness; refer again to the **Biennial Chart.** Plants that are hardy in your area can be added to the garden in early spring after the soil can be worked and the weather is settled. When plants are being used as two-season plants, they are usually planted from midsummer until about six weeks before the first autumn frost. The **Biennial Chart** outlines appropriate planting distances, but you can also check the seed packet or plant label.

Before planting, read the sections on **Soil** and **Planting.**

FERTILIZING BIENNIALS

Incorporate a balanced fertilizer such as 5-10-5 into the soil before planting; plants carried over the winter should be fertilized again when growth starts the following spring. See **Fertilizing.**

WATERING BIENNIALS

Biennials have varying water requirements (see the **Biennial Chart**). Plants with average moisture requirements need 1 inch (25 mm) of water per week; others need either more or less water. Water deeply and as infrequently as possible to encourage deep roots. Do not water biennials prone to diseases or to be used for cutting overhead. See **Watering.**

PRUNING BIENNIALS

After biennials bloom, they will set seed and die. Since many will sprout new plants from fallen seeds, wait until the seeds form and drop before cutting off the flowering stalks, or cut the flowers off as soon as they fade and leave them on the ground to set seeds for new growth.

PROTECTING BIENNIALS IN THE WINTER

Biennials that are being left in the ground over the winter may need winter protec-

BELOW: *A birdbath provides water for birds when a natural source is not available, and is a sure way to attract them to your garden.*

The correct selection of plants, such as mock orange (PHILADELPHUS CORONARIUS), ABOVE, will help you encourage birds to nest in your garden.

tion. Once they have died, biennials should be removed from the beds to remove breeding sites for insects and diseases, and for better visual appearance.

See also **Diseases and Disease Control, Insects and Insect Control, Mulching, Staking and Tying, Weeds,** and **Winter Protection.**

BIRDS

Birds are as much a part of a garden as fish are of a stream. It is delightful to wake up to the sounds of birds as dawn's first light appears, or watch them scurry about in late afternoon as the sun starts to set. Some gardeners keep records of the number of different bird species that are attracted to their feeders, and attempt to spy a little-known visitor to the neighborhood. Birds can be a great asset to the garden, as some of them dine on insects that would otherwise be dining on your plants.

ATTRACTING BIRDS TO THE GARDEN

Basically, to keep birds at home in your garden, you have to provide water, shelter, and food.

WATER
If you have a pond, brook, or swamp, you won't need to worry about providing supplemental water unless the source you have freezes in winter. Put out clean, fresh water every day if it is not otherwise available; you can use a birdbath, a shallow pan, or a pie plate. Birdbath heaters are also available to keep the water from freezing in winter. Set water in a protected spot, close to trees, shrubs, feeders, and bird houses.

SHELTER
Shelter, especially during breeding and nesting season, will keep the birds in your garden. Some birds will nest in trees and shrubs; however, over fifty different types of birds will nest in houses. It's a good idea to place birdhouses in natural settings, and to clean them after they've been vacated for the next generation of birds.

FOOD
A bird's high body temperature demands a constant supply of energy and food. During the growing season, much of this food can be obtained from plants and insects, although additional food is a good way to attract birds to your garden. In winter, when insects are not available, set out suet and chunky peanut butter in addition to seeds. Many birds also like dog biscuits, bread crumbs, apple peels, oranges, and raisins.

Birds eat a variety of seeds; each species has its favorite. Cardinals and finches like sunflower seeds, sparrows like millet, goldfinches like thistle, mourning doves and bluejays like buckwheat, and cardinals and red-winged blackbirds like cracked corn. You can buy ready-made bird seed mixtures, or buy the components and mix your own. Add sand, gravel, or grit to your mixture, as this aids digestion.

BIRD FEEDERS

Some birds, such as sparrows, cardinals, and thrushes, are ground feeders; others, such as grosbeaks, titmice, and mockingbirds, are not. Consequently, you should place food both on the ground and in feeders to attract the greatest number of birds. Additionally, different types of feeders attract different species; to that end, feeders for small birds may have crossbars to keep larger birds to their own sources of food. Set feeders in a warm spot, away from preying cats and squirrels, or near your windows so you can watch nature live in front of you. You can also place feeders on top of a smooth, greased pipe, which will certainly frustrate squirrels!

PLANTS THAT ATTRACT BIRDS

The right selection of plants may also increase the number of birds that visit your garden. If you want to encourage nesting, select dense evergreens such as spruce and hemlock, or deciduous trees and shrubs such as spirea, mock orange, viburnum, and privet. In summer, provide seed-producing annuals, and in the winter, provide berrying trees and shrubs. Birds don't like to fly over too much open space to get to their food and

PLANTS THAT ATTRACT BIRDS TO THE GARDEN

Latin Name	Common Name	Type of Plant
Amelanchier canadensis	Serviceberry	Shrub
Aquilegia species	Columbine	Perennial
Aronia arbutifolia	Red chokeberry	Shrub
Berberis species	Barberry	Shrub
Betula species	Birch	Tree
Campsis radicans	Trumpet vine	Vine
Celastrus species	Bittersweet	Vine, Ground cover
Celtis species	Hackberry	Tree
Cirsium species	Thistle	Perennial
Coreopsis species	Tickseed	Annual, Perennial
Cornus species	Dogwood	Tree, Shrub
Cosmos species	Cosmos	Annual
Cotoneaster species	Cotoneaster	Shrub
Crataegus species	Hawthorn	Tree
Forsythia species	Forsythia	Shrub
Helianthus annuus	Sunflower	Annual
Ilex species	Holly	Tree, Shrub
Juniperus virginiana	Red Cedar	Tree
Ligustrum species	Privet	Shrub
Lonicera species	Honeysuckle	Shrub, Vine
Malus species	Crabapple	Tree
Myrica pensylvanica	Bayberry	Shrub
Parthenocissus quinquefolia	Virginia creeper	Vine, Ground cover
Philadelphus species	Mock orange	Shrub
Phlox species	Phlox	Annual, Perennial
Picea species	Spruce	Shrub, Tree
Pinus species	Pine	Tree, Shrub
Pyracantha species	Fire thorn	Shrub
Quercus species	Oak	Tree
Rhus species	Sumac	Shrub, Ground cover
Rosa species	Wild rose	Shrub
Rudbeckia species	Gloriosa daisy	Annual, Perennial
Sambucus canadensis	American elder, Elderberry	Shrub
Sorbus species	Mountain ash	Tree
Spiraea species	Spirea	Shrub
Symphoricarpos species	Snowberry	Shrub
Tagetes species	Marigold	Annual
Tsuga species	Hemlock	Tree, Shrub
Viburnum species	Arrowwood, Virburnum	Shrub

shelter, so locate birdhouses and feeders near protective plants.

If you don't want the birds to feast on your crops, cover the plants with netting or cheesecloth at fruiting time.

Once you start feeding and providing water for birds, be sure to do it all year. It's very important to continue throughout the winter when natural food and water may not be available.

BONSAI

Bonsai is the art of dwarfing shrubs and trees. See **Pruning.**

BUDDING

Budding is a method of plant propagation in which a bud from one plant is grafted to another plant. See **Propagation**.

BULBS

Bulbs are among nature's unique creations. They are self-contained packages of foliage and flowers that burst into growth, bloom, die down, and then lay dormant until the next season. For some species, the blooming period is short, but their beauty is close to permanent, year after year.

True bulbs, including daffodils, lilies, hyacinths, tulips, and glory-of-the-snow, are complete plants. The dormant bulb contains the plant's future roots, stems, leaves, and flowers. Fleshy scales surround the potential growth organs and contain the food necessary for the bulb to grow and flower. After a bulb blooms, the leaves manufacture food for the next year and transfer it underground to renew the cycle the following season. Some bulbs are covered with a thin, brown, papery covering.

As bulbs grow, small bulblets form around their bases. These bulblets can be separated from the mother bulb to grow into new plants. A few bulbs, such as some lilies, form similar structures, bulbils, in their leaf axils.

TYPES OF BULBS

Several other structures, including corms, rhizomes, tubers, and tuberous roots, are commonly classified as bulbs although they differ from each other in some ways. They are grouped together because of their food-storing capabilities and similar growth habits.

CORMS

Corms, including crocus, freesia, and gladiolus, are modified stems filled with food-storage tissue. They are usually short and somewhat flat, and covered with a meshy material. Growth eyes appear at the top of dormant corms. After a corm blooms, it disappears, and is replaced by a new one to produce the following year's growth and flowers. Some corms produce cormels, which, like bulblets, can be separated from the mother plant and grown separately.

RHIZOMES

Rhizomes, such as cannas, are thick food-storage stems that grow along, or just below, the soil surface. Growth buds appear along the rhizome for the next year's leaves and flowers, but the original rhizome does not rebloom.

TUBERS

Tubers, including Grecian windflower, caladiums, and tuberous begonias, are thick, underground food-storing stems with growth buds at their tops. They do not creep as rhizomes do. They grow larger every year, and can be cut apart to form new plants every two to three years.

TUBEROUS ROOTS

Tuberous roots, which include the dahlia, are roots with thick, fleshy, food-storing structures that resemble tubers. They are depleted during the growing season, but replaced by new ones every year. They can be separated to grow new plants.

SPRING, SUMMER, HARDY, AND TENDER BULBS

Spring, summer, hardy, and tender are other terms used for referring to bulbs. Spring bulbs are winter-hardy; in other words, they are planted in autumn, grow

and flower in spring, and lie dormant until the following spring. Not all hardy bulbs, however, are spring-flowering; some, such as colchicum, bloom in autumn. Most summer-flowering bulbs are tender bulbs, which means that they cannot withstand frost and/or frozen ground. Most are planted in spring, bloom in summer, and are dug from the ground and stored indoors over the winter until they are replanted the following spring. In frost-free areas, tender bulbs may be left in the ground permanently.

Many spring bulbs need cold temperatures during the winter, or they will not grow and bloom satisfactorily. Gardeners in frost-free areas (Zones 9 and 10) often refrigerate these bulbs before planting.

SELECTING BULBS

With the proper selection, you can have bulbs in bloom from very early spring until frost (see the **Bulb Chart** for blooming times). For example, you can start with the earliest blooming winter aconite and snowdrops, follow with Grecian windflower and Siberian squill, then plan for daffodils and hyacinths, and end spring with late-blooming tulips. About this time, you can add gladiolus or dahlias for summer color.

Other considerations when choosing bulbs are hardiness, height, and flower color. These aspects are also outlined in the **Bulb Chart.** See also **Hardiness.**

DESIGNING WITH BULBS

Nothing greets spring better than a colorful display of bulbs. Long before color comes to the garden from shrubs and perennials, when days are bleak and there are still no leaves on the trees, early-blooming bulbs are poking their heads through the ground, or even the snow.

Early-blooming bulbs can be naturalized in the lawn to create a meadowlike effect. You can plant bulbs in front of flowering shrubs and under flowering trees, but be careful to choose bulbs that bloom at the same time and are of a complementary color. Perennial beds and borders, even rose beds, can be colorful with crocus and daffodils long before the later-blooming plants start to grow. Late-blooming spring bulbs, such as alliums, can be combined with early-blooming perennials, such as irises and peonies. Late-flowering spring bulbs also fill the void between the times when flowering trees, shrubs, and summer annuals bloom.

Almost without exception, bulbs look best when you plant them in clumps of at least three of the same variety, or at least three of the same color. The smaller the flower, the more bulbs you will need in the clump. Certainly, the least attractive way to design with bulbs is to plant them single-file across the front of the house.

Formal gardens are best planted with stately bulbs, such as tulips and hya-

Proper bulb selection can provide flowers from very early spring, such as iris (IRIS RETICULATA), LEFT, and Dutch crocus (CROCUS VERNUS), BELOW, until frost. BOTTOM: Informal gardens make the best use of bulbs planted in natural-looking drifts.

cinths, which are most effective in large beds of the same color. Geometric patterns are very effective in this type of planting, too. Informal gardens make the best use of bulbs planted in natural-looking drifts. Consider the view from both inside and outside the house to maximize the beauty of bulbs.

Bulbs can be "naturalized" into an informal look and left to increase on their own. Be sure to select a spot that will not be disturbed until the flowers and foliage have faded. To naturalize bulbs, toss them lightly onto the ground. Plant after making adjustments for bulbs that fall too close together. The effect will not be as contrived as if you tried to arrange them yourself.

Smaller spring bulbs should be planted where they will be noticed. They are pretty flanking the front door. They can also line pathways, the area later turned over to annuals, or tucked into numerous spots in the foundation planting or rock garden. Bulbs can smother rock walls with color, or turn a monotonous evergreen ground cover into a kaleidoscope of color.

Summer bulbs can be used in the garden on their own or combined with annuals and perennials. Many have exotic shapes and colors for landscape accent. They have a place in beds, borders, and containers.

Any bulb known for its fragrance should be situated near outdoor living spaces, along the path to the front door, or under windows so you can enjoy its rich aroma. See **Fragrance.** Many bulbs are grown for the beauty of their flowers which can be cut and enjoyed indoors. See **Cutting Flowers.**

For more information, read the section on **Landscape Design.**

GROWING AND MAINTAINING BULBS

PLANTING BULBS

The first step in growing a beautiful bulb garden is to start with good-quality bulbs. Make sure they are large and firm; "bargain" collections usually turn out to be disappointments. Until you plant the bulbs, store them in a dark, dry, cool, but not freezing, place so they will not grow, rot, or shrivel up.

Some summer bulbs, primarily tuberous begonias, caladiums, calla, and peacock orchids, benefit from being started indoors in flats or in pots of peat moss and perlite about four to six weeks before the last spring frost. Other bulbs are directly planted in the ground; refer to the **Bulb Chart** for planting times.

Before planting, read the sections on **Soil** and **Planting.** Since bulb roots grow deep in the ground, prepare the soil to a depth of 6 to 12 inches (15 to 30 cm), depending on the size of the bulb. You should also incorporate generous amounts of organic matter such as peat moss, compost, or leaf mold. To promote root growth, it is a good idea to incorporate bonemeal or superphosphate into the soil at the bottom of the planting hole or bed.

Bulbs generally prefer full sun to light shade. A bulb garden may be in heavy shade from nearby trees at planting time, but since most spring-flowering bulbs bloom before leaves are on the trees, this shouldn't be a problem. Bulbs planted in light shade bloom later and last longer than those that are planted in full sun. You should avoid planting bulbs in the heavy shade cast by buildings and solid fences.

Bulbs are often disturbed by small animals. Read the section on **Rodent and Animal Control** for methods to minimize this problem.

TOP: *Bulbs look best when planted in clumps of at least three of the same variety, or at least three of the same color.*

ABOVE: *The planting of bulbs is no simple matter. Here, a gardener transplants his hyacinth bulbs into the garden with great care.*

WATERING AND FERTILIZING BULBS

After planting, water the bulbs well; this should be sufficient moisture until growth starts. Mulch newly planted beds of spring-flowering bulbs, and remove the mulch when growth starts.

When bulbs start to grow, make sure they receive enough water to keep the soil evenly moist, but not wet, throughout the growing and flowering period. A mulch will help, and will also hold down weeds. When the foliage starts to yellow, apply a balanced fertilizer. Summer bulbs benefit from regular feeding during the growing and flowering period. Refer also to the sections on **Watering, Fertilizing, Mulching,** and **Weeds.**

Some tall plants will need support. See **Staking and Tying.**

PRUNING BULBS

When the blooms of large-flowered bulbs have faded, remove them to prevent seed formation (see **Deadheading**). This will target the energy of the plant to the bulb or, in the case of summer-flowering bulbs like dahlias, to promote new growth and flowering. Smaller bulbs can be allowed to go to seed, which will increase the size of the colony. See

Disbudding in the **Pruning** section.

Although the foliage of some bulbs remains green until it is killed by frost, the foliage of most bulbs naturally turns yellow after the blooming cycle is complete. During this time, the plant is producing food for the next season. For this reason, it is important not to remove the foliage until it has turned completely brown. If it is unattractive, it can be braided, or pushed under nearby plants. If bulbs are naturalized in the lawn, do not mow the grass until the foliage has completely "ripened."

DIVIDING AND STORING BULBS

The best time to divide spring-flowering bulbs is after the foliage has browned in the spring. It's easier to locate the bulbs at this time and you're less apt to do damage. You also know where gaps in the garden are to set the new divisions. Many small bulbs can be left in place for many years and do not need dividing. Other larger bulbs will need dividing when the clumps get too large and when the number of flowers starts to decrease. Summer bulbs can be divided before replanting in spring.

Tender bulbs should be lifted from the ground and stored indoors over winter. Tuberous begonias are best dug before the first autumn frost; others can wait until the foliage is blackened by frost. Be careful when digging not to do any damage. After digging the bulbs, wash off the soil and dry them in a sunny spot for several days. Store them in a dark, dry area at 40° to 50° F (4° to 10° C). Check the bulbs periodically to make sure they are not growing, rotting, or shriveling.

Tulips and hyacinths do not multiply in the environmental conditions found in most parts of North America. They diminish in size and need to be replaced every few years. For further information on division and replanting, see **Propagation** and **Transplanting**. The **Propagation** section also contains information on starting plants from seed, a method that can be used with some bulbs.

See also **Forcing** for information on bringing bulbs into bloom indoors in winter, and **Container Gardening** for growing bulbs in pots outdoors. If you encounter problems, refer to **Diseases and Disease Control** and **Insects and Insect Control.**

BULBS

	PD	PP	PL	PH	FC	L	HZ*	PT	BT
Acidanthera bicolor Peacock orchid	5"	2–3"	AF	24"	WHITE	S	7–10	C	Su
Agapanthus species Lily-of-the-Nile	1½'	1–2"	AF	1–3'	BLUE, WHITE	S,PSh	9–10	R	Su
Allium giganteum Giant onion	12"	10"	A	3–5'	PURPLE	S	5–10	B	LSp
Allium Moly Lily leek	4"	3"	A	12"	YELLOW	S	4–10	B	LSp
Alstroemeria species Peruvian lily	1–1½'	6"	AF	1–4'	MIX	S	9–10	R	Su
Anemone blanda Grecian windflower	4–6"	2"	A	2–6"	PINK, BLUE, WHITE	S,PSh	6–9	T	ESp
Anemone coronaria Poppy anemone	6"	3"	AF	1–1½'	MIX	S	7–10	T	Su
Begonia × tuberhybrida Tuberous begonia	8"	2"	AF	8–12"	MIX	Sh	9–10	T	Su
Caladium × hortulanum Fancy-leaved caladium	12"	1"	AF	8–36"	MIX (Foliage)	Sh	10	T	Su
Camassia species Camass	4–6"	4"	A	3'	BLUE	P,PSh	5–9	B	LSp
Canna species Canna	9–24"	1"	AF	1½–4'	MIX	S,PSh	9–10	R	Su
Chiondoxa Luciliae Glory-of-the-snow	3"	4"	A	4–5"	BLUE, PINK, WHITE	S,PSh	4–9	B	ESp
Clivia miniata Kaffir lily	12"	1"	AF	1–1½'	ORANGE, RED	Sh	10	B	Su
Colchicum autumnale Autumn crocus	4"	3–4"	A	4–12"	VIOLET, PINK, WHITE	S,PSh	4–10	C	A
Crinum species Spider lily	2–3'	1"	AF	1–4'	WHITE	LSh	9–10	B	Su
Crocosmia × crocosmiiflora Montebretia	4"	4"	AF	24"	ORANGE, RED, YELLOW	S	7–10	C	Su

*Hardiness Zone: The numbers given represent the range in which the particular bulb is hardy. If a bulb is hardy where you garden, it can remain in the ground all year, and may bloom at other times than stated. If it is not hardy, it must be dug up in autumn, stored indoors over winter, and replanted in spring.

BULBS cont.

	PD	PP	PL	PH	FC	L	HZ*	PT	BT
Crocus species Crocus	3"	3–4"	A	3–6"	PURPLE, WHITE, YELLOW	S,PSh	3–10	C	ESp or A
Dahlia hybrids Dahlia	6–24"	4"	AF	1–4'	MIX	S,LSh	9–10	TR	Su
Endymion hispanicus Wood hyacinth	6"	3"	A	1–1½'	BLUE	PSh	5–9	B	LSp
Eranthis hyemalis Winter aconite	3–4"	2"	A	2–4"	YELLOW	S,PSh	4–9	TR	VESp
Eremurus species Desert candle, Foxtail lily	24"	6"	A	4–8'	MIX	S	3–9	TR	LSp
Erythronium species Dog-tooth violet, Trout lily	4"	3"	A	6–12"	MIX	Sh	2–9	C	ESp
Eucharis grandiflora Amazon lily	2'	2"	AF	20"	WHITE	LSh	10	B	Su
Eucomis species Pineapple lily	10"	6"	AF	12–15"	WHITE	S	7–10	B	Su
Freesia × *hybrida* Freesia	2"	2"	AF	1–1½'	MIX	S	9–10	C	Su
Fritillaria imperialis Crown imperial	18"	5"	A	3–4'	YELLOW, RED, ORANGE	PSh	5–9	B	LSp
Fritillaria Meleagris Guinea-hen flower	5"	4"	A	6–12"	PURPLE	S,PSh	3–9	B	MSp
Galanthus species Snowdrop	2–3"	4"	A	4–6"	WHITE	S,PSh	3–10	B	VESp
Gladiolus × *hortulanus* Gladiolus	6"	4"	AF	1–3'	MIX	S	9–10	C	Su
Gloriosa species Gloriosa lily	6–8"	4"	AF	6–12'	YELLOW, RED	S	10	TR	Su
Hippeastrum hybrids Amaryllis	6"	**	AF	18"	MIX	S	10	B	Su
Hyacinthus orientalis Hyacinth	6"	6"	A	6–8"	MIX	S,LSh	6–9	B	MSp
Ipheion uniflorum Spring starflower	3"	3"	A	6–8"	BLUE	S	6–10	B	MSp

BULBS cont.

	PD	PP	PL	PH	FC	L	HZ*	PT	BT
Iris reticulata Netted iris	2–3"	4"	A	4"	PURPLE	S	5–10	B	ESp
Iris Xiphium Dutch and Spanish iris	3–4"	4"	A	24"	BLUE, WHITE, YELLOW	S	5–10	B	LSp
Leucojum aestivum Summer snowflake	4"	4"	A	8–18"	WHITE	PSh	4–10	B	MSp
Lilium species Lily	6–8"	8"	A	3–7'	MIX	S,LSh	4–10	B	Su
Muscari species Grape hyacinth	4"	3"	A	4"	PURPLE, BLUE	S,LSh	3–10	B	MSp
Narcissus species Daffodil	6–12"	6"	A	4–12"	YELLOW, WHITE	S,PSh	4–9	B	ESp MSp
Ornithogalum umbellatum Star-of-Bethlehem	3–4"	4"	A	6"	WHITE	S,PSh	5–10	B	MSp
Puschkinia scilloides Puschkinia	3"	3"	A	2–3"	BLUE	S,PSh	4–10	B	ESp
Ranunculus asiaticus Persian buttercup	8"	2"	AF	12–18"	MIX	S	8–10	TR	Su
Scilla siberica Siberian squill	3"	2–3"	A	4–6"	PURPLE	S,PSh	4–10	B	ESp
Sparaxis tricolor Wandflower, Harlequin flower	1–1½'	3–4"	AF	18"	MIX	S	9–10	C	Su
Sprekelia formosissima Aztec lily	12"	1"	AF	12"	RED	S	9–10	B	Su
Tigridia pavonia Tiger flower, Mexican shellflower	6"	2–4"	AF	24"	RED	S	7–10	B	Su
Tulipa species Tulip	4–6"	6"	A	6–36"	MIX	S	4–9	B	ESp MSp LSp
Zantedeschia species Calla lily	1–2'	3"	AF	1–5'	WHITE, PINK, YELLOW	S,PSh	10	R	Su

COLDFRAMES AND HOTBEDS

A coldframe is a bottomless box with an adjustable, transparent cover or lid. In essence, a coldframe is a type of miniature greenhouse. Covered with glass, fiberglass, acrylic, or plastic, a coldframe traps the heat of the sun inside of it, and warms the air and the soil. When the temperature drops at night, the coldframe can contain enough heat to keep the plants as much as 10° to 20° F (5° to 10° C) warmer than if they were outside.

The tops of coldframes are hinged at the back so that they can be propped open; this enables you to easily work inside of them. It's also a good idea to open them when the air inside becomes too hot (over 85° F [29° C]) during the day, and to provide good air circulation. Equip a coldframe with an outdoor thermometer so you know when to open and close it. Some coldframes are equipped with sensors that automatically open and close the lid in correspondence with temperature changes.

THE BENEFITS OF A COLDFRAME

The major uses of a coldframe are to protect plants from frost and to raise the temperature of the air inside of it enough so that you can grow plants when the outside temperature is too cold.

HOW TO USE A COLDFRAME

In spring, you can start seeds, or place young seedlings inside to be hardened off and to grow. When the time comes to move the seedlings to the garden, they will be much larger, and will mature more quickly than if they had not received this extra growing step. In autumn, and in milder areas throughout winter, plants such as lettuce and spinach can be grown and harvested from a coldframe.

Small plants grown near their hardiness limits can be overwintered in a coldframe to keep them warmer and to protect them from fluctuating temperatures. The warmth of a coldframe also speeds up the rooting of cuttings and the germination of seeds. In short, a coldframe allows you to grow plants you wouldn't ordinarily be able to grow and to extend the growing season into the spring and autumn.

You can remove the lid from a coldframe in summer and use the frame for starting seeds or cuttings. If the lid is left in place, it will be hot enough inside the frame to use it as a drying rack for herbs and vegetables.

BUILDING A COLDFRAME OR HOTBED

Although coldframes can be purchased, they are also easy to make. The size may be determined by what you have available; for example, you may want to use old windows for the lid, and build the box to fit those dimensions. If not, common dimensions are 3 feet (1 m) wide, 6 feet 1.8 m) long, 12 to 18 inches (30 to 45 cm) high at the back, and 6 inches (15 cm) high at the front, although you can adjust these measurements to your available space. It's important that the lid is 6 to 12 inches (15 to 30 cm) higher in the back that it is in the front in order to trap the maximum amount of heat. Use redwood, pressure-treated pine, cedar, or even cinder or cement blocks for the frame. Painting the inside and outside of the frame black will increase its ability to retain heat.

Orient the coldframe to face south or southwest. Sinking the frame several

BELOW: *Coldframes make it possible to grow plants when the outside temperature is too cold. Any coldframe that has an auxiliary source of heat is known as a hotbed.*

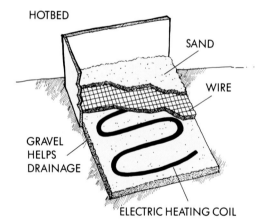

HOTBED

SAND

WIRE

GRAVEL HELPS DRAINAGE

ELECTRIC HEATING COIL

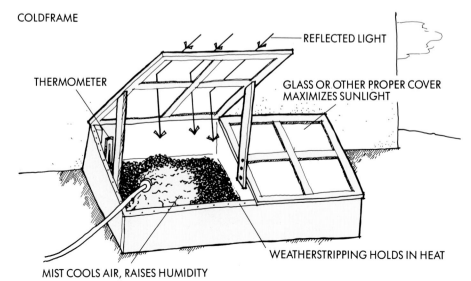

COLDFRAME

THERMOMETER

REFLECTED LIGHT

GLASS OR OTHER PROPER COVER MAXIMIZES SUNLIGHT

WEATHERSTRIPPING HOLDS IN HEAT

MIST COOLS AIR, RAISES HUMIDITY

inches (mm) into the ground helps it retain even more heat; just be sure that the drainage under the box is excellent. A fence, wall, or hedge at the backside will minimize the drying effects of the wind. Make sure the frame is tight, and place hooks on the front to hold the lid in place when it is shut. It is also a good idea to place the coldframe close to the house or a water source, so it will be easy to water the plants inside.

HOTBEDS

Any coldframe that has an auxiliary source of heat is known as a hotbed. Years ago, manure was used in hotbeds. While this is not so common today, heat is available from sources such as electrical warming cables and light bulbs. The uses and construction of a hotbed are the same as for a coldframe. In very cold climates, a hotbed is necessary to grow plants all winter. Leaves, straw, compost, or soil can be mounded up against the frame for additional protection in winter.

COMPOSTING

THE BENEFITS OF COMPOST

Compost is decayed organic material that is used to condition soil. There are other sources of organic matter that can be used to condition soil, such as peat moss, leaf mold, and dehydrated manure, but compost is one of the best and certainly the least expensive sources. Read about the benefits of organic matter under **Soil.** In addition, making your own compost also gives you the satisfaction of recycling organic wastes from the garden and kitchen.

HOW COMPOST IS MADE

Compost is created when waste materials properly decompose. Decomposition is effected by microorganisms such as bacteria and fungi; tiny insects and earthworms break up waste debris and

carry the microorganisms from one site to another. Both insects and microorganisms get their energy by digesting dead or decaying organic residues; this digestion process causes the organic debris to finely decompose. It is possible to purchase microorganisms for "compost starter," but this is usually unnecessary as microorganisms are always present on organic waste.

Microorganisms need a blend of protein and carbohydrates to do their work. High protein wastes are usually green vegetation (kitchen garbage and grass clippings), pulverized seeds, coffee grounds, and animal byproducts (manure). High carbohydrate wastes are dry, tough, former plant parts such as autumn leaves, straw, and sawdust. Both types of materials are needed to make a successful, quick-acting compost pile. You can also increase the rate of decomposition by grinding your compost items into small pieces.

MAKING AND MAINTAINING YOUR OWN COMPOST PILE

To make a compost pile, select an out-of-the-way place. You can make the pile in a heap, a pit, as well as in a variety of enclosures and open bins. The size of the pile is limited only by available space, the amount of material you will have to place in it, the amount of organic matter you need for your garden, and the time you have to devote to cultivating the pile. If space is no problem, a pile that measures 3 to 10 feet (1 to 3 m) wide,

Making compost. 1: A compost shredder makes it possible to chop tough material into small pieces so that it will decay more readily. Always use gloves and protect your eyes when feeding materials into the shredder. 2: Sift compost through a 1-inch (25-mm) wire screen or sieve for garden use; you can use a thinner screen if you want the compost to have a finer texture for other purposes.

3 to 5 feet (1 to 1.5 m) high, and the length you desire is the easiest to work with. Experts say that a pile should be no less than 3′×3′×3′ (1×1×1 m) to attain the necessary heat for decomposition. If compost is made in a container, be sure there are holes in it for aeration and drainage. Double bins are often used to transfer materials from one side to the other to stimulate aeration, or to have compost "cooking" in various stages. While helpful, double bins are not necessary.

The easiest way to start a compost pile is to alternately layer a nitrogen source, such as grass clippings, with a carbohydrate source, such as dried leaves. Later, as other materials become available, they can be added to the pile, but should be placed in the middle, where there is the most heat. As the material decays, it becomes hot; when the temperature in the center of the pile reaches 150° F (65° C) (you can check this with a meat thermometer), it should be turned. If the pile is decomposing properly, you'll turn the pile every three to four days. Usually four turnings are necessary to complete the cycle. If a pile does not get hot enough, it needs more nitrogen from a protein source.

When turning a pile, place the material that was in the center of the pile on the outside, and vice versa. Turning a pile also aerates it, and oxygen is necessary for decomposition. Water also is a necessary element, but the water released from a green nitrogen source is usually sufficient. Water the pile only if it is dry—too much water kills the microorganisms.

You can add commercial fertilizer such as 5-10-5 to a compost pile to provide a source of nitrogen for decomposition and to increase the nutrient level of the finished product. Because organic matter decomposes best in a neutral pH range, adding limestone, crushed clam or oyster shells, egg shells, ashes, or bone meal can help neutralize the acidity present in organic wastes. The heat of a compost pile generally destroys disease organisms, insects, and weed seeds; however, it is a good idea not to add any known diseased or infested materials or weeds in seed to the pile.

When a pile is complete, it will be dark and crumbly, its components will not be recognizable, it will cool down to the air temperature, and it will shrink to about half its original size. When compost is finished, it can be mixed with soil to condition it, used as a mulch, or screened for potting soil or starting seeds.

CONIFERS

Conifers are trees that produce cone fruits. Although some conifers are deciduous, most are evergreen and narrow-leaved, such as pine, fir, spruce, and cedar.

COMPOST BIN

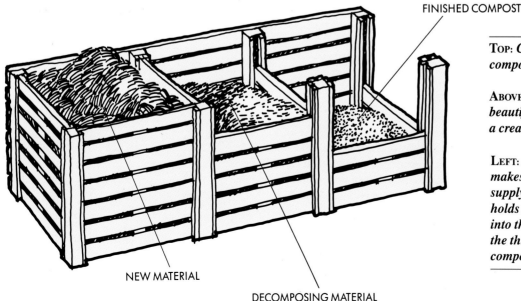

FINISHED COMPOST

NEW MATERIAL

DECOMPOSING MATERIAL

TOP: *Compost at different stages of composition.*

ABOVE: *This swimming pool is beautifully and dynamically edged with a creative selection of conifers.*

LEFT: *A three-sectioned compost bin makes it easy to maintain a constant supply of compost. The first section holds new material, which is placed into the middle section after it rots; the third section holds the finished compost.*

CONTAINER GARDENING

TOP: *This mixed variety of begonias* (BEGONIA × TUBERHYBRIDA), *planted in window boxes, is just one of the many creative ways to garden in containers.*

ABOVE: *This imaginative container garden features a barrel planted with water plants as its main accent, surrounded by annuals (such as petunias) and succulents (mostly varieties of sedum) in terra-cotta pots. A small basket and an old pair of boots also serve as ornamental planters, while a background of ornamental grasses creates a decorative screen for privacy.*

BENEFITS OF CONTAINER GARDENING

Petunias in a bird bath, marigolds in a washtub, impatiens in a hanging basket—these are examples of container gardening. While the most important use of containers may be for gardeners who don't have any land, landscaping with containers can be a creative way to garden. In addition to using containers in soilless areas such as balconies and rooftops, you can use them on patios and decks, on doorsteps, at streetside, or by the front door.

If the soil is poor, and improving it involves more work than you want to do, grow your plants in containers instead. Tall or elevated containers are perfect for gardeners who can not bend or stoop to the ground. Additionally, the movability of containers lets you change your landscape plan as often as you change your mind.

TYPES OF CONTAINERS

Just about anything that will hold growing medium can be used as a container, if it is large enough to hold the plants you want to grow and has drainage holes in the bottom, or preferably at the sides near the bottom. If a prized container does not have drainage holes and you don't wish to put holes in it, you can use it as an outside pot, and place your plants in a second container that fits

inside of it. An alternative way to handle this problem is to place a 1-inch (25-mm) layer of gravel or stones in the bottom of the container before adding growing medium. All containers with bottom drainage holes will drain better if they are raised off of the ground slightly with small "feet." You can also place large and heavy containers on casters to facilitate moving them.

Purchased, found, or made, containers can be made of plastic, wood, fiber, clay, stone, paper, or rubber—even an old tire or shoe, or a used bushel basket. You can preserve wood containers with copper naphthenate, but don't use creosote or pentachlorophenol, as they damage the plants. The only material not recommended for containers is metal because it gets too hot in the sun. Wash whatever you use well before planting into it.

You can use specialty containers, too. Try strawberry jars, hanging baskets, window boxes, or PVC pipe dotted with planting holes. If you grow fragrant plants in containers near windows and doors, their aroma is more likely to fill inside rooms. Where space is severely limited, container gardens can be grown vertically. You can hang pots on fences, or grow plants in a vertical frame made of supports and chicken wire.

POTTING MEDIUM FOR CONTAINER PLANTS

Garden soil should not be used in containers, because it is heavy and will not properly aerate or drain in the limited space of a pot. Use a soilless mixture that is 50% organic material (compost, peat moss, or leaf mold) and 50% inert material (coarse sand, perlite, or vermiculite). Adding a wetting agent will help to keep the medium evenly moist. Soilless mixtures are also more weed-free.

CONTAINER GARDENS

You can use flower containers to house a massed bed of color from one variety of one plant, or a mixed bouquet of similar or contrasting colors. For a mixed container, it's often best to combine various plant shapes—try a tall, spiked plant at the center, underplanted with mounds of color, and trimmed with a vining plant at the edges. Foliage plants such as dusty miller and trailing vinca can add different texture or color, or soften the edges of the container.

ANNUALS AND PERENNIALS

Container gardens can work for flowering annuals and perennials. For the longest display, choose plants that bloom for many months, such as coreopsis and gaillardia, or use pots of biennials or perennials for seasonal color—creeping phlox or English daisy in spring, and mums in autumn. Pots of bulbs are a welcome sight in spring. Treat them as you would bulbs in the ground; plant them in autumn and plunge the pots in a coldframe or in the ground over winter for necessary chilling.

ROSES AND HARDY SHRUBS

You can also grow roses and other hardy shrubs in containers. Choose types and varieties that will stay in proportion to the size of the container. When the flowers outgrow their space, you can move them to a larger container, or remove them from the container, root-prune them, and return them to their home.

HERBS AND VEGETABLES

You can grow a kitchen garden in containers. Many herbs, especially parsley, sage, rosemary, and thyme, do very well in containers. Any small growing vegetable, such as carrots, lettuce, and beets, is suited for container growing, as are the dwarf and bush varieties of tomato, cucumber, squash, and other vegetables available today.

WINTER PROTECTION FOR CONTAINER PLANTS

Plants will be more subject to winter damage in a container because the soil freezes faster than it does in the ground. Where container plants are not hardy, you can move them into a sunroom or greenhouse. You can also allow the plants to go dormant; water them well, cover them with a black plastic bag, and place them in an unheated, but not freezing, garage or shed. As soon as it warms up in spring, return them to the outdoors. Most conifers, especially *Taxus* and *Juniperus* species, can with-

stand winters outdoors in containers in areas where they are hardy. Move them out of the sun and wind in autumn, and make sure the medium is well watered before it freezes. An antidesiccant spray will further reduce winter injury.

TIPS FOR CONTAINER GARDENS

Here are a few tips to keep your containers as attractive as possible:

• Choose plants whose size is in proportion to the size of the container, and set plants closer together than you would in the ground.

• Be aware of light, moisture, and other growing requirements of the plants you use and combine plants with similar needs.

• Water container plants as soon as the top of the growing medium starts to dry out. Plants in containers dry out more quickly than the ground does and will need more frequent watering, especially if they are in porous containers or exposed to the wind.

• Fertilize plants regularly with a balanced, water-soluble plant food. Nutrients leach quickly from a container due to the more frequent watering container plants need.

• Place plant containers, especially window boxes, so the view from inside the house is as attractive as it is from outside.

• If plants are growing unevenly, rotate the containers regularly.

Plants in containers are prone to insects and diseases, just as plants in the ground are, although the use of soilless medium will eliminate or reduce soil-borne diseases. Read about **Diseases and Disease Control** and **Insects and Insect Control.**

CORMS

Corms are modified stems filled with food storage tissue. See **Bulbs.**

TOP: *Wood containers such as this tub are a good place to grow roses and hardy shrubs, and can be preserved with copper napthenate; don't use creosote or pentachlorophenol, as they damage plants.*

ABOVE: *An attractive container garden consisting of chrysanthemums, geranium, cyclamen, and tulips planted in redware pots.*

RIGHT: *A cutting garden of tulips and grape hyacinth.*

CUTTING FLOWERS

One of the joys of gardening is being able to cut flowers for your home or to give to your friends. Many annuals, biennials, perennials, bulbs, roses, and even trees and shrubs have flowers that can brighten up the indoors.

Flowers grown for cutting can, if space permits, be relegated to a cutting garden. This is a non-decorative garden that is laid out in rows or blocks, and is usually out of sight. However, any plant grown for its flowers can be intermingled into flower beds and borders, so a cutting garden is not necessary.

The life of a cut flower depends on how the plant was grown and, more importantly, on how the flower is treated after it is cut. Healthy plants that receive proper fertilizing, watering, pruning, disbudding, and other care will produce larger, more colorful, longer-lasting flowers. Flowers that are properly treated after they are cut can last for a week or more indoors.

HOW TO CUT FLOWERS

Flowers should be cut in the afternoon. This is when their sugar content is highest; additionally, the heat of the day has passed, and the plants are less dehydrated. When you cut, have ready a bucket of 100° F (38° C) water to which a floral preservative has been added. Place the stems in the bucket immediately after you cut them. If you don't have floral preservative, you can use one tablespoon (15 ml) of household bleach and one tablespoon (15 ml) of sugar for each quart (950 ml) of water. This will inhibit disease and provide the flowers with added energy.

After you're done cutting, recut all of the stems in the water so that they can absorb the maximum amount of moisture. Flowers with woody stems, such as those on trees and shrubs, benefit from making several cuts into the end of the stem to increase the surface area for water intake. Flowers with hollow stems or milky sap will quickly wilt unless the end of the stem is seared with a flame before being plunged into water.

STORING CUT FLOWERS

Place the flowers in a cool, dark area for several hours to condition them. Flowers may be placed in a 33° to 35° F (0.5° to 1.6° C) refrigerator if they are not going to be used immediately. Do not store fruits or vegetables in the same refrigerator as the flowers, because the fruits and vegetables release ethylene gas that can damage flowers.

ARRANGING CUT FLOWERS

When arranging flowers, place them in a clean container that has been rinsed with a bleach solution, and always use water than contains a floral preservative or a bleach/sugar mixture. Cut off any leaves that will be submerged below the water as they will decompose quickly and sour the water. Change the water every few days, recutting the stems under water every time you do so. Cut flowers like to be kept out of direct sun and away from heat and drafts.

The type of floral arrangement you make depends on your taste, the style of your home, and the way the arrangement will be used. In general, centerpieces should be low enough so you can see over them. If the arrangement is for a formal occasion, use subtle colors and close harmonies; bolder, brighter, and more varied colors are more appropriate for informal gatherings. These guidelines are true for other types of plant and flower arrangements as well.

Long-stemmed flowers can be put in a vase, but this is not necessary. With the aid of florists' foam or a pinholder,

flowers can be arranged in the shallowest of containers. Ensure that the container is in scale with the flowers, and that the material and texture of the container corresponds to the style of the flowers.

Start with an imaginary line for your arrangement; it could be a triangle or an S-curve. Use branches or prominent flowers to establish the line, and then fill in the remainder of the arrangement. The finished product can be filled with flowers, as in a mass arrangement in the Victorian style, or achieved with only a few flowers in the Japanese tradition. When you are finished, your eye should move easily from one side of the arrangement to the other, without any distractions caused by colors or flower size. Remember the flower designers' credo: "When in doubt, leave it out."

If the arrangement is going to be viewed from more than one side, make sure it is equally attractive from every angle.

CUTTINGS

Cuttings of stems, leaves, or roots are a common method used to increase plants. See **Propagation.**

DEADHEADING

Deadheading is the removal of faded flowers from a plant. See **Pruning.**

DECIDUOUS

Deciduous is a term that describes those woody plants—trees, shrubs, vines, and ground covers—that lose their leaves during the winter.

DISBUDDING

Disbudding is the removal of small, side flower buds to achieve a larger size in the plant's main flower. See **Pruning.**

FLOWERS FOR CUTTING

Latin Name	Common Name	Type of Plant
Achillea species	Yarrow	Perennial
Antirrhinum majus	Snapdragon	Annual
Aquilegia × hybrida	Columbine	Perennial
Baptisia australis	False indigo	Perennial
Calendula officianalis	Pot marigold	Annual
Callistephus chinensis	China aster	Annual
Calluna vulgaris	Heather	Shrub
Campsis radicans	Trumpet vine	Vine
Celosia cristata	Cockscomb	Annual
Centaurea cyanus	Cornflower, Bachelor's button	Annual, Perennial
Chrysanthemum species	Chrysanthemum	Annual, Perennial
Consolida ambigua	Rocket larkspur	Annual
Coreopsis species	Tickseed	Annual, Perennial
Cornus species	Dogwood	Shrub, Tree
Cosmos species	Cosmos	Annual
Dahlia hybrids	Dahlia	Bulb
Daucus Carota Carota	Queen Anne's lace	Perennial wildflower
Delphinium species	Delphinium	Perennial
Dianthus barbatus	Sweet William	Biennial
Dianthus caryphyllus	Carnation	Annual, Perennial
Digitalis purpurea	Foxglove	Biennial
Echinops humilis	Globe thistle	Perennial
Gerbera Jamesonii	Transvaal daisy	Annual
Gladiolus hybrids	Gladiolus	Bulb
Gypsophila elegans	Baby's breath	Annual, Perennial
Helichrysum bracteatum	Strawflower	Annual
Kalmia latifolia	Mountain laurel	Shrub
Lathyrus odoratus	Sweet pea	Annual vine
Lavandula angustifolia	English lavender	Perennial
Lunaria annua	Honesty, money plant	Biennial
Magnolia species	Magnolia	Tree
Matthiola incana	Stock	Annual
Myosotis species	Forget-me-not	Tree
Nicotiana alata	Flowering tobacco	Annual
Paeonia officinalis	Peony	Perennial
Papaver species	Poppy	Annual, Perennial
Phlox paniculata	Perennial phlox	Perennial
Rosa species	Wild rose	Shrub
Rudbeckia species	Gloriosa daisy	Annual, Perennial
Salpiglossis sinuata	Painted tongue	Annual

FLOWERS FOR CUTTING cont.

LATIN NAME	COMMON NAME	TYPE OF PLANT
Salvia splendens	Scarlet sage	Annual
Syringa species	Lilac	Shrub
Tagetes species	Marigold	Annual
Tithonia rotundifolia	Mexican sunflower	Annual
Valeriana officinalis	Heliotrope	Annual
Vitex Angus-castus	Chaste tree	Shrub
Wisteria species	Wisteria	Vine
Zinnia elegans	Zinnia	Annual

DISEASES AND DISEASE CONTROL

When a plant becomes diseased, it is imperative that it be cured if possible, and that the spread of the disease to other plants be stopped. It is almost always easier to prevent a disease from occurring than it is to cure it once it has taken hold.

Several cultural practices will reduce the incidence of disease. Diseases are carried by water, air, and insects. Mulch will prevent water from splashing onto plants from the ground during rain or irrigation, as the water carries the disease spores. Plants should be watered in the morning so they are not wet all night, as diseases grow quickly under wet conditions.

Diseased parts of plants should be pruned away, then destroyed or discarded so that the disease does not spread. Diseased leaves should be cleaned up as soon as they fall. Some diseases are soil-borne and can not be cured; unfortunately, replacing the plant and soil under severe disease conditions is the only cure. Rotating plants that are disease prone to a different location in the garden each year will lessen many soil-borne diseases. In some cases, adjusting the soil pH will reduce disease.

Some diseases can be minimized if air circulation is good; therefore, do not plant disease-susceptible plants too close together. Where diseases are carried by insects, controlling the pests will lessen or eliminate the disease. Many diseases harbor in weeds, thus eliminating weeds will eliminate the disease breeding grounds.

In addition to cultural practices, diseases can be controlled with fungicides. In many cases, preventive spraying will give better results than waiting until the disease occurs.

Most plant diseases are caused by fungi, but they can also be caused by viruses or bacteria.

Proper diagnosis of a disease is necessary to initiate the right control measures. The following descriptions will help you to do this. If you have a problem you cannot identify, your garden center or county extension agent will be able to help. Specific product names are not given for fungicides because their availability varies from location to location, and new ones are introduced as older ones are taken from the market each year. Once you know what disease you are attacking, the garden center or supply store can recommend what fungicide to use. Read also about **Spraying**.

COMMON PLANT DISEASES

ANTHRACNOSE

Symptoms: Sunken black or purple spots on foliage, vegetables, and fruit. Leaves turn black and shrivel, especially in wet weather. Flowers may not develop. Spots may also develop on stems.
Treatment: Buy varieties of vegetables with anthracnose resistance, or buy treated seeds (seeds coated with fungicide). Prune away any damaged plant parts, and remove fallen leaves from the garden. Spray with a fungicide.

ASTER YELLOW

Symptoms: Leaves suddenly turn yellow; flowers are misformed and greenish in color. Annuals and perennials are chiefly affected by this disease.
Treatment: Control leafhoppers, which spread the disease. Remove and destroy infected plants. Do not use the same type of plant in the same spot the following year. Keep the garden well weeded. There are no chemical controls for aster yellow.

BOTRYTIS BLIGHT (OR GREY MOLD)

Symptoms: Leaves and growing tips turn black. Flower buds turn black and may not open; if they do open, the flowers may be streaked with brown and covered with a gray fuzzy growth.
Treatment: Avoid watering at night and improve air circulation. Cut away any infected plant parts. Spray with a fungicide to prevent or control the disease.

CANKER

Symptoms: Red, brown, or black sunken and elongated spots appear along stems and branches of woody plants. Cracks may appear within the spots. The spots enlarge and eventually encircle the stems.
Treatment: There are no chemical controls for canker. Prune away the stems below the infection.

CROWN GALL

Symptoms: Brown, woody growths appear on the roots, or on the stem near the ground. Plants may fail to grow and die.
Treatment: There are no chemical controls for crown gall. Galls can be pruned out. In serious cases, discard the plant.

DAMPING OFF

Symptoms: Seeds rot before they germinate, or new seedlings suddenly fall over and die.
Treatment: Only use sterile, unused, soilless medium before starting seeds. Treat the medium with a fungicide before sowing seeds. Be sure the growing medium has excellent drainage, and do not overwater.

Top: *A marigold (*Tagetes spp.*) suffers from aster yellow.*

Middle: *Botrytis blight has injured the leaves of this geranium (*Pelargonium spp.*).*

Bottom: *The mildew on this lilac (*Syringa spp.*) leaf can be eradicated with a sulfur-containing fungicide.*

Fire Blight

Symptoms: Leaves at the ends of the branches suddenly wilt, turn black, and look like they were scorched by fire. Stems may also turn black.

Treatment: Prune out damaged branches, and dip the pruning shears in alcohol between cuts. Antibiotic sprays can be used to prevent the disease.

Leaf Spot

Symptoms: Spots appear on the upper and/or undersides of leaves; the spots may be black, brown, or purple, and are often surrounded by yellow halos.

Treatment: Remove damaged leaves and spray with a fungicide to prevent or control the disease. Water plants early in the day. Discard fallen leaves. Prune plants back, as disease spores live on the stems.

Mildews, Powdery, and Downy

Symptoms: Powdery mildew is characterized by a white or gray dusty powder that coats leaves, stems, and flower buds. Downy mildew is characterized by gray or tan fuzzy growths on the undersides of the leaves. With both diseases, leaves and flowers become distorted, turn yellow, and fall.

Treatment: Remove and destroy infected leaves. Treat plants with a fungicide to prevent spread of the disease. Fungicides containing sulfur will eradicate mildew. Improve air circulation, and water early in the day.

Mosaic

Symptoms: Leaves become mottled or streaked with yellow or light green. Leaves may curl, and plants are often stunted. Vegetables may be discolored or streaked.

Treatment: There are no chemical controls for this virulent disease. Remove and discard severely infected plants. Control insects that spread the disease. Sometimes the symptoms disappear by themselves.

Root Rots

Symptoms: Leaves turn yellow and become wilted; entire plants may wilt and die. Plants can easily be pulled from the soil, revealing soft, wet, black, or brown roots.

Treatment: Remove and discard infected plants. Drench the soil with a fungicide. Improve drainage if necessary.

Rust

Symptoms: Upper leaf surfaces turn pale; lower leaf surfaces are covered with orange powder.

Treatment: Water early in the day. Remove infected leaves and clean up any fallen leaves and stems. Spray with a fungicide to prevent or control the disease. Some varieties of plants are rust-resistant.

Scab

Symptoms: Gray or black sunken spots or raised, sometimes corky, growths appear mostly on fruits and vegetables, although leaves may also show some spotting.

Treatment: Remove and destroy infected fruit and vegetables. Spray with a fungicide to prevent the disease.

Wilt, Fusarium Wilt, Verticillium Wilt

Symptoms: Vegetable plants suddenly wilt and die. Foliage of trees, shrubs, perennials, and annuals turns yellow, then brown, then wilts and drops.

Treatment: There are no cures for wilt diseases, which are soil-borne. Prune out any infected plant parts. Totally diseased plants should be removed and destroyed. Soil replacement is necessary in severe cases. There are varieties of vegetables, perennials, and annuals that are wilt-resistant.

See **Lawns** for disease identification and control of turfgrasses.

DIVISION

Division is the process of separating plant roots, or cutting a plant in half to make two or more plants. See **Propagation.**

DRAINAGE

Drainage is the process by which water moves through the soil. See **Soil.**

DROUGHT RESISTANCE

Water is one of our most valuable resources. Unfortunately, it has taken severe shortages and droughts for us to realize the extent to which we must conserve it. Many gardeners do not realize that it is possible to have a beautiful garden and not use excessive amounts of water. The following are principles of wise water usage that can be applied during periods of drought, in dry areas, and by gardeners who realize the need to conserve this precious liquid.

Landscaping to conserve water is known as **xeriscaping,** which comes from the Greek word for "dry." The seven principles of xeriscaping are:

1. Planning and Design: Group plants by their water needs, not only by how they appear together.

2. Limited Turf Areas: Locate lawns only in areas where they provide functional benefits. Turf should be separated from other plantings so it can be watered separately from the rest of the garden, or replaced with drought-resistant ground covers and perennials, or mulches. Water turf only when necessary, not when your calendar or clock says so. Aerate lawns for better water penetration.

3. Efficient Irrigation: Landscape plants should be grouped according to their water needs so they can be watered separately from other plants. Irrigation methods, such as drip and trickle irrigation and soaker hoses, conserve large amounts of water. Proper irrigation can save as much as half a household's water consumption. Water plants in the morning to avoid evaporation loss. Install timers on irrigation systems.

4. Soil Improvement: Improving soil with organic matter allows it to better absorb water and improves its water-holding capacity.

5. Use of Mulches: Mulches can be used instead of lawns, and around trees, shrubs and flower beds. Mulches cover and cool soil, which minimizes evaporation, reduces weed growth, and slows erosion.

6. Use Drought-Resistant Plants: Select plants with low water needs. See **Drought-Resistant Plants Chart.**

7. Appropriate Maintenance: Regular maintenance, including pruning, weeding, proper fertilizing, pest control, and watering preserves the beauty of the garden and saves water.

OTHER WATER-SAVING TIPS

The following tips will also conserve water:

- Water plants only deeply enough to wet the entire root area, and do not water again until needed. Extend the time between watering periods.

- Create a basin around individual plants to prevent run-off during watering.

- Avoid overfertilizing; excessive growth requires more water in addition to causing plants to burn.

- Remove sick plants from the landscape.

- Mow the lawn slightly higher than usually recommended.

- Use rinse water as long as it does not contain bleach, harmful detergents, or water softeners, which can damage plants.

- Make sure hoses and faucets do not leak.

- Save rainwater.

- Adjust watering systems so water does not fall onto sidewalks and driveways.

- Prune back and thin out trees and shrubs with heavy foliage.

- Use anti-transpirant sprays.

Remember, however, that even drought-resistant plants need frequent watering until they become established. At that

TOP: *Drought-resistant plants, such as rosemary (ROSMARINUS OFFICINALIS), not only grow well in dry areas, but also help conserve water due to their low moisture needs.*

ABOVE: *Though this drought-tolerant rock garden in Tucson, Arizona, features mostly cacti and succulents for water conservation, the design also includes a small, decorative reflecting pool for the benefit of birds.*

Bearberry (ARCTOSTAPHYLOS UVA-URSI), TOP, *and Siberian carpet* (MICROBIOTA DECUSSATA), MIDDLE, *are both hardy, drought-resistant shrubs.* BOTTOM: *This sunny, exposed garden features terraces planted with English lavender, silvery lamb's ears, and chives among its drought-tolerant plants.*

DROUGHT-RESISTANT PLANTS

LATIN NAME	COMMON NAME	TYPE OF PLANT
Achillea species	Yarrow	Perennial
Aegopodium Podagraria	Goutweed	Ground cover
Albizia Julibrissin	Silk tree	Tree
Antennaria dioica rosea	Pussy-toes	Ground cover
Arctostaphylos Uva-ursi	Bearberry	Ground cover
Armeria maritima	Thrift	Perennial
Artemisia species	Wormwood	Perennial
Asclepias tuberosa	Butterfly weed	Perennial
Atriplex species	Saltbush	Perennial, Shrub
Baccharis pilularis	Coyote brush	Ground cover
Berberis species	Barberry	Shrub
Calandrina umbellata	Rock purslane	Perennial, Annual
Callirhoe species	Poppy mallow	Perennial
Caragana species	Pea shrub	Shrub
Cassia species	Senna	Shrub, Tree
Catharanthus roseus	Vinca, Periwinkle	Annual
Ceanothus species	Wild lilac	Shrub
Cerastium tomentosum	Snow-in-summer	Perennial
Cercis occidentalis	Western redbud	Tree
Cercocarpus species	Mountain mahogany	Tree
Chamaebatiaria millefolium	Fernbush	Shrub
Chrysothamnus nauseosus	Rabbitbrush	Shrub
Cistus species	Rock rose	Shrub
Cleome Hasslerana	Spider flower	Annual
Coreopsis species	Tickseed	Annual, Perennial
Coronilla varia	Crown vetch	Ground cover
Cortaderia Selloana	Pampas grass	Ornamental grass
Cotoneaster species	Cotoneaster	Shrub
Cytisus and *Spartium* species	Broom	Shrub
Echinacea purpurea	Purple coneflower	Perennial
Elaeagnus angustifolia	Russian olive	Shrub, Tree
Ephedra species	Mormon tea	Shrub
Eschscholzia californica	California poppy	Perennial
Eucalyptus species	Gum tree	Tree
Euphorbia species	Spurge	Perennial, Ground cover
Festuca species	Fescue	Lawn and ornamental grass
Forestiera neomexicana	Desert olive	Shrub
Gaillardia species	Blanket flower	Perennial, Annual
Gazania rigens	Treasure flower	Annual
Helianthus annuus	Common sunflower	Annual

DROUGHT-RESISTANT PLANTS cont.

LATIN NAME	COMMON NAME	TYPE OF PLANT
Helichrysum bracteatum	Strawflower	Annual
Hippophae rhamnoides	Sea buckthorn	Shrub
Ilex vomitoria	Yaupon holly	Shrub
Juniperus species	Juniper	Shrub, Tree
Kniphofia Uvaria	Red-hot poker	Perennial
Kochia scoparia	Summer cypress	Annual
Koelreuteria paniculata	Golden-rain tree	Tree
Lantana species	Lantana	Annual, Perennial
Lavandula species	Lavender	Perennial
Leontopodium alpinum	Edelweiss	Perennial
Ligustrum species	Privet	Shrub
Limonium latifolium	Sea lavender	Perennial
Lonicera japonica	Japanese honeysuckle	Vine
Mesembryanthemum species	Ice plant	Ground cover
Microbiota decussata	Siberian carpet	Ground cover
Mirabilis Jalapa	Four-o'clock	Annual
Monarda species	Bee balm	Herb, Perennial
Nerium Oleander	Oleander	Tree
Opuntia humifusa	Prickly pear	Perennial
Papaver species	Poppy	Perennial, Annual
Petunia × hybrida	Petunia	Annual
Phellodendron amurense	Amur cork tree	Tree
Phlox stolonifera	Creeping phlox	Ground cover
Pinus species	Pine (some species)	Shrub, Tree
Polygonum Aubertii	Silver lace vine	Vine
Portulaca grandiflora	Moss rose	Annual
Potentilla species	Cinquefoil	Shrub, Perennial
Ratibida columnifera	Prairie coneflower	Perennial
Rhus species	Sumac	Shrub
Robinia species	Locust	Tree, Shrub
Rosmarinus officinalis	Rosemary	Herb
Rudbeckia species	Black-eyed Susan	Perennial, Annual
Santolina Chamaecyparissus	Lavender cotton	Perennial
Schinus Molle	Pepper tree	Tree
Sedum species	Stonecrop	Perennial, Ground cover
Senecio Cineraria	Dusty miller	Annual
Solidago species	Goldenrod	Perennial
Stachys byzantina	Lamb's ears	Perennial
Symphoricarpos species	Snowberry	Shrub
Yucca species	Yucca	Perennial

point, you can decrease the amount of water you give them. Also read the section on **Watering.**

DRYING PLANTS

Even after the freshness of spring, the warmth of summer, and the brilliance of autumn have faded from the garden, you can enjoy the beauty of flowers and foliage indoors by drying plants. Herbs and many vegetables can be dried for use in the kitchen all year.

DRYING METHODS

☐ AIR DRYING

Most flowers that can be dried can be air-dried. After cutting them, strip the leaves from the stems and tie the stems together in small bunches. Hang them upside down in a dark, airy room that is not too hot. They will be ready in two to three weeks. Flowers with thin stems should have florists' wire wrapped around the stems before drying; these can be air-dried head up in a coffee can or other container.

DESICCANTS

Flowers can also be dried with a desiccant; silica gel is the most popular. After placing 2 inches (5 cm) of silica gel in a container big enough to fully accommodate the flowers, put the flowers on top of the gel, face up. Sprinkle more silica gel on the flowers until they are covered, and cover the container. They should be ready in two to six days. Flowers may also be dried in borax or fine sand; in this case, they should be dried face down and left uncovered. Flowers take twice as long to dry with borax or sand as they do with silica gel.

MICROWAVE OVENS

Flowers can be dried in a microwave, too. Using silica gel, start with one minute on high and adjust as necessary. Foliage can be dried in a microwave after wrapping it in a paper towel; start with two minutes on high and increase or decrease as needed. Since individual ovens vary, you'll need to experiment.

Marigolds (TAGETES **spp.**), BOTTOM, *and peonies* (PAEONIA LACTIFLORA), OPPOSITE PAGE, *are just a couple of the many annuals and perennials that are excellent for drying.*

BELOW: *A simple rack for drying herbs. The wide spacing allows air to circulate freely, thus drying the herbs quickly and effectively.*

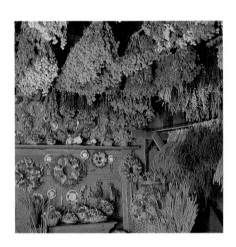

PRESSING

Foliage for arrangements can be dried by pressing it, either with a purchased press, or by placing it between waxed paper and weighting it with heavy books. Peony, oak, beech, eucalyptus, holly, laurel, magnolia, dogwood, and rhododendron leaves can be preserved with glycerine. Cut branches and let them stand in a two-to-one water/glycerine solution for ten to fourteen days. Some flowers that become brittle when they are dried can also be dried with glycerine.

DRYING HERBS

Herb foliage can be dried by hanging stems upside down in a dry, dark, well-ventilated spot, on a drying rack, or a screen. Basil, burnet, chervil, chives, and fennel do not air-dry well and are best frozen; parsley is best dried in the refrigerator; leaves should be stored whole and chopped or grated as used.

DRYING VEGETABLES

Vegetables can be dried in a pan in a single layer in a 140° F (60° C) oven; the process will take one to four hours depending on the vegetable. They can also be dried in a dehydrator, which takes much longer. Sun-drying is possible only when temperatures are around 100° F (38° C) and the humidity is low.

When the weather isn't hot enough, vegetables can be dried in a coldframe during the summer, provided adequate ventilation can be supplied. Vegetables should be washed, and most need to be blanched, before drying. You should restore the lost moisture by soaking the vegetables in water before using them.

Seeds may be dry enough as they fall from the plant. If not, spread them on a screen or piece of cheesecloth to dry.

Most flowers, leaves, vegetables, and seeds that have been dried will absorb moisture in a humid room. Therefore, store them in an airtight container when they are not in use. If moisture collects inside the container, they need further drying. Do not store herbs near the stove as the heat will accelerate their loss of flavor.

POTPOURRI

Potpourri is a mixture of dried flowers, leaves, essential oils, spices, and a fixative that retains its fragrance for many years. Although rose petals are traditional in making potpourri, you can use any other fragrant petals or leaves. To make dry potpourri, dry petals or leaves on a screen until crisp. To each quart (950 ml) of dried material, add one ounce (30 ml) of orrisroot or other fixative, which will retain the scent. Add spices, such as cloves or cinnamon, to obtain the desired scent, and a few drops of essential oil, which you can purchase. Mix everything together well and store the potpourri in an airtight jar.

Wet potpourri, which holds its scent longer than dry potpourri, is made with partially dried petals or leaves. You can make wet potpourri by alternating layers of petals or leaves with a sprinkling of table salt in a non-metallic container until it is full. Add fixative, spices, and essential oil, then place a weight on the mixture for several weeks. You can then mix your ingredients.

FLOWERS FOR DRYING

ANNUALS

Acrolinium, ageratum, bells of Ireland, cockscomb, globe amaranth, immortelle, marigold, snapdragon, strawflower, zinnia.

Plant selection and protective devices such as a cloche, BELOW, make it possible to extend the gardening season.

BIENNIALS

Money plant (honesty), winged everlasting.

PERENNIALS

Baby's breath, Chinese lantern, chrysanthemum, cupid's dart, delphinium, feverfew, goldenrod, pearly everlasting, peony, Queen Anne's lace, ranunculus, sea holly, statice, thistle, yarrow.

SHRUBS AND TREES

Acacia, heather, hydrangea, lilac, rose.

ESPALIER

Espalier is the method of training plants to grow on a flat plane, often in an intricate or attractive design. See **Pruning.**

EVERGREEN

Evergreen is a term used to describe those woody plants—trees, shrubs, vines, and ground covers—that do not lose their leaves during the winter. Evergreens may be broad-leaved or narrow-leaved, depending on the size and shape of the foliage.

EXTENDING THE SEASON

Gardening is not just a summer activity. By extending the season into early spring and late autumn, it is possible to have colorful flowers and bountiful fruits for many more months of the year than the summer.

PLANT SELECTION

One way to extend the season is through plant selection. Choose annuals, perennials, bulbs, trees, and shrubs that bloom from spring through autumn. Annuals that prefer cool climates can be planted for either spring or autumn color where summer temperatures are hot. Vegetables that prefer cool weather can be planted to harvest crops long before and after the tomatoes are ripe.

PROTECTIVE DEVICES

Another way to extend the season is by fooling Mother Nature. These tech-

CLOCHE

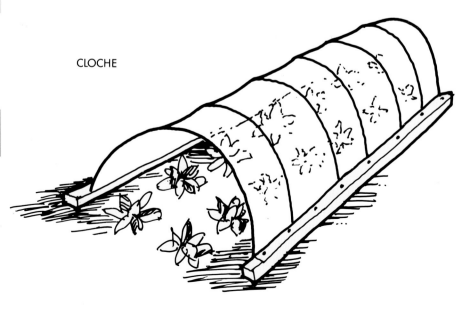

niques are primarily used in vegetable gardens, but can be applied to some other plants. By warming the soil and the air around plants, it is possible to grow them even though the outside temperature is too low. Protective devices such as hotkaps and cloches are transparent coverings which are placed over individual plants to absorb the rays of the sun. They trap heat so the air inside them remains warmer than the surrounding outside air.

You can stretch clear plastic over a row of plants in a tentlike fashion and support it with wire or bamboo stakes to achieve the same results. You can also place a pane of glass on the south side of a plant to warm the soil and the air behind it. A large box with the bottom cut out of it can be placed around a plant; leave the box open during the day and close it at night to retain heat.

Using these techniques, plants can be set into the ground earlier than usually recommended in spring, and continue to grow after autumn frost. These same techniques can also be applied to perennials and small shrubs that are grown at the lower limits of their hardiness. The coverings can be used as temporary

measures, set in place only if frost threatens, and removed when not needed. Raised beds also warm up earlier in spring and stay warm longer in autumn.

Coldframes and Hotbeds can also be used to extend the season. Read this section for further information.

FERTILIZING

Most plants need food to survive, grow, and flower or fruit properly. Although a small amount of nutrients is available in soil and air, supplemental fertilizing is almost always essential. It is important when fertilizing to use the right fertilizer, in the right amount, and at the right time.

NITROGEN, PHOSPHORUS, AND POTASSIUM

Fertilizers contain three basic elements for plant growth, nitrogen (N), phosphorus (P), and potassium (K). These elements are marked on fertilizer labels as N-P-K, and as a series of numbers such as 5-10-5 or 10-6-4. The first number indicates the percentage of nitrogen, which promotes stem and leaf growth, and deep green color, in the mix. The second number shows the percentage of phosphorus, which stimulates root growth and is necessary for photosynthesis. The third number is the percentage of potassium, which contributes to a plant's metabolism, hardiness, and disease resistance. When a fertilizer contains all three elements, it is said to be a complete, or balanced, fertilizer.

Ten other elements are needed for growth, but in small amounts; these elements are called trace elements. Most of these are already present in soil, air, or water in sufficient amounts, but occasionally calcium, magnesium, sulfur, or iron need to be added; the other trace elements are boron, chlorine, copper, zinc, manganese, and molybdenum. Some fertilizers contain trace elements, which the label will indicate; it is also possible to buy mixtures of trace elements, iron, or sulfur. Calcium is obtained from limestone, or gypsum (also a source of sulfur), and dolomitic limestone contains magnesium. Also read about **Soil.**

The source of the nitrogen in a fertilizer determines if it is organic or inorganic. Inorganic fertilizers, such as potassium nitrate, are highly water-soluble and release nutrients to the plant quickly. They are less expensive than organic fertilizers, but are subject to rapid leaching and may cause burning. They need to be applied more often than organic fertilizers.

ORGANIC FERTILIZERS

Organic fertilizers, with few exceptions, are more slowly available to plants (urea, although organic, is highly water-soluble). Some organic fertilizers, such as bone meal and cottonseed meal, are natural; others, such as IBDU and Nitroform, are manufactured. Natural organic fertilizers are bulky, and do not contain as high a percentage of nutrients as manufactured organic and inorganic fertilizers. While organic matter is essential as a soil conditioner, organic fertilizers are no more beneficial to plants than inorganic ones.

SLOW-RELEASE FERTILIZERS

As their name indicates, slow-release fertilizers release their nutrients over a long period of time, and are sometimes activated by moisture, or by temperature. Some are labeled as to the number of months they will last. A good clue as to whether a fertilizer is slow-release is to look on the label for the percentage of water-insoluble nitrogen (WIN). If the WIN number is 15% or less, the fertilizer is a fast-acting one. If the WIN number is 30% or more, the fertilizer is considered slow-release.

LIQUID VS. DRY FERTILIZERS

Dry fertilizers can either be fast-acting or slow-release. Liquid fertilizers are always fast-acting, and are best for container plants, or for giving plants a "boost." Liquid fertilizers can be applied to the ground and/or the foliage. Because they release nutrients quickly, they must be applied often.

SELECTING FERTILIZER

The type of fertilizer to use in the garden depends on plant type. Lawns need fertilizers high in nitrogen to promote leaf growth, such as 10-6-4, 23-7-7, and 16-4-12. Flowering and fruiting plants need a fertilizer where the ratio of N-P-K is 1:2:1, 1:2:2, or similar; 5-10-5 and 5-10-10 are typical formulations. One of the fertilizers used when planting, especially when planting bulbs, superphosphate, is 0-45-0; only phosphorus is needed by the plant at this time to develop strong roots.

TIMING FERTILIZATION

Timing fertilization is critical, as the nutrients must be available to be absorbed by the roots when the plant needs them most, during its most active stage of development. As a general rule, incorporate fertilizer into the soil at planting time. Annual plants, including vegetables, that produce heavy growth during a growing season may need additional feeding during the year. Perennials should be fertilized when growth starts in spring. Feed trees and shrubs when they are most actively producing new growth; sometimes this occurs before the plants flower, but can occur afterwards. Roses are heavy feeders and require fertilization several times a year. Refer to the entries on **Annuals, Herbs, Trees,** etc. for specifics.

Many experts now recommend dormant feeding. This is the application of fertilizer during late autumn or winter when the plants are not growing. Since roots start to grow in spring before top growth appears, the fertilizer will be in the soil for the roots to absorb as soon as they can use it.

APPLYING FERTILIZER

Always follow label directions regarding the amount of fertilizer to apply, as the amount will depend on the fertilizer's formulation. For example, you need half as much 10-10-10 to give you the same amount of nitrogen that you'd get from 5-10-5.

Always apply fertilizer to moist soil, and spread it over the entire area in which the roots grow underground. Generally, this soil is under the spread of the plant. Work the fertilizer lightly into the top of the soil and water again. Do not allow fertilizer to accumulate near the main trunk or stems.

LEFT: *Raised beds help extend the gardening season because they warm up earlier in spring and stay warm longer in autumn than the ground does.*

BELOW, TOP TO BOTTOM: *Some gardening essentials: fertilizer, lime, and compost.*

FORCING PLANTS

Forcing is a term used to describe the process by which plants are made to bloom at a time other than their normal flowering period. You can accomplish this by manipulating either temperature, light, or a combination of both.

FORCING BULBS

A group of plants commonly forced is bulbs, for they bring spring cheer indoors long before the weather permits them to bloom outside. You can force one bulb, such as one hyacinth, or a group of bulbs, such as tulips, crocuses, or daffodils, for an indoor garden. Bulbs are planted in autumn for bloom in late winter or early spring.

A 6-inch (15-cm) container will accommodate six tulips; three daffodils or hyacinths; fifteen crocuses, grape hyacinths, or small irises. A 10- to 12-inch (25- to 30-cm) pot will hold sixteen paperwhite narcissi. Select a clean container that is at least twice as deep as the bulbs, and fill the pot three-quarters full with a lightweight, soilless medium, such as 50% peat moss and 50% perlite or vermiculite. Place bulbs a pinkie's width apart on top of the medium so that the growing tip or nose of the bulbs is even with the top of the pot. When planting tulips, set the flat edge of the bulbs against the outside of the container. Add more medium around the bulbs to fill the pot to within 1/4 inch (6 mm) of the rim. Water thoroughly and label with the variety and the date.

Next, place the container in a dark location where it is between 35° and 45° F (1.6° and 7° C) for twelve to fourteen weeks. This simulates an out-of-doors winter environment for the bulbs. You can do this in a refrigerator, unheated garage or porch, cool basement or coldframe, or by plunging the pots into the ground. If you place pots in the ground, place the top of the pot below ground level and apply 3 to 4 inches (8 to 10 cm) of mulch.

When roots appear from the bottom of the pot and shoots are 2 to 3 inches (5 to 8 cm) tall, bring the pots inside. For the first ten days, keep them in indirect sun at a temperature between 55° and 60° F (13° and 15° C). After that, you can move them to a sunny window, but avoid drafts and heat. To provide adequate humidity, place the pots on pebbles in trays of water. Within three to four weeks, the flowers will appear. Prolong blooming by keeping the plants as cool as possible.

After the flowers fade, move the pots to a cool, sunny spot so the leaves can naturally ripen. Most bulbs that have been forced cannot be forced again, but they can be planted into the outdoor garden. The major exception to this is the paperwhite narcissus, which will never bloom satisfactorily again, and should be discarded.

FORCING FLOWERING TREES AND SHRUBS

A second major group of plants that can be forced is flowering trees and shrubs. Branches can be cut in late winter or early spring and forced into bloom before the plants will flower outdoors. The most commonly used plants for this purpose are pussy willow, forsythia, redbud, dogwood, witch hazel, andromeda, quince, magnolia, viburnum, and flowering cherry and crabapple.

To force flowering trees or shrubs, cut branches in late winter or early spring any time after the flower buds start to swell; place them indoors in a container of water in a warm room in bright light, but not in full sun. The branches will come into bloom, depending on the time that they were cut and the indoor temperature, within a few days to a month.

FORCING HOUSEPLANTS

The third group of plants commonly forced is a group of houseplants such as poinsettia, Thanksgiving and Christmas cacti, chrysanthemums, and kalanchoe. These plants are photoperiodic, which means that their bloom cycle depends on the length of the day. Unless you properly manipulate the duration of light and darkness they receive, these plants will not be in bloom for the holidays with which they are associated.

To force these plants to bloom, they must be totally excluded from light for a specific number of hours each night over a specific number of weeks. This can be done by covering a plant with black cloth or plastic, by placing a box over a plant, or by placing a plant in a dark closet every night. During the day, you must return the plant to normal light conditions.

Poinsettias require darkness for fifteen hours per night for five weeks beginning in late September to ensure that they bloom for Christmas. Thanksgiving cacti must receive sixteen hours of darkness for four weeks starting in mid-August if they are to bloom by Thanksgiving. Christmas cacti also need sixteen hours of darkness for four weeks starting in mid-September for Christmas bloom. Kalanchoe needs fourteen hours of darkness for six weeks, beginning six weeks before the

ABOVE: *A beautiful window box of houseplants containing amaryllis, poinsettia, gerbera, and window-snow.*

BELOW: *Forcing bulbs. By forcing bulbs, you can bring spring cheer into your home during the winter. 1: Select a container that is twice as deep as the bulbs, and fill the pot three-quarters full with lightweight, soilless medium. 2: Place bulbs a pinkie's width apart. Put flat side of tulips out. Set bulb tips even with pot rim. 3: Cover with more medium and pat down gently with your hands. 4: Water thoroughly, and label with the variety and date.*

desired bloom date. Chrysanthemums need ten-and-a-half to twelve hours of darkness per night for five weeks, beginning about seven weeks before the desired bloom date.

FRAGRANCE

For some gardeners, fragrance is a bonus in the garden; for others, it is the reason for the garden. Fragrance enhances the beauty of the flowers, foliage, fruit, or form of the plants that you have chosen for your garden, or it can be the chief reason you select a particular plant.

Most scents are essential oils and are produced by glands in flowers, leaves or bark. Fragrance is one of the factors, in addition to color and form, that attracts insects to flowers and ensures pollination.

Fragrance should be considered when designing a garden. Fragrant trees and shrubs planted near windows allow a delicious aroma to pervade the house. Fragrant plants provide a nice welcome when planted by the front door or walkway. Flowering plants near patios, decks, and other outdoor living spaces increase the livability and enjoyment of those areas.

Scents can be enhanced by still, warm air, brought closer to you by a gentle breeze, or dissipated by strong winds. Keep these factors in mind when designing a fragrant garden. You may need a wall or solid fence to increase the enjoyment of the aromas.

As with any other element of garden design, plant for a succession of fragrances through the seasons. It is also a good idea to keep plants with competing fragrances away from each other.

Some plants are fragrant only at night, or more highly fragrant at night, a point that should be remembered when designing a garden. Pay attention to these plants when selecting candidates for an area that will be used in the evening. The most common of these include honeysuckle, gardenia, stock, flowering tobacco, and evening primrose.

The following chart outlines the most common plants with fragrant flowers. Keep in mind that many herbs have a highly fragrant foliage and can be included in a fragrant garden.

FRAGRANT PLANTS

Latin Name	Common Name	Type of Plant
Albizia Julibrissin	Mimosa	Tree
Buddleia Davidii	Butterfly bush; Summer lilac	Shrub
Calycanthus floridus	Carolina allspice	Shrub
Cheiranthus Cheiri	Wallflower	Biennial
Clematis paniculata	Sweet autumn clematis	Vine
Clethra alnifolia	Summer-sweet	Shrub
Convallaria majalis	Lily of the valley	Ground cover
Corylopsis species	Winter hazel	Shrub
Daphne species	Daphne	Shrub
Dianthus species	Pinks, Carnations, Sweet William	Annual, Perennial
Dictamnus albus	Gas plant	Perennial
Elaeagnus angustifolia	Russian olive	Tree
Fothergilla species	Fothergilla	Shrub
Galium odoratum	Sweet woodruff	Perennial, Herb
Gardenia jasminoides	Gardenia	Shrub
Hamamelis mollis	Chinese witch hazel	Shrub
Hesperis matronalis	Sweet rocket	Perennial
Hosta plantaginea	Fragrant plaintain lily	Perennial
Hyacinthus species	Hyacinth	Bulb
Hydrangea species	Hydrangea	Shrub, Vine
Ipomoea alba	Moonflower	Vine
Jasminum officinale	Jasmine, Poet's jessamine	Vine
Lathyrus odoratus	Sweet pea	Annual
Lavandula species	Lavender	Perennial
Lilium species	Lily	Bulb
Lindera Benzoin	Spicebush	Shrub
Lobularia maritima	Sweet alyssum	Annual
Lonicera species	Honeysuckle	Shrub, Vine
Magnolia species	Magnolia	Shrub, Tree
Malus species	Apple, Crabapple	Tree
Matthiola species	Stock	Annual
Mirabilis Jalapa	Four-o'clock	Annual
Myrtus communis	Myrtle	Shrub
Narcissus species	Daffodil	Bulb
Nicotiana alata	Flowering tobacco	Annual
Oenothera species	Evening primrose	Perennial
Osmanthus species	Devilweed	Shrub
Paeonia species	Peony	Perennial

FRAGRANT PLANTS cont.

LATIN NAME	COMMON NAME	TYPE OF PLANT
Philadelphus species	Mock orange	Shrub
Phlox species	Phlox	Perennial
Polianthes tuberosa	Tuberose	Bulb
Primula species	Primrose	Annual, Perennial
Prunus species	Cherry	Tree
Reseda odorata	Mignonette	Annual
Rosa species	Wild rose	Shrub
Skimmia japonica	Skimmia	Shrub
Styrax Obassia	Fragrant snowball	Shrub
Syringa species	Lilac	Shrub
Tilia species	Linden	Tree
Valeriana officinalis	Heliotrope	Annual, Perennial
Viburnum species	Arrowhead, Viburnum	Shrub
Viola odorata	Sweet violet	Perennial
Wisteria species	Wisteria	Vine

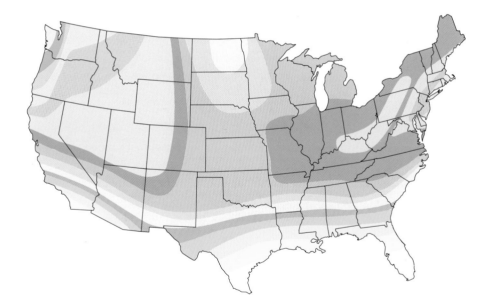

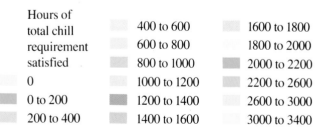

Hours of total chill requirement satisfied		
0	400 to 600	1600 to 1800
0 to 200	600 to 800	1800 to 2000
200 to 400	800 to 1000	2000 to 2200
	1000 to 1200	2200 to 2600
	1200 to 1400	2600 to 3000
	1400 to 1600	3000 to 3400

This Fruit Chill Requirement Map is based on the number of hours that temperatures are between 32° and 45° F (0° and 7° C).

FRUIT TREES

The home orchard, even if it consists of only a few trees, will delight you for years with fresh produce, and be a feast for your eyes in the landscape. Fruit trees do not need to be planted in regimented rows, although you can do this if space allows. Two or three trees can frame the house or be used as lawn specimens; they will be a delight when their white, pink, or red flowers appear in spring.

SELECTING FRUIT TREES

Climate plays a big role in selecting fruit trees. Fruit trees require cool temperatures during winter dormancy in order for them to set flower buds, and this will vary from variety to variety. All fruit varieties have known chill requirement ratings, which are the number of hours when the temperature is between 32° and 45° F (0° and 7° C). Fruit varieties also differ in hardiness, which differs from variety to variety as well as from type to type. This information is available from mail-order catalogs, garden centers, or your local county extension agent. (See **Fruit Chill Requirement Map.**)

Even if a fruit variety is hardy in your area, it may not flower and fruit if late spring frosts kill the flower buds. Where late spring frosts are common, do not choose early-blooming varieties.

Pollination requirements must also be considered when selecting fruit trees. Some trees are self-fruitful, which means they can be fertilized by blossoms from the same plant. Others need a second variety within 100 feet (30 m) for cross-pollination to take place. Self-pollinating fruits include some apples, pears, and plums, most peaches and apricots, and all nectarines and sour cherries. Those fruits that need a cross-pollinator include most apples, some pears, peaches, apricots, plums, and all sweet cherries. Cross-pollinating varieties must also bloom at the same time, and there should be plenty of bees. It is possible to buy fruit trees that have been grafted with more than one variety. These requirements are spelled out in the **Fruit Tree Chart.**

Where space is limited, there are a large number of semidwarf (12 to 15 feet [3.5 to 4.5 m] high) and dwarf (8 to 10 feet [2.5 to 3 m] high) varieties. The fruit is the same, the plants are just smaller. Semidwarfs can be planted in the ground or in containers.

Finally, some fruit varieties are best used for eating, while others are better for cooking and preserving. This information is also provided in the **Fruit Tree Chart.**

GROWING AND MAINTAINING FRUIT TREES

PLANTING FRUIT TREES

While it is possible to propagate your own fruit trees by grafting, most gardeners purchase fruit trees from their local nurseries or from mail-order sources. Fruit trees may be bought bare-root, balled and burlapped, or containerized. Plant fruit trees in full sun and protect them with a windbreak, such as an evergreen hedge, if winds are high in your area. For directions, read about **Planting** and **Soil.** Most fruit trees require a slightly acidic soil with excellent drainage.

FERTILIZING FRUIT TREES

Fruit trees like a total of 2 to 4 pounds (0.9 to 1.8 kg) of 5-10-5 per inch (25 mm) diameter of trunk, measured 4 feet (1.2 m) above the ground, with the fertilizer evenly divided over two to four feedings. The first feeding should be applied in early spring when leaf buds are first opening; the last feeding should be applied in midsummer. Be observant about the growth of your fruit trees and adjust your fertilizing practices accordingly. If new growth is poor or the leaves are yellow, increase the amount of fertilizer. If the tree is very leafy or growing very rapidly and not as much fruit is forming as expected, cut down on the amount of fertilizer. If fruit trees become susceptible to fire blight, reduce the amount of fertilizer. Also read the section on **Fertilizing.**

WATERING FRUIT TREES

Fruit trees need a deep supply of water. For effective watering, dig a ditch 6 to 12 inches (15 to 30 cm) wide around the plant at the most outward point that the branches reach. Allow water to run into the ditch from the garden hose and soak into the ground to a depth that is as deep as the root system. For young trees, this depth is 2 to 3 feet (.6 to 1 m); for large trees, the measurement is 4 to 5 feet (1.2 to 1.5 m). Penetrate the soil with a probe to test how long it will take for the water to reach the desired level, and to see how often the soil will dry out and need to be watered. Read about **Watering.**

MULCHING FRUIT TREES

Fruit trees also benefit from mulching. Spread an organic mulch 2 inches (5 cm) thick over the entire area under the branches. Do not place mulch within 6 inches (15 cm) of the trunk, or it may have problems with rot.

PRUNING FRUIT TREES

Read the section on **Pruning** as it relates to fruit trees. In addition to regular pruning, especially when trees are young, fruit trees should also be thinned to prevent overbearing, excessive disease, heavy branches, and poor, small fruit. For apple trees, fruit should be thinned every 6 inches (15 cm) along the branches after the natural fruit drop occurs in early summer. For pear trees, remove damaged or undersized fruit several weeks before harvest. Thin peaches when the fruit reaches thumbnail size; leave 6 to 8 inches (15 to 20 cm) between fruit for early-bearing varieties and 4 to 5 inches (10 to 12.5 cm) between fruit for late-bearing varieties. Apricots should be thinned so that 1 to 2 inches (25 to 50 mm) remains between fruit. Cherries and European and American hybrid plums need no thinning; Japanese plums should be thinned to one fruit every 4 to 6 inches (10 to 15 cm) when the fruit is thumbnail size.

PROTECTING FRUIT TREES

Fruit trees are subject to a number of insects and diseases and must be sprayed regularly throughout the season. Avoid applying insecticides when the plants are in bloom to prevent killing the bees; if the bees die, there will be no pollination and consequently, no fruit. Read about **Diseases and Disease Control, Insects and Insect Control,** and **Spraying.**

TOP: *Bing cherries* (PRUNUS AVIUM) *on the tree.*

MIDDLE: *It is important to prune regularly, especially when fruit trees are young, to prevent overbearing, excessive disease, heavy branches, and poor, small fruit. Always use scissors; pulling fruit off the tree can damage the spur.*

BOTTOM: *A harvest of apricots, plums, blueberries, and raspberries.*

TOP: *Moorpark apricots on the tree.*

ABOVE: *The McIntosh apple is a popular dessert-quality variety. Bearing clusters of red fruit with crisp white flesh and a sweet flavor, it is delicious for eating fresh off the tree or for making into cider. It also keeps very well.*

FRUIT TREES

APPLES

VARIETY	USES	POLLINATION
Cortland	Eating, cooking, sauce	Cross-pollinating
Empire	Eating	Cross-pollinating
Golden Delicious	Eating, cooking, sauce	Self-pollinating
Jonalicious	Eating, baking, cider	Cross-pollinating
Jonathan	Eating	Cross-pollinating
Lodi	Baking, sauce	Cross-pollinating
McIntosh	Eating, baking, cider, sauce	Cross-pollinating
Northern Spy	Eating, baking	Cross-pollinating
Red Delicious	Eating	Cross-pollinating
Rome Beauty	Baking	Self-pollinating
Stayman	Eating, cooking	Self-pollinating; doesn't pollinate other varieties

APRICOTS

Two varieties of apricots, even though they are self-pollinating, will increase your yield.

VARIETY	USES	POLLINATION
Early Golden	Eating, canning	Self-pollinating
Moorpark	Eating, canning	Self-pollinating
Riland	Cooking	Self-pollinating
Scout	Eating, canning	Self-pollinating

CHERRIES

There are two types of cherries: sweet and sour. Sweet cherries need another variety of sweet cherry as a pollinator, but not all varieties are compatible. Sour cherries are self-pollinating.

VARIETY	USES	POLLINATION
Bing (sweet)	Eating, cooking	Cross-pollinating with Windsor or Black Tartarian
Black Tartarian (sweet)	Canning	Cross-pollinating with any variety
Lambert (sweet)	Eating, canning, freezing	Cross-pollinating with Windsor
Meteor (sour)	Cooking	Self-pollinating
Montmorency (sour)	Cooking, preserving	Self-pollinating
Royal Ann (Napolean) (sweet)	Eating, canning, candy	Cross-pollinating with Windsor or Black Tartarian
Schmidt (sweet)	Eating, cooking	Cross-pollinating with Windsor or Black Tartarian
Windsor (sweet)	Cooking, canning	Cross-pollinating with any variety

FRUIT TREES cont.

PEACHES

VARIETY	USES	POLLINATION
Elberta	Eating, canning, preserving	Self-pollinating
Georgia Belle	Eating	Self-pollinating
Golden Jubilee	Eating, canning, freezing	Self-pollinating
Hale Haven	Eating, canning, freezing	Self-pollinating
J.H. Hale	Eating, canning, freezing	Cross-pollinating
Raritan Rose	Eating, canning	Self-pollinating
Red Haven	Eating, freezing	Self-pollinating
Sunhaven	Eating, canning	Self-pollinating

PEARS

VARIETY	USES	POLLINATION
Anjou	Eating, canning	Cross-pollinating
Bartlett	Eating, canning	Cross-pollinating (not Seckel)
Bosc	Eating, canning, cooking	Cross-pollinating
Clapp's Favorite	Eating, canning	Cross-pollinating
Duchess	Eating, canning, cooking	Self-pollinating
Gorham	Eating, canning	Cross-pollinating
Kieffer	Canning, cooking	Self-pollinating
Seckel	Eating, canning, cooking	Cross-pollinating (not Bartlett)

PLUMS

There are three different types of plums. The European (E) plums are mostly blue-fruited, and are used to produce prunes. The Japanese (J) plums are mostly red-fruited. The American hybrids (AH) grow well in cold climates. Most Japanese and American hybrid plums require cross-pollination, while most European plums are self-pollinating. Japanese and European plums will not pollinate each other, but American hybrids will cross pollinate with Japanese varieties.

VARIETY	USES	POLLINATION
Burbank (J)	Eating, canning	Cross-pollinating with Santa Rosa or Early Golden
Damson (E)	Jam, jelly, preserves	Self-pollinating
Early Golden (J)	Canning, cooking	Cross-pollinating with Burbank or Shiro
Green Gage (E)	Eating, cooking, preserves	Self-pollinating
Italian (E)	Eating, canning, drying	Self-pollinating
Santa Rosa (J)	Eating, canning	Self-pollinating, but gives higher yields if cross-pollinated
Shiro (J)	Eating, cooking	Cross-pollinating with Santa Rosa or Early Golden
Stanley (E)	Eating, canning, drying	Self-pollinating
Superior (AH)	Eating, canning, drying	Cross-pollinating
Underwood (AH)	Eating, canning, drying	Cross-pollinating

TOP: *Seckel pears* (PYRUS 'SECKEL').

MIDDLE: *Damson plums* (PRUNUS INSITITIA).

BOTTOM: *Peach 'Redskin' is an attractive freestone peach with rosy-red skin, orange flesh, and a delicious sweet flavor.*

FRUIT, SMALL

Small fruit are a group of plants that include cane and bush fruit: blackberries, blueberries, currants, gooseberries, raspberries, grapes, and strawberries. Small fruit are a tasty solution for gardeners who don't have the room for fruit trees. Some small fruit can be integrated into the landscape as their flowers and berries are quite showy. Grape vines can double as shading devices when grown on arbors or trellises, and strawberries make attractive ground covers.

SELECTING SMALL FRUIT

☐

BLACKBERRIES

(Rubus allegheniensis) Blackberries are a different fruit from black raspberries, although the two are often confused. Blackberries are larger and more elongated, and grow on either tall, erect canes or on trailing vines. Cane varieties thrive in cooler climates (Zones 4–8), while vining types are limited to warmer regions (Zones 8–10). Boysenberries, dewberries, and loganberries are all varieties of trailing blackberries.

BLUEBERRIES

(Vaccinium corymbosum) Blueberries are tall shrubs that have pinkish-white flowers in early spring, and produce blueberries in early summer. You should plant several plants for cross-pollination. Blueberries grow best in Zones 5–8.

CURRANTS

(Ribes sativum) Currants are shrubby plants that grow to be 5 feet (1.5 m) high. Currants have large clusters of drooping whitish flowers in mid-spring that are followed by large clusters of red berries in early summer. They are suited for Zones 5–8. Black currants are outlawed in many states because they are an alternate host for white pine blister rust.

GOOSEBERRIES

(Ribes uva-crispa) Gooseberries are tart, yellowish green, pink, or red, round fruit that are produced on thorny bushes. Because the gooseberry is an alternate host for white pine blister rust, its cultivation is banned in certain states. It grows best in Zones 5–8.

WINE GRAPES

(Vitis vinifera) Wine grapes are vining plants that can be grown on trellises, arbors, or fences. The fruits form during summer and autumn. Even though most grapes are self-fertilizing, the clusters will be larger if cross-pollination takes place; this is why it is a good idea to plant at least two varieties. Combining varieties that are early-bearing with mid- and late-season varieties also ensures a longer supply of fruit. Grapes are suited for culture in Zones 6-10.

RASPBERRIES

(Rubus spp.) Raspberry varieties fall into two categories: summer fruiting, which produce berries on the previous season's canes in early to midsummer; and everbearing, which bear fruit in early summer on the previous season's growth and rebear in autumn on the current year's growth. Red and black raspberries are the most common types of this small fruit, although there are purple and yellow varieties. Red raspberries *(Rubus idaeus)* grow on erect canes, and black raspberries *(Rubus occidentalis)* have arching canes.

BELOW: *Gooseberries* (RIBES UVA-CRISPA).

BOTTOM: *Blackberries* (RUBUS ALLEGHENIENSIS).

LEFT: *Currants* (RIBES SATIVUM).

BELOW: *Earliglow strawberries* (FRAGARIA 'EARLIGLOW').

BOTTOM: *Raspberry 'Black Hawk'* (RUBUS 'BLACK HAWK').

Raspberry canes are biennial, which means they live for two years and die after they produce fruit. Red raspberries spread by underground runners, while black raspberries form new plants wherever the tip of an old stem touches the ground. Red raspberries grow best in Zones 3-7, and black raspberries do better in Zones 4-8.

STRAWBERRIES

(*Fragaria* × *Ananassa*) Strawberries can be grown from plants or from seeds, in the ground or in containers. There are several types of strawberries. The everbearing types produce fruit in early summer and again in autumn; the autumn crop is heavier, but the berries are smaller. Everbearing strawberries require a long growing season and are not recommended for gardens in northern areas that have early frosts. June-bearing strawberries produce fruit only once in early summer, but the crop is larger than that of everbearing types. Day-neutral strawberries (strawberries that are not dependent on day length) produce berries all summer. Most strawberries reproduce by forming new plants at the ends of runners. Strawberries grow in Zones 5-10.

GROWING AND MAINTAINING SMALL FRUIT

PLANTING SMALL FRUIT

Most small fruit prefer to be planted in full sun, although currants and gooseberries like partial shade. Read about **Soil** and **Planting** before planting small fruit. Raspberries and blackberries should be planted in early spring as soon as the soil can be worked. Space raspberries and cane blackberries 30 inches (75 cm) apart in rows that are 6 to 8 feet (1.8 to 2.4 m) apart. Set plants 2 to 3 inches (5 to 7.5 cm) deeper than they grew the year before. For support, grow plants between double wires stretched along the length of the row. After planting, cut the canes back to a height of 6 to 8 inches (15 to 20 cm).

Blueberries are planted in spring or autumn, 4 to 7 feet (1.2 to 2.1 m) apart, in rows 8 feet (2.4 m) apart. Set them into the ground at the level that they previously grew. After planting, cut the tops back to 6 to 10 inches (15 to 25 cm). Birds love blueberries, so protect the fruit with a covering of netting, cheesecloth, or chicken wire.

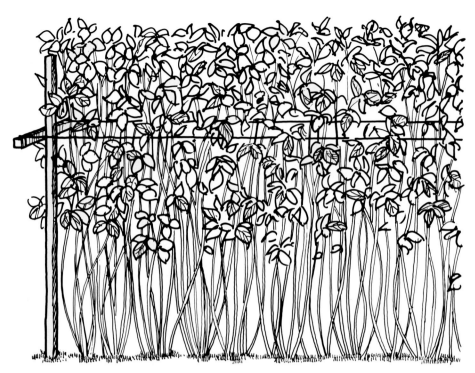

RIGHT: *Raspberries* (**RUBUS spp.**) *grow best in a row, with their canes trained against parallel wires. The wires provide needed support, and can easily be stretched along the length of the rows in which the raspberries are planted.*

BELOW: *Concord grapes* (**VITIS 'CONCORD'**).

Currants and **Gooseberries** are best planted in autumn but can be planted in spring. Set plants slightly deeper than they grew before; space them 4 to 5 feet (1.2 to 1.5 m) apart. After planting, cut the branches back to 12 inches (30 cm).

Grapes can be planted in spring or autumn, and should be placed where air circulation is good to prevent diseases. If possible, run the vines in an east/west orientation to take full advantage of the sunlight. Before setting new plants into the ground, cut the roots back to 8 to 12 inches (20 to 30 cm) and cut the tops back to the second or third set of buds.

Strawberry plants are set out in spring. Plant them so the crown of the plant is just above the soil line. There are two different methods of laying out a strawberry patch. In one, called the hill method, plants are set 12 inches (30 cm) apart in rows 18 inches (45 cm) apart, and all runners are removed as they grow. The plants grow larger, as do the strawberries, but the yield is lower. The second method, called the matted row method, calls for plants to be set 18 to 24 inches (45 to 60 cm) apart. Runners are allowed to form, and eventually the planting becomes a solid mass. The berries are smaller using this method, but the yield is higher.

PRUNING SMALL FRUIT

Cane fruit must be pruned every year to keep them in fruiting condition, and to prevent them from becoming a tangled thicket of brambles. Grapes also need yearly pruning. See **Pruning** for specific directions. Prune out old and weak branches of blueberries, currants, and gooseberries every winter before growth starts. Thin out strawberry plantings as they become crowded.

FERTILIZING SMALL FRUIT

All small fruit should be fertilized each year in early spring as growth starts (see **Fertilizing**).

WATERING SMALL FRUIT

Small fruit like regular, deep watering. A deep mulch which will protect their roots, and keep them cool and moist.

Winter protection is necessary in the colder limits of a fruit's hardiness zone. See **Winter Protection.**

FUNGICIDE

Fungicide is a chemical that kills plant diseases or prevents their spread. See **Diseases and Disease Control.**

GRAFTING

Grafting is a method of propagation in which a stem or bud from one plant is joined to the stem or roots of a second plant. See **Propagation**.

GROUND COVERS

Ground covers are low, spreading or mat-forming plants, mostly perennials, vines, or small shrubs, which are used to stabilize and beautify areas where there is little or no foot traffic. Ground covers are used as alternatives to lawns as they generally require less care. Ground covers are also useful on slopes that are difficult to mow. Many ground covers tolerate adverse growing conditions, such as poor soil and shade, that grass will not tolerate. Ground covers can also be used to unite different sections of the landscape.

SELECTING GROUND COVERS

When selecting ground covers, choose those that correspond to your garden's light and soil conditions. Not all ground covers have showy flowers, but if a flowering carpet is desired, pick plants with the bloom color and time you desire. It is wise to pick a ground cover that blooms at the same time as the trees and shrubs above it if the colors are complementary. Ground covers in the front part of the landscape will make a larger contribution to the total picture if they are evergreen. Some ground covers have attractive autumn berries, and can be used to increase the seasonal interest of the garden.

GROWING AND MAINTAINING GROUND COVERS

Ground covers can be purchased at garden centers and are usually sold in small pots or flats. Some ground covers are easy to propagate from seeds, division, or cuttings. Before planting, read the sections on **Soil** and **Planting**. When setting ground covers into a slope, stagger the plants to help prevent soil erosion.

It is difficult to set rules as to how far apart ground covers should be planted. If an immediate effect is needed, you would plant them closer together than if you have the time to wait. However, you can estimate that vining plants can be spaced 6 to 12 inches (15 to 30 cm)

apart, and perennials and shrubs at a distance equal to their ultimate width.

Ground covers, depending on the type, may need yearly thinning and heading back, or may not need attention for several years. Keep ground covers trimmed, especially at the point where they meet the lawn or walkway. An edging of brick or a metal barrier will help keep ground covers out of places where they don't belong. Most ground covers will be happy with an annual fertilizing and routine watering. Those tolerant of dry soil are indicated in the **Ground Cover Chart**.

Once ground covers have become established, weeds will have a hard time growing through their thick carpeting. However, until this has occurred, be sure to keep the planting weed-free. An attractive mulch will not only keep weeds to a minimum, it will also fill in the spaces between the plants until they mature.

BELOW: *Some ground covers, such as Cotoneaster (*Cotoneaster horizontalis*), have attractive autumn color, and can be used to create seasonal interest in the garden.*

GROUND COVERS

	PH	FC	BT	BC	L	MO	PT	HZ
Aegopodium Podograria Goutweed	12"	WHITE	ESu	—	PSh,Sh	D–M	HP	4–10
Ajuga reptans Carpet bugleweed	3"	BLUE	LSp	—	S,PSh	A	HP	3–10
Arabis caucasica Wall rock cress	6"	WHITE, PINK	MSp	—	S,LSh	A	HP	4–8
Arctostaphylos uva-ursi Common bearberry	4"	—	—	RED	S,PSh	D	ES	2–7
Calluna vulgaris Heather	10"	MIX	MSu	—	S,LSh	M	ES	4–7
Cerastium tomentosum Snow-in-summer	6"	WHITE	ESu	—	S	D	HP	2–10
Convallaria majalis Lily of the valley	6"	WHITE	MSp	—	PSh,Sh	M	HP	4–8
Cotoneaster horizontalis Rock cotoneaster	36"	WHITE	MSp	RED	S,PSh	A	ES	5–9
Epimedium species Barrenwort	9"	PINK, YELLOW	MSp	—	PSh	A–M	HP	4–10
Erica carnea Spring heath	6–18"	MIX	ESp,MSp	—	S	A	ES	3–9
Euonymus Fortunei radicans Wintercreeper	1–2'	—	—	PINK	S,Sh	A	EV	5–9
Gaultheria procumbens Wintergreen	4"	WHITE	LSp	RED	PSh	M	ES	3–10
Hedera Helix English ivy	3"	—	—	—	S,Sh	D–M	EV	6–10
Hosta species Plantain lily	1–2'	WHITE, BLUE, LAVENDER	MSu	—	PSh,Sh	A–M	HP	4–9
Iberis sempervirens Edging candytuft	12"	WHITE	MSp	—	S,PSh	A–M	EP	4–10
Juniperus chinensis Chinese juniper	18"	—	—	—	S	A–D	ES	4–9
Juniperus conferta Shore juniper	12"	—	—	—	S	A–D	ES	6–9
Juniperus horizontalis Creeping juniper	1–3'	—	—	—	S	A–D	ES	3–9

GROUND COVERS cont.

	PH	FC	BT	BC	L	MO	PT	HZ
Lamium species Dead nettle	12″	PURPLE	ESu	—	PSh,Sh	A–M	HP	4–9
Liriope species Lily turf	12″	PURPLE, WHITE	LSu	—	S,Sh	M	EP	5–10
Mesembryanthemum *crystallinum* Ice plant	4″	MIX	LSp	—	S	D	EP	9–10
Microbiota decussata Russian cypress, Siberian carpet	24″	—	—	—	S,Sh	D	ES	2–10
Pachysandra terminalis Japanese spurge	12″	WHITE	LSp	—	PSh,Sh	M	EP	5–8
Parthenocissus tricuspidata Boston ivy	9″	—	—	—	S,PSh	M	DV	4–9
Paxistima Canbyi Canby pachistima, Cliff-green, Mountain-lover	12″	WHITE, RED	ESu	—	S,PSh	M	ES	4–9
Phlox stolonifera Creeping phlox	10″	MIX	MSp	—	PSh	M	HP	4–9
Phlox subulata Moss pink, Mountain pink	6″	MIX	LSp	—	S	D	HP	3–9
Sedum species Stonecrop	2–10″	MIX	LSp,LSu	—	S,LSh	D	HP	3–10
Sempervivum tectorum Hen and chickens	6″	PINK	MSu	—	S	A–D	HP	4–10
Stachys byzantina Lamb's ears	8″	PINK, PURPLE	ESu	—	S,LSh	A	HP	4–10
Thymus species Thyme	1–2″	MIX	MSu	—	S	D	HP	4–10
Tiarella cordifolia Foamflower	6″	WHITE	MSp	—	PSh	M	HP	5–10
Vaccinium Vitis-idaea Cowberry	6″	PINK	LSp	RED	S,PSh	M	ES	3–9
Veronica repens Creeping speedwell	2″	BLUE	LSp	—	S,PSh	M	HP	5–10
Vinca minor Periwinkle, vinca	6″	BLUE	MSp	—	S,PSh	M	EV	5–10

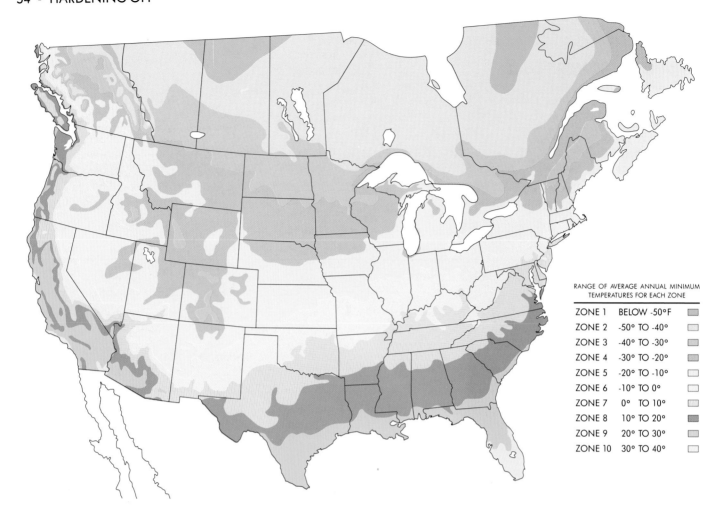

RANGE OF AVERAGE ANNUAL MINIMUM TEMPERATURES FOR EACH ZONE		
ZONE 1	BELOW -50°F	
ZONE 2	-50° TO -40°	
ZONE 3	-40° TO -30°	
ZONE 4	-30° TO -20°	
ZONE 5	-20° TO -10°	
ZONE 6	-10° TO 0°	
ZONE 7	0° TO 10°	
ZONE 8	10° TO 20°	
ZONE 9	20° TO 30°	
ZONE 10	30° TO 40°	

The U.S.D.A. Hardiness Zone Map, divided into ten zones, indicates the minimum temperature plants can withstand.

HARDENING OFF

Hardening off is the process of acclimating seedlings that were started indoors to the outdoor environment. See **Propagation**.

HARDINESS

Hardiness refers to a plant's ability to flourish within certain climatic conditions. Hardiness almost always refers to the minimum winter temperature that a plant can withstand, although other factors, such as the amount of moisture, exposure to wind and sun, soil conditions, and length of the growing season, can contribute to hardiness.

HARDINESS ZONES

The U.S. Department of Agriculture Zone Map has been developed to indicate the minimum winter temperature plants can withstand. The United States and Canada have been divided into ten zones. Zone 1 is the coldest, with winter minimum temperatures of below -50° F (-45° C); Zone 10 is the warmest, with winter minimum temperatures of 30° to 40° F (-1° to 4° C), and is often frost-free. By noting the zone in which you live, you will be able to determine which plants will grow best for you.

Throughout this book, ranges from 1 to 10 are used to indicate plant hardiness. The lower number in the range indicates the minimum winter temperature a plant can withstand, and the upper number indicates the maximum winter temperature it can withstand. For example, if a plant is hardy in Zone 5–9, it cannot withstand temperatures lower than -20° F (-29° C) but must have temperatures of at least 30° F (-1° C) in winter to force dormancy, or set growth, and/or flower buds.

Zone information, however, is only based on average winter temperatures. In any year, the winter minimum may be 5° to 10° F (3° to 6° C) higher or lower than average. As you approach the boundary lines between zones, the differences become less distinct.

MICROCLIMATES

Additionally, any given zone may have a microclimate; this is a climate that differs from the one that prevails in the zone. For example, cities with large buildings trap heat and are warmer than the surrounding suburbs. This same heat entrapment occurs in gardens surrounded by a solid wall or fence. It is also warmer on a slope with southern exposure, or where heat reflects off a south wall or the pavement. If your plants bloom in spring earlier than those in the rest of the neighborhood, your garden or yard is a warm microclimate. If they bloom later, or if you get frost when your neighbors don't, you have a cool microclimate.

It is possible, with the right microclimate and with mulching, to grow a plant that is one zone less hardy than your garden. Where snowfall is heavy, plants may survive better outside their hardiness limits, because snow is an excellent insulator. Plants can sometimes be grown in warmer climates than are ideal, if they are grown in more shade than is normally recommended.

Hardiness affects plants in other ways, too. A plant that is a shrub in the colder climates of Wisconsin may grow to be tree-size in Kentucky. A shrub that is deciduous in New York may be evergreen in Virginia. Spring naturally comes earlier in the warmer zones, and therefore, so does growth and flowering. Some shrubs that are hardy in the north may not bloom as well as in the south because their flower buds may be damaged by early spring frosts.

When selecting plants, in addition to their size, shape, use, flower color, and other aspects, consider their hardiness. No amount of care will make a plant succeed if it is grown too far out of its hardiness zone.

HEDGES

A hedge is a planting of shrubs or trees that is usually set in a straight line. A hedge can be used as a living fence to define a lot line, or divide property; it can be used for privacy, or to screen an unsightly view. Tall hedges can be used as a backdrop for lower-growing shrubs, bulbs, annuals, and perennials. Lower-growing hedges can be used to define an

Hedges can be used for a variety of purposes, from creating comfort to marking boundaries to establishing privacy. **TOP:** *This winged spindle tree serves as a windbreak for this property located along the coast.* **MIDDLE:** *This laurel hedge, fronted by short eugenia plants, was planted to provide a barrier between the house behind it and the street in front.*

ABOVE: *Purple lilac* (**SYRINGA VULGARIS**).

LEFT: LONICERA HECKROTTII *is one of the 150 or more species of the honeysuckle family.*

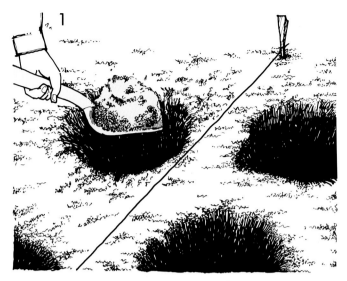

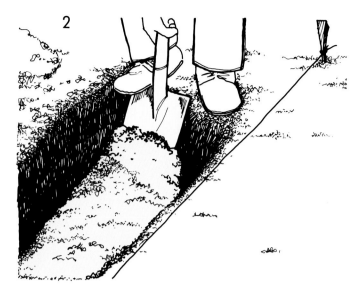

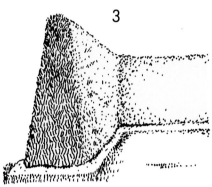

ABOVE: *Planting a hedge. 1: To create a dense hedge, set plants a little closer together than suggested, or in a double, staggered row. 2: To create a straight hedge, use the trench method. A trench the width of two shovel blades is suitable for most young plants. 3: Mature hedges should be trimmed so that they taper from top to bottom.*

area without blocking a view. Hedges also act as windbreaks and buffer street noise. Flowering shrubs and trees can add a wall of color, too.

SELECTING HEDGES

Almost any tree or shrub can be used as a hedge, but for the best results, you should choose a plant with a uniform growth habit, heavy branching, and dense foliage. Where year-round privacy or screening is needed, choose evergreen rather than deciduous plants. When the hedge is made from thorny plants such as barberry, pyracantha, or rose, it discourages trespassing. Where space is tight, pick an upright, columnar plant rather than one with a wide, spreading base.

Hedges may be either informal or formal in character; this look depends on the plant you select and the way you prune it. The style of your home and the rest of your garden largely determines the type of hedge to choose.

GROWING AND MAINTAINING HEDGES

Caring for a hedge is almost the same as caring for a shrub or tree. Read the growing and maintenance sections under **Trees** and **Shrubs** to find out specifics on fertilizing and watering.

PLANTING HEDGES

When planting a hedge, set several stakes along the hedge line, and tie string between them to make sure the hedge is straight. To create a dense hedge, set plants a little closer together than ordinarily suggested, or set the plants in a double, staggered row.

PRUNING HEDGES

Newly planted deciduous hedges should be pruned back by about one-third to encourage compact, dense growth. While informal hedges may not require any more than an annual trimming, a formal hedge will need more constant pruning, perhaps several times a year, to keep it trim and neat. When pruning a hedge, make sure the base of the hedge is wider than the top so that sun will fall on the bottom branches and keep them full and dense.

HERBACEOUS

Herbaceous describes plants whose tops die to the ground during the winter, as opposed to woody plants like trees and shrubs, whose tops remain alive even though they are dormant.

HERBICIDE

Herbicides are chemicals used to destroy plant material, and usually refer to weed killers, although herbicides can kill any type of plant. Herbicides are classified as pre-emergent, which means that the seeds are killed before they germinate, or post-emergent, which means that the plant is destroyed while in active growth.

HEDGES

Latin Name	Common Name	Type of Plant
Berberis Thunbergii	Japanese barberry	Deciduous
Buxus species	Boxwood	Evergreen
Camellia species	Camellia	Evergreen
Carpinus betulus	European hornbeam	Deciduous
Chaenomeles species	Flowering quince	Deciduous
Chamaecyparis species	False cypress	Evergreen
Cotoneaster species	Cotoneaster	Deciduous, Evergreen
Crataegus monogyna	English hawthorn	Deciduous
× *Cupressocyparis Leylandii*	Leyland cypress	Evergreen
Elaeagnus angustifolia	Russian olive	Deciduous
Euonymus japonica	Spindle tree	Evergreen
Fagus sylvatica	European beech	Deciduous
Forsythia species	Forsythia	Deciduous
Hydrangea species	Hydrangea	Deciduous
Ligustrum species	Privet	Deciduous, Evergreen
Lonicera tatarica	Tatarian honeysuckle	Deciduous
Mahonia Aquifolium	Oregon grape holly	Evergreen
Osmanthus species	Devilweed	Evergreen
Philadelphus species	Mock orange	Deciduous
Pyracantha species	Fire thorn	Evergreen
Rhamnus Frangula	Buckthorn	Deciduous
Rosa species	Wild rose	Deciduous
Spiraea species	Spirea	Deciduous
Syringa species	Lilac	Deciduous
Taxus species	Yew	Evergreen
Thuja species	Arborvitae	Evergreen
Tsuga canadensis	Canada hemlock	Evergreen
Viburnum species	Arrowwood, Viburnum	Deciduous

HERBS

An herb is any plant that is valued for its medicinal, flavorful, or aromatic qualities. Herbs are used as seasonings in food and drink and as garnishes. They are also used as dried flowers, in cosmetics and soaps, and to repel insects. Herbs are classified as being annual, biennial, or perennial. Whether the leaves, flowers, seeds, roots, or stems are harvested for use depends on the plant.

Annual herbs may be either hardy or tender. Hardy annuals will withstand light frost; tender annuals are killed by frost and must not be planted until all danger of frost has passed in spring. Some herbs that are perennials in warm climates may be grown as annuals in colder areas. Additionally, some herbs that are biennials can also be grown as annuals.

SELECTING HERBS

When selecting herbs, you should choose plants that can thrive in the climate and growing conditions of your garden, as well as consider whether you want to grow annuals or perennials. Then you should also consider their visual impact and what you would like to use them for.

Herbs have definite climatic preferences. Some herbs prefer cool growing conditions, while others must have hot climates. Each biennial and perennial herb has a range of hardiness zones in which it will grow; there is a minimum winter temperature each will endure, and some must have freezing temperatures in winter to grow well. Herbs also have preferences for sun or shade, and although most prefer dry soil, some need moist soil conditions. The **Herb Chart** outlines the environmental needs for the most popular herbs. See also **Hardiness**.

DESIGNING WITH HERBS

If you have space in your garden, you can easily design an herb garden. Traditional designs include knot gardens and wagon wheels, although herbs can be planted in beds and borders like other plants. Where space is limited, herbs can be mixed into flower beds and borders, integrated into vegetable gardens, grown in pots, or as edgings, depending on their size and growth habit. Most herbs are delightfully fragrant and can be used near outdoor living spaces or open windows. Many have gray or colored foliage that can be used to accent or buffer other plants. Caraway and dill have attractive, finely cut foliage that makes a nice contrast to coarser plants. Low-growing thyme and mint can be used as ground covers. Basil, chives, marjoram, and parsley can be grown indoors on a windowsill.

For more information, read the section on **Container Gardening**, **Fragrance** and **Landscaping Design**.

GROWING AND MAINTAINING HERBS

PLANTING HERBS

Depending on the individual plant, herbs are propagated by seeds, cuttings, divisions, or layering. The **Herb Chart** outlines the various methods of propagation for each herb; read the appropriate sections under **Propagation** for specific instructions.

If an herb can be propagated by seed, you can start your own seeds indoors in early spring, or sow them directly into the garden, depending on the plant. Cumin, germander, lemon balm, rosemary, savory, sesame, and wormwood should be started indoors; borage, caraway, and horehound should be started in the garden. Other herbs can be seeded as desired.

If you do not wish to propagate your own herbs, you can buy plants at the garden center or from mail-order catalogs. Select plants that are healthy in appearance and preferably not in bloom; smell or taste a little piece of the leaf if it is an herb whose foliage is used to make sure you like its aroma or flavor. Be sure to water plants regularly until planting time.

As for planting, hardy annuals can be planted as soon as the soil can be worked in early to mid-spring, about four weeks before the last frost. Those herbs that are tender annuals can not be planted until the spring when all danger of frost has passed. Perennials and bien-

nials can be added to the garden any time from mid-spring until about six weeks before the first autumn frost. If you are growing the plants as annuals, they should be planted in spring. The **Herb Chart** outlines planting distances, but you can also check the seed packet or plant label.

Before planting, read the sections on **Soil**, **Planting**, and **Transplanting**.

HERBS' SOIL AND FERTILIZATION NEEDS

Herbs vary in their need for rich or poor, fertile or infertile soil. Too much organic matter and/or fertilizer can ruin the flavor of some herbs (see the **Herb Chart** for individual soil and moisture requirements). If an herb needs poor soil, add no organic matter when preparing the soil; if it needs rich soil, be extremely generous with organic matter. If an herb likes infertile soil, never add fertilizer. Otherwise, incorporate a bal-

BELOW: *Anise hyssop* (AGASTACHE FOENICULUM).

RIGHT: *A traditional herb knot garden.*

anced fertilizer such as 5-10-5 into the soil before planting herbs; no further feeding will be necessary during their growing season. Feed biennial and perennial herbs as long as they don't prefer infertile soil at the beginning of each growing season. See also **Fertilizing**.

WATERING HERBS

Many herbs like dry soil; soil that is too wet can ruin their flavor or cause them to rot. Herbs with average moisture requirements should receive 1 inch (25 mm) of water per week; adjust the amount of water for those that prefer dry or moist soils. Refer to **Watering.**

PRUNING HERBS

If an herb is growing too tall and lanky, pinch out the central growing tip to keep it compact and bushy. If an herb is being grown for its foliage, remove flower buds to keep the leaves more flavorful. Some herbs are invasive growers, but this tendency can be kept in check by removing flowers before they drop seeds, or by installing edgings of metal or stone as barriers.

PROTECTING HERBS IN THE WINTER

Herbs may need winter protection if grown near their hardiness limit. Some herbs are damaged by poorly drained soil during the winter; improve drainage if you encounter this problem.

In autumn, after herbs are killed by frost, they should be removed from the beds to remove breeding sites for insects and diseases, and for a better visual appearance of your garden.

Most herbs are relatively problem-free, but you may want to refer to **Diseases and Disease Control** and **Insects and Insect Control**. Also read **Mulching, Staking and Tying**, and **Weeds**.

HARVESTING HERBS

Fresh herb leaves have more flavor than dried leaves, and are usually most flavorful before the plants bloom. Harvest leaves for fresh or dried use whenever they are large enough; cut them off the plant on a dry, sunny morning after the dew has dried. If you are harvesting flowers, cut them off when they are one-third to two-thirds open and dry. Several weeks after the flowers have faded, the seeds will be ready for harvest, and often change color at this point. As seeds begin to form, cut the stems and hang them indoors, upside down in a paper bag, so the seeds will fall into the bag. You should cut stems or dig roots at the end of your herbs' growing season.

To learn how to dry your herbal bounty, read **Drying Plants**.

TOP: *Scented-leaf geranium* (PELARGONIUM GRAVEOLENS).

MIDDLE: *Variegated sage* (SALVIA OFFICINALIS VARIEGATA).

BOTTOM: *Island beds of summer annuals in a formal courtyard garden. The beds are edged with dwarf red barberry and dwarf Japanese holly. Junipers have been pruned to topiary shapes for an old-fashioned American Colonial look.*

HERBS

Herb	PT HZ	PH	FC BT	PPH	U	P	PD	L	T	S
Agastache Foeniculum Anise hyssop	P 3–10	3–4'	BLUE ASu	L,R	D,M	S,D,C	18"	S,LSh	A	D,A I
Allium sativum Garlic	TA	36"	WHITE MSu	R	C	S, Cl	3–4"	S	A	M
Allium Schoenoprasum Chives	P 3–10	8–24"	PURPLE MSp	L,F	C	S,D	6–8"	S,LSh	A	M R
Aloysia triphylla Lemon verbena	P/A 9–10	36"	WHITE, LILAC LSu	L	D,P	C	2–5'	S	A	M R
Anethum graveolens Dill	HA	24–36"	YELLOW MSu	L,S	C	S	4–8"	S	A	M
Angelica Archangelica Angelica	B 4–10	5'	WHITE ESu	L,St,S,R	C	S	3'	S,LSh	H	M
Anthriscus Cerefolium Chervil	HA	24"	WHITE MSp	L	C	S	6–8"	LSh, PSh,Sh	C	M R
Armoracia rusticana Horseradish	P 4–10	24"	WHITE ESu	R	C	C	12"	S,PSh	A	M R
Artemisia Absinthium Absinthe, Wormwood	P 2–10	36"	YELLOW LSu	L	I	S,D,C	18"	S	A	D–M
Artemisia Dracunculus var. *sativa* Tarragon	P 5–8	36"	RARE MSu	L	C	D,C	12–24"	S,LSh	A	A R
Borago officinalis Borage	HA	2–3'	BLUE ASu	L,F	C,G	S	12"	S,LSh	A	D I,P
Calendula officinalis Pot marigold	HA	6–24"	YELLOW, GOLD, ORANGE MSp,Su	F	F,G,C, D,P	S	12–15"	S,LSh	C	M R
Carthamus tinctorius Safflower	TA	36"	YELLOW ASu	F	C,P,F	S	10"	S	A	A
Carum Carvi Caraway	B 3–10	24–30"	WHITE ASu	L,S,R	C	S	6–9"	S	A	D
Chamaemelum nobile Russian Chamomile	P 4–10	6"	WHITE LSu	F	D,M, Co	S,C	3–4"	S,LSh	C	D–M P
Coriandrum sativum Coriander	HA	30"	WHITE, PINK LSu	L,S	C	S	8–10"	S	A	M
Crocus sativus Saffron	P 6–10	6–8"	LAVENDER A	F	C	Co	3–4"	S,LSh	A	M
Cuminum Cyminum Cumin	TA	6"	WHITE, ROSE ASu	S	C	S	6"	S	H	A

HERBS cont.

HERB	PT HZ	PH	FC BT	PPH	U	P	PD	L	T	S
Cymbopogon citratus Lemongrass	P/A 10	6'	—	L	C,D,P	D	3'	S	H	M
Foeniculum vulgare Fennel	P/A 9–10	4–5'	YELLOW ASu	L,S,St	C	S	8–12"	S	A	D-M
Galium odoratum Sweet woodruff	P 4–10	6–8"	WHITE LSp	L	D,P	D,C	12–15"	PSh,Sh	A	M R,I
Hedeoma pulegioides American pennyroyal	HA	12"	BLUE ASu	L	P,I	S	12–24"	S,LSh	C	M R
Hyssopus officinalis Hyssop	P 3–7	18–24"	VIOLET ESu	L,F	D,M,H	S,D,C	12–18"	S,LSh	A	D
Lavandula angustifolia English lavender	P 5–10	18–24"	VIOLET ASu	F	C,P,Co	S,C	12"	S	A	D I
Levisticum officinale Lovage	P 3–8	36"	YELLOW ASu	L,S,St	C	S,D	12–15"	S,LSh	A	M R
Marrubium vulgare Horehound	P 3–10	18–24"	WHITE ASu	L,F	D,M	S,D,C	8–10"	S	A	D,A P
Matricaria recutita Sweet false chamomile	HA	24–30"	WHITE ASu	F	D,M	S	8"	S,LSh	C	D-M P
Melissa officinalis Lemon balm	P 4–10	24"	WHITE ASu	L	D,C	S,D,C	18"	LSh	A	D-M P
Mentha species Mint	P 3–10	12–18"	PURPLE MSu	L	C,D	S,D,C	12–24"	S,LSh	A	A,M R
Mentha Pulegium English pennyroyal	P 3–10	6"	BLUE ASu	L	P,I	D,C	12–24"	S,LSh	C	M R
Monarda didyma Bee balm	P 4–10	2–4'	MIX ASu	L	D	S,D,C	12"	S,LSh	A	D,A I,P
Myrrhis odorata Sweet cicely	P 3–8	24"	WHITE LSp	L,S,St	C,D	S,C	2'	Sh	A	M R
Nasturtium officinale Watercress	B 6–10	3"	YELLOW LSp	L	C,G	S,D	12–15"	Sh	C	M
Nepeta Cataria Catnip	P 3–10	24–48"	VIOLET ESu	L	D	S,D	18–24"	S,PSh	A	D I,P
Ocimum Basilicum Basil	TA	18–24"	WHITE, PURPLE ASu	L	C	S	10–12"	S	A	A
Origanum species Oregano	P,A 5–10	18–24"	PURPLE, PINK MSu	L	C	S,D,C	12"	S	A	A I,P

HERBS cont.

HERB	PT HZ	PH	FC BT	PPH	U	P	PD	L	1	S
Origanum Majorana Sweet marjoram	P/A 9–10	8–10″	PINK MSu	L	C	S,C	6–8″	S	A	A
Pelargonium species Scented geranium	P/A	12–48″	WHITE LSp–A	L	C,D	S,C	12–24″	S	A	A
Perilla frutescens Beefsteak plant	TA	18–36″	LILAC LSu	L,F	C	S	12–15″	S,LSh	A	D R
Petroselinum crispum Parsley	B/A 3–10	8–12″	GREEN LSp	L	C,G	S	6–8″	S,LSh	A	A R
Pimpinella Anisum Anise	HA	18–24″	WHITE ESu	L,S	C	S	6–9″	S	A	D
Poterium Sanguisorba Burnet	P 3–10	18–24″	WHITE, PINK ESu, MSu	L	C,D	S,D	15″	S	A	D I,P
Rosmarinus officinalis Rosemary	P/A 8–10	1–5′	BLUE ESp	L	C,Co	S,D,C,L	12–18″	S,PSh	A	A
Ruta graveolens Rue	P 4–10	18–36″	YELLOW MSu	L	H,I	S,D,C	6–12″	S	A	M P
Salvia officinalis Sage	P 3–10	18–24″	VIOLET, PINK ESu	L	C,D	S,D,C	12–18″	S,LSh	A	A,M
Santolina Chamaecyparissus Lavender cotton	P 6–10	18–24″	YELLOW LSu	L,F	P,H,I	S,D,C	18″	S	A	D P
Satureja hortensis Summer savory	HA	12–18″	LILAC ASu	L	C	S	4–6″	S	A	M P
Satureja montana Winter savory	P 5–10	6–12″	PINK, WHITE LSu	L	C	S,D,L	12–15″	S	A	M P
Sesamum indicum Sesame	TA	24–36″	WHITE, ROSE ASu	S	C	S	6″	S	H	A
Tanacetum vulgare Tansy	P 3–10	48″	YELLOW LSu	L,F	F,I,P	S,D	12–18″	S	A	M R
Teucrium Chamaedrys Germander	P 5–10	10–12″	PURPLE LSu	—	H	S,D,C	12″	S,PSh	H	D,A
Thymus vulgaris Thyme	P 5–10	6–12″	BLUE ASu	L	C	S,D,C,L	10″	S	A	D P

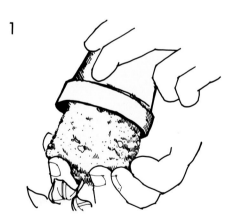

ABOVE: *This creative container garden includes orchids, dracaena, asparagus, and false aralia.*

BELOW: *Repotting houseplants. 1: Being careful not to disturb roots, remove plant from pot. 2: Loosen roots before repotting to ensure new growth. 3: Hold plant at proper level in new pot; fill in under and around roots with potting medium. 4: Hold plant loosely by stem; pack soil with fingers.*

HOTBEDS

Hotbeds are coldframes equipped with heating systems. See **Coldframes and Hotbeds**.

HOUSEPLANTS

About 150 years ago, gardeners discovered that they could grow plants inside to bring color and liveliness into their homes. Houseplants allow you to garden all year, and their flowers or diverse foliage can enhance your home's interior decor.

SELECTING HOUSEPLANTS

Like garden plants, houseplants vary in their requirements for light, temperature, and humidity, so you need to choose those that will grow well in your home. The **Houseplant Chart** outlines the various environmental conditions that houseplants need. You can place houseplants almost anywhere that their

growing conditions are met. If appropriate light is not available, however, you can grow them under fluorescent lights.

When you buy houseplants at a garden center or greenhouse, look for healthy plants that have no signs of insects and diseases. Once you bring the plant home, it may take several weeks for it to acclimate to its new surroundings; it may lose leaves, but will recover as it adjusts to the lower light of your house. It's a good idea to keep the humidity high during this transition period.

It is easy to increase your houseplant collection by propagating your own. Depending on the specific plant, you can do this by division, stem cuttings, leaf cuttings, air layering, offshoots, or seeds. Read about these different methods under **Propagation**.

GROWING AND MAINTAINING HOUSEPLANTS

HOUSEPLANTS' SOIL NEEDS

Most houseplants should be grown in a soilless medium of 50% organic matter and 50% inorganic matter. The organic portion can be made up of peat moss or bark; the inorganic portion can be made up of perlite, vermiculite, or coarse sand. You can either make your own, or purchase potting medium. Houseplants that like moist soil will benefit from a potting medium that is higher in organic matter than normal, while those that like dry soil should have more inorganic matter added to their potting medium.

CONTAINERS FOR HOUSEPLANTS

Containers for houseplants can be plastic, clay, ceramic, or metal. The most important things to consider when choosing a container are its size (keep it in proportion to the size of the plant) and drainage holes. If a decorative pot has no drainage holes, use it only as an outside container, or fill the bottom of it with several inches (mm) of coarse gravel.

REPOTTING HOUSEPLANTS

When plants outgrow their containers, you'll need to repot them. Select a new or clean pot that is slightly larger than the original one. Remove the plant care-

1

2
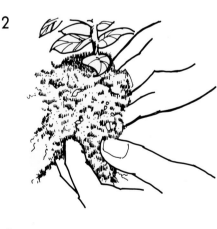

3
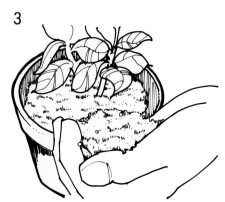

4

RIGHT: *Lipstick plant* (AESCHYANTHUS PULCHER).

BELOW: *Zebra plant* (APHELANDRA SQUAROSSA).

BOTTOM: *A collection of potted tulips, hyacinths, and narcissus.*

fully from the pot so as not to disturb the roots too much and, holding the plant at the right level in its new pot, fill in under and around the roots with potting medium. When repotting plants, loosen the roots before repotting to ensure new, free root growth. Most plants need watering immediately after repotting to eliminate air pockets, although cacti and succulents should sit for a few days before watering to prevent rot.

HOUSEPLANTS' LIGHT REQUIREMENTS

Houseplants need varying amounts of light. A sunny windowsill without curtains that supplies at least four hours of sun each day is considered a source of direct light. In winter, only south-facing windows will supply direct light. East-, west-, and south-facing windows supply direct light the rest of the year. Bright light, between one and four hours of direct sun each day, can be supplied in north-facing, uncurtained windows in summer and in east- and west-facing windows in winter. With indirect light, direct sun never hits the plant's leaves. In summer, plants requiring indirect light should be up to 5 feet (1.5 m) from an unobstructed window, or grown on the sill of a curtained window. In winter, indirect light is found on north-facing windows.

WATERING HOUSEPLANTS

Watering is probably the largest cause of houseplant problems. Plants can suffer equally from either too much or too little water. It is best not to water on a reg-

ular schedule, because variables such as temperature, light, and humidity change from day to day. In fact, two identical plants will have different water needs if their containers are of a different size. Plants need less water in the short days of winter than they do when they are actively growing the rest of the year. You must feel the planting medium to determine when to water.

Water requirements are outlined in the **Houseplant Chart.** Plants that require dry soil should not be watered until the top 1/2 inch (12.5 mm) of the medium is dry. Plants with average water needs should be watered when the medium surface becomes dry. Plants that like moist conditions should always have a moist surface, but you should never allow the medium to be soggy. Water your plants with warm water, and be careful not to wet the leaves. You should water until the water flows from the drainage holes at the bottom of the pot. Empty the saucer after the water has drained so that the roots do not sit in water. You can also water your plants by placing them in a sink or bucket of water; they'll absorb water from the bottom.

HOUSEPLANTS' TEMPERATURE NEEDS

Temperature needs for houseplants also vary. Refer to the **Houseplant Chart** for specifics. Plants generally prefer it if night temperatures are about 10° F (6° C) lower than daytime temperatures. Plants should be kept out of drafts, away from radiators and air conditioners, and from cold windows in winter.

HOUSEPLANTS

	PT	L	T	MO	HU	P
Abutilon species Flowering maple	Fl	D	A	M	H	SC,S
Achimenes hybrids Magic flower	Fl	B	W	M	H	S,SC
Adiantum Capillus-Veneris Southern maidenhair fern	Fo	I	A	M	H	D
Aechmea fasciata Urn plant	Fl	B	A	A	M–H	O
Aeschynanthus species Lipstick plant	Fl	D	W	M	H	SC
Agave Victoriae-Reginae Century plant	Fo	D	A	D	L	S,O
Aglaonema species Chinese evergreen	Fo	I	A	D	M	D,A
Aloe species Aloe	Fo	D	A	D	L	O
Anthurium species Tailflower	Fl	I	A–W	M	H	D
Aphelandra squarrosa Zebra plant	Fl	B	A	M	A–H	SC
Ardisia crenata Coralberry	Fl	B–D	C	M	H	S
Asparagus species Asparagus fern	Fo	B	A–C	M	M	D
Aspidistra elatior Cast-iron plant	Fo	I–B	C	D	M	D
Asplenium nidus Bird's nest fern	Fo	I–B	A–C	M	H	D
Aucuba japonica Japanese aucuba	Fo	B	C–A	M	L–M	SC
Beaucarnea recurvata Ponytail plant	Fo	D	A	D	L	O
Begonia species Begonia	Fo,Fl	B–I	A–W	A	M–H	S,D,LC,SC
Brassaia actinophylla Australian umbrella tree	Fo	B–I	W	D	H	S,A
Various genera of the family *Cactaceae* Cactus, varied	Fo,Fl	D	A–W	D	L	S,O

HOUSEPLANTS cont.

	PT	L	T	MO	HU	P
Calceolaria species Pocketbook flower	Fl	B	C	A–M	M	S,SC
Chamaedora elegans Parlor palm	Fo	B	W	M	H	D,O
Chlorophytum comosum Spider plant	Fo	B	A	A	M	D,O
Chrysanthemum × morifolium Chrysanthemum	Fl	D	A	M	M	LC
Cissus rhombifolia Grape ivy, Venezuela treebine	Fo	B–I	A	D	M	SC
Clerodendrum species Glory bower	Fl	B	W	A–M	A	SC
Columnea species Columnea	Fl	B	A–W	M	H	SC,D,S
Cordyline terminalis Ti plant	Fo	D	A–W	A	H	SC,A
Crassula argentea Jade plant	Fo	D	A	D	L	SC
Croton variegatum pictum Croton	Fo	D	W	M	M–H	SC,A
Cycas revoluta Sago palm	Fo	B	A	M	L–M	S
Cyclamen persicum Florist's cyclamen	Fl	D	C	M	M–H	S
Dieffenbachia species Dumb cane	Fo	B	A	A	M–H	SC,A
Dizygotheca elegantissima False aralia	Fo	B	W	A	H	S
Dracaena species Dracena	Fo	B	A–W	D	M–H	SC,A,O
Epipremnum aureum Pothos	Fo	B	A	D	M	SC
Episcia species Carpet plant	Fl	B	W	M	H	SC
Euphorbia pulcherrima Poinsettia	Fl	D	A	M	M	SC
Exacum affine Persian violet	Fl	B	A	M	A–H	S

HOUSEPLANTS cont.

	PT	L	T	MO	HU	P
Fatsia japonica Japanese fatsia	Fo	B–D	C–A	D	L–M	S,SC
Ficus benjamina Weeping fig	Fo	D	A–W	D–A	M	SC
Ficus elastica Rubber plant	Fo	D	A–W	D–A	M	A
Fittonia Verschaffeltii Nerve plant	Fo	I–B	W	M	M–H	SC
Fuchsia hybrids Fuchsia	Fl	D	A	M	H	SC
Gardenia jasminoides Gardenia	Fl	D	C	M	H	SC
Gynura aurantiaca Purple passion plant	Fo	B	W	M	H	SC
Hedera species Ivy	Fo	B	C–A	M	M	SC
Hippeastrum hybrids Amaryllis	Fl	D	A–W	M	A	O
Hoya carnosa Wax plant	Fo,Fl	D	A	D	L	SC
Iresine herbstii Bloodleaf	Fo	D	A	A	M	SC
Kalanchoe species Kalanchoe	Fo,Fl	D	A	D	L	S,SC,LC
Lilium longiflorum eximium Easter lily	Fl	B	C	M	M	O
Maranta leuconeura Prayer plant	Fo	B	A	M	M–H	D
Monstera deliciosa Swiss-cheese plant	Fo	B	W	A	M–H	SC,A
Nephrolepis exaltata Boston fern	Fo	B	A	M	H	D
Pelargonium species Geranium	Fl,Fo	D	A	M	M	S,SC
Peperomia species Radiator plant	Fo	B	A–W	A	M–H	LC,SC,D
Philodendron species Philodendron	Fo	B	A–W	A	M	SC,A

HOUSEPLANTS cont.

	PT	L	T	MO	HU	P
Pilea species Pilea	Fo	I–B	W	A	M–H	SC
Pittosporum Tobira Pittosporum	Fo	B	C	D	L–M	SC
Plectranthus australis Swedish ivy	Fo	B	A	D–A	M	SC
Primula species Primrose	Fl	B	C	M	H	S
Saintpaulia species and hybrids African violet	Fl	B	A	A–M	H	SC,LC,D,S
Sansevieria trifasciata Snake plant	Fo	B–D	A–W	D	M	O,LC,D
Schlumbergera Bridgesii Christmas cactus	Fl	B	C–A	M	H	SC,S
Schlumbergera truncata Thanksgiving cactus	Fl	B	C–A	M	H	SC,S
Sedum Morganianum Burro's tail	Fo	D	A–W	D	M	D,LC,SC
Senecio × hybridus Cineraria	Fl	D	C	M	M	S,SC
Sinningia speciosa Gloxinia	Fl	B	W	M	M	LC,S
Solanum Pseudocapsicum Jerusalem cherry	Fl	D	A	D	M	S
Spathiphyllum species Spathe flower	Fl,Fo	I	A	M	M	D
Streptocarpus species and hybrids Cape primrose	Fl	B	W	M	M–H	D,S,LC
Syngonium podophyllum Arrowhead vine	Fo	B	W	D	M–H	SC
Tolmiea Menziesii Piggyback plant	Fo	B	C–A	D	M	O
Tradescantia fluminensis, *Zebrina pendula* Wandering Jew	Fo	B	A	D	M	SC

Two methods of creating humidity. Place damp moss between potted plant and larger pot, FAR LEFT, *or set plant on pebbles in dish or tray of shallow water,* LEFT.

BELOW: *Many houseplants, among them this Barbados aloe (*ALOE BARBADENSIS*), thrive when placed outdoors for summer.*

BOTTOM: *A terrarium planting of various carnivorous plants.*

HOUSEPLANTS' HUMIDITY NEEDS

Houseplants whose native habitats are tropical jungles need a high humidity level, or more than 50%. Moderate humidity needs are in the 30% to 50% range, while low humidity levels, required by plants native to deserts, are less than 30%. Heated homes in winter have low humidity. To raise the humidity to its needed level, use a humidifier, or grow plants on trays filled with pebbles and water. Misting plants in order to raise humidity has very limited effectiveness. If foliage turns brown from heat or dry conditions, cut it off with a sharp scissors.

FERTILIZING HOUSEPLANTS

Houseplants do not have constant nutritional needs. If plants are actively growing or flowering, they should be fertilized with a soluble fertilizer such as 20-20-20. It is best to feed houseplants at quarter strength every week than to feed them once a month, as this encourages a more even growth. When plants stop growing, particularly during the short days of winter, fertilizing should stop, too. These rules do not apply to plants grown under fluorescent lights, as they have no summer or winter as such. If you accidentally overfeed a houseplant, flush the medium with water until the runoff water is colorless. See **Fertilizing**.

CLEANING HOUSEPLANTS

Large, smooth-leaved plants collect dust and should be wiped clean on a regular basis. Fuzzy-leaved plants will also collect dust and can be cleaned with a small paintbrush. Flowers of blooming houseplants should be removed as they fade.

BRINGING HOUSEPLANTS OUTDOORS

Many houseplants benefit from being moved outdoors for the summer. Place them in a partially shaded spot and continue to give them regular care. Move them back indoors in early autumn, and inspect them carefully for any signs of insects and/or diseases; treat your plants if necessary.

TREATING DISEASED HOUSEPLANTS

Insects and diseases can trouble houseplants. Keeping water off of the leaves, and ensuring that the air circulation is good will reduce many diseases. If insects or diseases attack, and treatment is necessary, spraying indoors is not recommended. Make a solution of insecticide or fungicide in a bucket and plunge the entire plant into it, rinsing it with clear water afterwards. In summer, plants can be taken outside to be sprayed. Always move an infested or infected plant away from the others until the problem has been corrected. Read about **Diseases and Disease Control** and **Insects and Insect Control**.

USING FLUORESCENT LIGHTING TO GROW HOUSEPLANTS

Fluorescent lights allow you to grow plants anywhere in your home. Plants need cool blue and violet light to grow

foliage, and warm red and orange light to produce flowers; this is why you should use cool white fluorescent lights for foliage plants, and a combination of both cool white and warm white bulbs for flowering plants.

You can also use special fluorescent lights for growing plants instead of regular bulbs. Wide-spectrum lights should be used for flowering plants. Incandescent lights give off a lot of red light, but they are usually not recommended for plants as they also emit a lot of heat.

CHOOSING APPROPRIATE LIGHT INTENSITY

You need to experiment to determine if your plants are receiving the right amount of light. If the light level is too low, growth will be leggy, leaves will turn yellow, and flowering will be poor. If the light is too high, growth will be compact and the foliage may burn. To increase intensity, you can use longer tubes and reflectors, install more tubes, or place them closer together. You can also try moving the plants closer to the tubes, or burning the lights longer. It is helpful to remember that light intensity is higher at the center of fluorescent

tubes than it is at the ends. Old lights may not be giving off enough light, even though their loss of light is not visible to the eye, so you should replace the tubes. To decrease light intensity, you may want to try the opposite of the measures just discussed.

Flowering plants need more light than foliage plants. Foliage plants will grow well if the lights are on for twelve hours a day. Flowering plants need fourteen to sixteen hours of light each day. Some plants will flower only when the day-length is a certain number of hours; read about **Forcing** for specifics. A timer is the most efficient way to make sure your plants have the proper light exposure.

Otherwise, all aspects of caring for plants grown under fluorescent lights are the same as caring for houseplants grown in natural light.

HYBRID

A hybrid is the product of two different species or varieties that have been crossed to produce a third plant with the best qualities of both.

BELOW: *A bromeliad* (AECHMEA FASCIATA).

BELOW RIGHT: *A healthy monkey-faced pansy* (ACHIMENES **spp.**).

INSECTS AND INSECT CONTROL

Unfortunately, insects like to feast on plants, which causes varying amounts of damage. They may chew holes in leaves and flowers, spread disease, and can even kill a plant. Insects must be controlled if you are to have a healthy, productive garden.

METHODS OF INSECT CONTROL

Many insects are large enough to be visible, and identifying them is usually easier than diagnosing the diseases they cause, which allows easier control.

WEEDING

Several cultural practices can reduce the chances of insect attack. Keeping your garden weed-free is the primary way to fight insects. Because insects often lay eggs and live in weeds, their elimination frees the garden of breeding sites. It is also wise to keep a close eye on the garden to catch early infestations, or signs of egg sacs before the insects do serious damage.

INSECTICIDES—CONTACT AND SYSTEMIC

Insecticides are another method used to control insects. Some insecticides are organic or biological, and will not harm birds or pets. Other insecticides are toxic, and should be treated with care. Do not use insecticides unless you have to.

Insecticides are classified as being either contact or systemic. Contact insecticides kill the insect on contact and must be sprayed directly onto it. Systemic insecticides are taken up by the plant and poison the insects as they eat plant parts. Other insecticides, such as dormant oil and insecticidal soap, kill insects by smothering them with a film, or destroying their eggs.

Proper diagnosis of an insect problem is necessary to initiate the right control measures. If you have an insect you cannot identify, contact your garden center or county extension agent. Specific product names are not given for insecticides because their availability varies from one section of the country to another; additionally, new ones enter the marketplace as older ones are removed. Check product labels, or inquire at the garden center as to which product to purchase.

MITICIDES

Mites, which technically are not insects, but treated as such in discussions like this, are treated with miticides. Mites thrive in hot, dry weather, so you can control them somewhat by misting the foliage, especially the undersides, with water on a regular basis.

Below are some common garden pests, and what to do about them. Refer to **Spraying** for more information.

APHID

Symptom: Leaves curl, wither, may turn yellow, and a clear, shiny substance appears on them. A black, sooty mold is sometimes present. Small, semitransparent, green, yellow, black, red, or brown insects cluster on buds, leaves, and stems.
Treatment: A strong stream of water will knock some of the insects off the plants. Spray with a contact or systemic insecticide, or insecticidal soap. Spraying with dormant oil in the spring will smother aphid eggs.

BEETLE

Symptom: Small, round holes appear in leaves and sometimes in flowers. Insects with hard shells of green, red, brown, or black are visible.
Treatment: Small infestations can be controlled by picking them off by hand. Traps are available, but have limited effectiveness. Systemic insecticides can be used. Keep the garden weed-free.

BORER

Symptom: Foliage and stems of vegetables suddenly wilt; leaves of woody plants are small or sparse, and they turn yellow and die. Growth slows or stops. A caterpillarlike insect can be located within the stems.
Treatment: Cut back vegetable stems until you locate the borer and discard it.

TOP: *An insecticide sprayer.*

MIDDLE: *Aphids in the process of destroying a leaf.*

BOTTOM: *Damage done to foliage by Japanese beetles.*

Wrap tree trunks and shrub branches with paper or plastic. Borers can sometimes be cut out of woody branches, and the affected plant parts also can be pruned away. Insecticides are available for borer control, and are painted on trunks and branches where the entry holes of the borer appear.

CATERPILLAR

Symptom: Large holes appear in leaves; sometimes the entire leaf is consumed. Buds, flowers, fruit, and stems may also be stripped from the plant. Long, thin insects of varying sizes are visible.
Treatment: Large caterpillars can be hand-picked and destroyed. Use a contact or systemic insecticide, or spray with *Bacillus thuringiensis*, a bacterium that kills caterpillars, but is harmless to plants and animals.

LEAFHOPPER

Symptom: Leaves turn yellow, starting at the edges, or are speckled with dots, and eventually curl up and die. Light green or grey wedge-shaped insects are visible.
Treatment: Remove damaged leaves and spray plants with insecticidal soap, or a contact or systemic insecticide.

LEAF MINER

Symptom: Leaves are marked with white, yellow, or tan serpentine trails. Insects are not visible.
Treatment: Prune out and destroy damaged leaves and use a systemic insecticide. Keep the garden weed-free.

MITE

Symptom: Leaves become speckled with yellow, and take on a dull bronze sheen. Small black spots are evident on the undersides of the leaves. Webbing becomes evident on the leaves and flower buds.
Treatment: Mist the undersides of the leaves with water on a daily basis. Over a nine-day period, spray with a miticide three times, three days apart. Spray woody plants with dormant oil in the early spring.

NEMATODE

Symptom: Plants suddenly lose their color, wilt, and die. If you dig up the plants, you'll see swollen and knotted roots. Insects are invisible as they are microscopic in size.
Treatment: There are no effective chemical controls available to the homeowner, but a licensed exterminator can treat the soil. Remove and destroy infested plants and the surrounding soil. Large plantings of marigolds will deter nematodes.

SCALE

Symptom: Plants stop growing and growing tips die back. Leaves turn yellow and fall from the plant. Clusters of insects are visible on trunks, stems, and branches. The insects are round, oval, or crescent-shaped; some have a soft shell, while others have a hard shell.
Treatment: Prune out any dead or severely infested branches. Spray with dormant oil in the spring and with a contact or systemic insecticide or insecticidal soap during the growing season.

SLUGS AND SNAILS

Symptom: Holes appear in the leaves; entire young plants may disappear almost overnight. Silvery trails are present on the leaves and along the ground. Long dark insects are visible at night.
Treatment: Bait can be set out at dusk. Slugs and snails can also be trapped with

BELOW: *The leaf miner is not visible, but it does mark leaves with its serpentine trail.*

BOTTOM: *The gardener's revenge on slugs—slug bait.*

RIGHT: *Labels, simple or intricate, are essential to continued gardening success.*

BELOW: *Gaping holes in leaves are a sure sign of slugs and snails.*

shallow saucers of beer or inverted grapefruit halves.

THRIP

Symptom: Leaves curl, and the leaf margins turn white, yellow, or brown. Flower buds are discolored and may not open; if they do open, the petals are streaked with brown. The insects are tiny and invisible.
Treatment: Remove and destroy any affected plant parts. Spray with insecticidal soap or a systemic insecticide.

WHITEFLY

Symptom: Leaves are mottled in yellow and curl up. Small white insects are found on the undersides of the leaves, and fly up in clouds when the plant is disturbed.
Treatment: Spray plants with an insecticidal soap or with a contact insecticide. Systemic insecticides may be applied to the soil.

LABELING

As good as you think your memory might be, it is unlikely that you will remember the name of every variety of annual, vegetable, or rose in your garden. If you had good results with a particular plant, you'll need to be able to identify it so you can grow it again.

Label or keep a record of every plant in the garden. Then, when you need to transplant, fertilize, or otherwise care for it, you'll be able to refer to gardening information if you don't know or remember its specific needs. You can use labels to mark the location of dormant bulbs and perennials so that you do not disturb them when working in the garden. Be sure to label seeds when sowing them, indoors or outdoors, so you know what you've planted, and when you should expect to see growth.

Labels can contain as much information as you want them to. In addition to the plant name, you can include the plant's sowing or planting date, as well as its propagation date. You can also include when the plant last bloomed or was fertilized. This information will be helpful in the future.

Plant labels can be purchased, or you can make your own. You can inscribe information on them with waterproof pen, pencil, or plastic tape from a labeling machine, or you can etch them in with a burning device or sharp-pointed object. Just be aware that pencil marks often fade or wash away, and plastic tape sometimes falls off. It's also a good idea to keep a separate record book of plant locations and names in case the labels break or are lost.

You can stick labels into the ground, or tie them around a stem or branch. If you are doing the latter, be sure to tie them loosely with soft string, not around the main trunk; heavy wire can do harm.

LANDSCAPE DESIGN

A landscape often benefits from an accent, such as the natural-looking planting around the sundial in this specially designed garden area, BELOW, *and the pool in this relatively formal garden,* BOTTOM.

The purpose of a landscape is to create a setting for a home that complements and enhances its architecture. With the proper selection and placement of plants, as well as walkways, driveways, and fences, you will add beauty, function, and value to the outside of your home. Landscape design is as important to your home as the interior design and decoration.

The landscape provides shade, color, privacy, and noise abatement. A well-designed landscape can facilitate access to various parts of your home and its outdoor areas as well as increase outdoor living space by creating areas for relaxation and recreation.

Think of the landscape of your home in the same way as you would its interior: both have floors, walls, and a ceiling. The lawn, ground covers, or paving materials are your landscape's floor. An expanse of lawn is no different than a wall-to-wall carpet, and smaller plantings of ground covers are like accent rugs. Hedges, shrubs, walls, and fences are like walls; they define boundaries, separate one area of the garden from another, direct traffic, or block unsightly views; they can be used as backgrounds for low shrub borders or flower gardens.

The ceiling of your landscape is the sky, in addition to the overhead canopy created by trees, which contribute shade, structure, and strength. Vines can create ceilings when grown on overhead structures. Hanging baskets suspended overhead add color, and can visually tie the ceiling and floor together.

THE PRINCIPLES OF LANDSCAPE DESIGN

Landscape design is both an art and a science. To be effective, a landscape design must follow certain basic artistic principles. You must work within your space, and fill it without overcrowding it. The design must have lines that visually lead the eye from one part of the garden to another, and unify the design within its space. These lines can be straight, which are the basis of the formal garden, or curved, which impart an informal, more natural feeling.

SHAPE

The three-dimensional shapes of the landscape make up its form. Plants may be upright, spreading, arching, weeping, round, or pyramidal. The combination and repetition of different forms, without using so many as to be visually disturbing, can create a pleasing whole. Consider not only the individual shape of a plant, but also how the shapes of the various plants in the landscape will look together.

TEXTURE

Texture is the surface finish of plants and other materials in the landscape. The size, shape, and finish of foliage,

LEFT: *The fluid, almost curving arrangement of plantings gives this landscape a natural, informal feeling.*

BELOW: *Plants can easily be incorporated with furniture, statuary, and other accents in almost any setting, from the very formal to the highly informal.*

BOTTOM: *Hedges such as azalea (RHODODENDRON spp.) can be used to create patterns and lend structure to the landscape.*

smoothness or roughness of bark, outline of tree and shrub branches, size and shape of the flowers, as well as surface of paving materials all contribute to the landscape's texture. You might want to combine and contrast plants with different textures for visual appeal, but again, do not use so many different types that you create visual disharmony. Fine-textured plants appear further away and are calming. Bold-textured plants appear closer, and make a stronger impact. You can make small spaces appear larger if you use fine-textured plants.

COLOR

Color comes from flowers, foliage, berries, bark, and construction materials. Repetition of color is pleasing and unifying, while too many different colors will make your garden lose its unity and pattern, and are too busy. Warm colors (red, orange, gold, and yellow) are bold and exciting, but they make the garden look smaller. Cool tones (green, violet, and blue) are relaxing and make an area appear larger. It is best to select a dominant color and combine it with one or two complementary colors, rather than

use every color of the rainbow in a design. A color wheel may be a helpful way to choose contrasting and complementary colors.

PATTERN

Pattern is the arrangement and use of solid and open space; it creates structure in the landscape. A design that utilizes only solid space appears confining and small. To avoid this, choose plants of different heights and shapes, and combine them in such a way that there are open spaces between solid masses.

BALANCE

Balancing the landscape creates visual stability. This does not imply that a landscape should be symmetrical, although a formal garden usually is. You can achieve balance through size, texture, or color. One side of a landscape can be heavy due to large plants, strong colors, or rough textures, and be balanced by its other side if that side is larger and filled with plants of lighter texture, smaller size, or more subtle colors.

A landscape often benefits from a dominant feature used as an accent. Sample accents include a magnificent tree in the middle of the lawn, or a garden statue.

SCALE AND PROPORTION

The final principle of design is scale and proportion. The size and shape of the plants you choose must be in the proper relationship to the size of your home and the property. In other words, don't use very large trees around a small cottage, or you will end up visually dwarfing the house. When all the design elements are used properly, the result will be a pleasing landscape that has contrast, yet is unified so that the eye moves easily from one section to another.

LANDSCAPE COMPONENTS

PLANT SELECTION

Choosing plants for your landscape is critical to your end result. Trees provide shade, framing, and sometimes color. Shrubs unite the house with the rest of the garden, create a line, make up living fences, and add seasonal interest; they frame the house, outline windows, and soften corners. Where year-round effect is needed, evergreens are a better choice than deciduous shrubs. Lawns give a feeling of spaciousness to the garden, unify it, and are practical as they can be walked and played upon. Ground covers also unify the design, while requiring lower maintenance than lawns. Vines can screen areas, cover fences, soften walls, and act as insulation. Flowering plants—annuals, perennials, and bulbs —provide masses or accents of color.

BEDS AND BORDERS

Shrubs and flowering plants can be used effectively in beds or borders. A bed is a free-standing area, such as an island in the middle of the lawn. Beds should be in proportion to the rest of the landscape; it is a good rule to have a bed fill no more than one-third of the lawn area to keep it in proper proportion. It is best to have an anchoring structure in a bed, such as a specimen shrub, so it is not an empty space when the flowers are not in bloom.

A border is not accessible from all sides, and it backs up to the house, a fence, wall, or property line. The depth of borders should be in proportion to their length.

CONSTRUCTION MATERIALS

Construction materials, such as gravel, bluestone, brick, wood, concrete, and stone should blend in with the garden plants and tone of the landscape in terms of color and texture. When using these materials in walkways, driveways, steps, patios, and decks, consider how they will look in relation to the rest of the house and the garden. Walkways do not have to be straight lines, and patios do not have to be rectangular; in fact, they usually look better if they are not.

DESIGNING YOUR LANDSCAPE

Before you design a landscape, ask yourself some questions. How can you best frame the house and make its first impression a pleasing one? Is there a nearby eyesore that needs to be screened? Do you need privacy from close neighbors? Are there children that need a play area? Do you do a lot of outdoor entertaining? How much time can you spend maintaining the garden? Do you want a swimming pool? A vegetable

TOP: *Ground covers, such as sweet alyssum* (LOBULARIA MARITIMA), *help to unify a landscape; they also require a low level of maintenance.*

ABOVE: *This collection of useful herbs is displayed in ornamental terra-cotta pots and clustered around stone sculptural accents to create a decorative courtyard garden.*

RIGHT: *Hedges can be used to define the landscape by creating borders.*

BELOW: *In addition to their culinary uses, herbs can provide decorative and protective edgings in the garden.*

garden? A flower garden? Do you want to attract birds to the garden? Is there a view that should be enhanced? Do you need to create shade or light?

Make a list of the plants you would like to include in your design. Consider hardiness, size, shape, color, and function. Study the amount of light the garden receives at different times of the day, and the nature of your soil. Visit your local garden center to see what is available. Then plan the landscape out on paper before you buy or plant *anything*. Position trees for framing and shade, and shrubs for their specific use. Situate plants with their mature size in mind to avoid overcrowded or empty spaces.

It is easiest to start a landscape design with a plan of your plot; if you don't have a plan, measure the property and locate the site of the house. Mark the location of windows and doors. Consider the best places for walkways to facilitate access to the front and back doors and the backyard. Do several designs on tracing paper until you come up with the one you like.

If you feel uneasy about designing your own landscape, there are many books available with sample landscape designs. If you can afford it, you can hire a professional to design the landscape for you.

LAWNS

A lawn is a green carpet that surrounds and frames many of our homes. While it is not necessary to have a lawn (homes in woodland settings or in city gardens generally have little, if any), lawns are used at suburban and rural homes to cover the ground, provide a place to walk and play, and allow for open spaces that enhance the view of the house and the rest of the landscape.

SELECTING LAWN GRASSES

The selection of lawn grasses (sometimes called turfgrasses) depends primarily on the climate and the amount of maintenance that you wish to do.

Lawn grasses are divided into cool-season and warm-season grasses. Cool-season grasses are winter-hardy, make most of their growth in spring and autumn, and burn out during the summer in very hot areas. Warm-season grasses are intolerant of cold winters, but grow well during the summer heat. See the map on p. 81 for an indication of the different zones where cool-season grasses and warm-season grasses grow. In the transition zone between these two areas, warm-season grasses are often combined or overseeded with cool-season grasses each autumn so that the lawn is green all year.

See the **Lawn Grass Chart** for information on required maintenance of the various types of lawn grasses. The chart also spells out light and moisture needs as well as wear tolerance. If the lawn will be used as a recreation area by you or your children, select a grass with high wear tolerance.

GROWING AND MAINTAINING LAWN GRASSES

RENOVATING OR STARTING A LAWN

Before renovating or starting a new lawn, you must properly prepare the soil (see **Soil**). The soil should be free of debris such as stones, have a pH in the range of 6.0 to 7.0, and be fertile. Heavy clay soils benefit from an application of gypsum (calcium sulfate), a neutral salt which does not change the pH, but supplies necessary calcium and conditions the soil. Before seeding or sodding, rake the soil so it is level. Early autumn is the best time to start or renovate a lawn. The grass will grow and develop better in the cool weather, and there is less competition from weeds. However, if necessary, you can also start your lawn in early to mid-spring.

SEEDS, SOD, AND PLUGS

There are three ways to start or renovate a lawn: seeds, sod, or plugs. Seeding is the most inexpensive method, but using sod gives more instant results. When seeding, apply seed at the rate specified on the bag or box. Heavy seeding results in overcrowding and poor germination.

1: To start grass from seed, grade soil to slope slightly away from your house and ensure good drainage.

2: Till soil enough to loosen it. Remove stones and other debris. Grade soil once more, then wet it to firm it down.

3: Spread grass seed with lawn spreader.

4: Rake seed lightly with back of bamboo rake.

5: Apply fertilizer on same day seed is spread.

6: Keep grass moist for at least two weeks, or until it is established.

7: Mow grass as soon as it is about 2½ inches (6.25 cm) high. Mow only when lawn is completely dry.

8: Don't worry if weeds appear. Most soils contain the seeds of various weeds, which usually die off after you begin to mow weekly.

Sprinkle seeds by hand on prepared soil and keep the area constantly moist until the new grass is 3 inches (7.5 cm) tall, which is when it can be mowed.

Some grasses, such as zoysia, are usually available only in plugs. Plugs are planted about 1 foot (30 cm) apart and will eventually spread to fill in the entire area.

Using mixtures of different types of grasses is better than planting only one variety. The strengths of one type or variety make up for the weaknesses of another, as grasses vary in their tolerance to drought, or resistance to insects and disease.

THATCHING A LAWN

Thatch is the dense layer of undecomposed organic material that lies on the soil surface at the base of the grass plants. A little thatch does no harm and, in fact, helps keep the soil cool and evenly moist. However, when thatch becomes more than 1/2 inch (12.5 mm) thick, it should be removed, as it prevents water and nutrients from reaching the plants' roots. This process is called thatching.

Thatch may be manually removed with a special tool called a thatching rake; if you have a lot of thatch, or a large area to thatch, it is easier to do the job with a power rake, which is available for rent in most areas.

Contrary to the popular notion, thatch is not caused by the accumulation of uncollected grass clippings. Grass clippings are made up mostly of water and some nutrients, including nitrogen, so leaving them on the lawn, if they are not so long as to smother the grass, is beneficial. You can control the accumulation of thatch by avoiding overfertilization, keeping the soil pH close to neutral, and minimizing the use of pesticides. Thatch is kept under control to some degree by bacterial action and earthworms, too.

It is best to thatch in spring as growth

starts, but you can do it at any time of the growing season.

AERATING A LAWN

Lawns that are growing on compacted or heavy clay soils should be regularly aerated. This is the process of making small holes in the lawn surface to allow air, water, and nutrients to reach the roots. Small areas can be handled with a digging fork, but the tines of the fork, while making holes, actually compact the soil around the edges of the holes even more. It is better to buy or rent a power aerator that removes small plugs of soil. The plugs can be left on the soil surface until dry and then raked, or they can be removed.

WATERING A LAWN

The amount of watering you should do depends on the type of grass you have and the climate you live in. See the **Lawn Grass Chart** for specific requirements. Average moisture requirements are 1 inch (25 mm) of water per week. You can apply water manually with sprinklers, or use an automatic sprinkler system. If you use an automatic system, choose one that works on a sensor for soil moisture, rather than on a timer, so you don't waste water. It is better to water deeply, but as infrequently as possible; this encourages deep roots, which help the grass to better withstand drought and heat.

FERTILIZING A LAWN

The amount of fertilizing you do also depends on the type of grass you grow. See the **Lawn Grass Chart** for the total amount of nitrogen that each type of grass needs each year. Never apply more than 1 pound (.45 kg) of nitrogen per feeding; take the total nitrogen amount needed per year and spread it out over several applications. If only one application is necessary, employ it in early spring or late autumn. If two treatments are needed, do them in late autumn and mid-spring. If three applications are needed, put them down in mid-spring, early autumn and late autumn. If more treatments are required, space them evenly over spring and autumn. It is best not to fertilize during the high heat of summer.

The easiest way to fertilize is with a spreader. For even application, apply half the fertilizer in one direction of the lawn, and then apply the other half in a crosswise direction.

Buy a fertilizer specifically for lawns where the percentage of nitrogen is higher than the percentages of phosphorus and potash.

MOWING A LAWN

Mowing is important to keep lawns healthy and attractive. Mow often enough that you never cut off more than one-third of the leaf blade. Each different lawn grass has a recommended mowing height. In the hottest part of summer, raise these heights by $1/2$ inch (12.5 mm). It is also very important to keep your mower's blades sharp enough to prevent fraying the grass blades.

WEEDING A LAWN

For appearance's sake as well as for the health of the lawn, it is important to keep it weed-free. Lawns that are properly maintained are less likely to be invaded by weeds than those that are not. If you have only a few weeds, it is better to spot-treat the lawn than to apply herbicides to the entire area. However, the entire lawn can be treated if weeds are widespread. Check with your local garden center or county extension agent for recommendations on correcting specific weed problems, as available materials vary from place to place. Herbicides that kill grassy weeds usually will not kill broad-leaved weeds such as dandelions, and vice versa.

Crabgrass and its close relative, goosegrass, are both annual grassy plants, and are two of the most common lawn weeds. It is easier to prevent the germination of crabgrass and goosegrass seeds in the spring than it is to kill the plants after they are in active growth. Chemicals known as pre-emergent herbicides are applied to prevent the weed seeds from germinating. Some of these herbicides can be used if you are putting down grass seed, while others cannot. Check with your garden center or county agent for recommendations regarding products and timing of application.

Lawns have their own set of insect and disease problems. Of course, proper diagnosis is critical to applying the proper treatment. Once proper diagnosis is made, check with your garden center or county agent for specific insecticide and fungicide recommendations.

For your lawn's appearance and health, it is important to keep it weed-free.

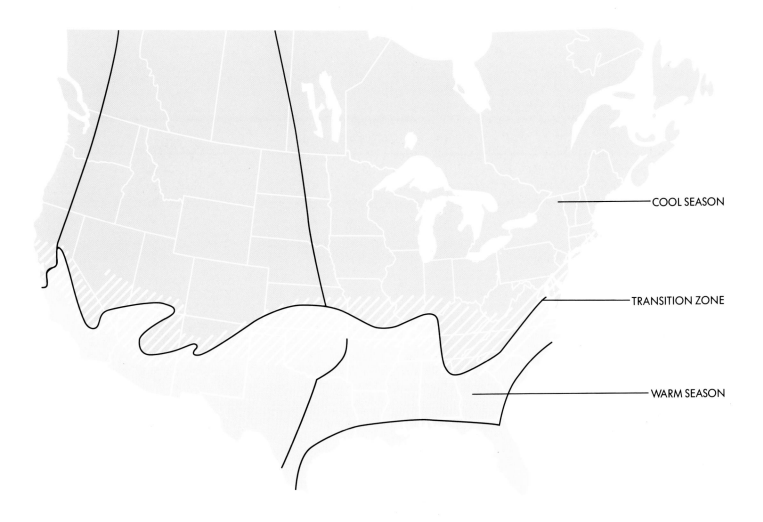

COOL SEASON

TRANSITION ZONE

WARM SEASON

LAWN DISEASES

COPPER SPOT

Symptoms: The lawn is spotted with small, copper-colored patches during cool, damp weather.
Treatment: Apply a fungicide until the symptoms disappear.

DOLLAR SPOT

Symptoms: The lawn is spotted with silver dollar-size patches. Individual grass blades have yellow or tan spots with reddish-brown borders. Warm, humid weather encourages the disease.
Treatment: Apply a fungicide twice, allowing seven days between applications. Water only in the morning.

FAIRY RING

Symptoms: Rings of lush, dark-green grass appear in the lawn. Mushrooms often grow within the rings.

Treatment: There are no chemical controls. Remove excess thatch.

FUSARIUM BLIGHT

Symptoms: Round patches of light-green grass develop and eventually turn brown and die. This disease occurs in hot, humid weather.
Treatment: Employ a fungicide three times, allowing seven days between applications.

LEAF SPOT
(HELMINTHOSPORIUM, MELTING OUT)

Symptoms: Spots of brown grass eventually cover the whole lawn. The grass blades have oval or round spots with tan centers, and black or purple borders. Leaf spot occurs in moderate temperature and high humidity.
Treatment: Apply a fungicide four

times, allowing seven days between applications. Water only in the morning.

POWDERY MILDEW

Symptoms: Grass is covered with a white powder and eventually turns yellow and dies. Symptoms appear when nights are cool and damp, and when days are hot and humid.
Treatment: Apply a fungicide every week until symptoms disappear. Water only in the morning, and do not mow wet grass.

PYTHIUM BLIGHT

Symptoms: The lawn is spotted with 1- to 3-inch (25- to 75-mm) patches of brown, wilted grass blades during warm, humid weather.
Treatment: Apply a fungicide every week until symptoms disappear. Do not mow wet grass.

RED THREAD

Symptoms: The lawn is spotted with irregular patches. Thin, red threads intertwine with the grass blades. Red thread is most prevalent in cool, humid weather.
Treatment: Apply fungicide four times; wait seven days between applications.

RHIZOCTONIA BLIGHT

Symptoms: Large, brown, 2-foot (60-cm) patches turn yellow, then brown. The lawn border may be purple, and sometimes the center of the patch is unaffected. The disease appears in hot, humid weather.
Treatment: Apply a fungicide and continue application throughout hot, humid weather.

RUST

Symptoms: Grass blades are mottled with yellow, and eventually wither and die. Blades are coated with orange powder. Rust is most prevalent in warm, humid weather.
Treatment: Apply a fungicide every week until symptoms disappear. Collect grass clippings.

SNOW MOLD

Symptoms: As snow melts, the lawn is spotted with yellow or tan areas and the grass blades within are matted together.
Treatment: Apply a fungicide in early spring and rake the grass to break up the mat.

STRIPED SMUT

Symptoms: Patches of yellow grass appear in the lawn. The blades are covered with stripes of black, sooty powder. It usually occurs in spring and autumn.
Treatment: Apply a fungicide when symptoms appear.

YELLOW TUFT (DOWNY MILDEW)

Symptoms: Tufts of stunted, thick, yellow grass blades are scattered through the lawn, mostly in cool, humid weather.
Treatment: Apply a fungicide as soon as symptoms appear. Mow only when grass is dry.

LAWN INSECTS

☐ CHINCH BUGS

Symptoms: Circular or irregular patches several feet (m) across appear during the summer, especially when the weather is hot and dry. Placing a bottomless can into the lawn and filling it with water will reveal the insects' presence.
Treatment: Apply insecticide as soon as symptoms appear, then every three weeks until they disappear.

GRUBS

Symptoms: Irregular patches of several inches (mm) to several feet (m) may appear throughout the lawn in early spring and late summer. Grass is easily pulled up and can be rolled back, which often reveals white insects with curled bodies.
Treatment: Treat with an insecticide for grubs or milky spore disease.

SOD WEDWORMS

Symptoms: Small patches of dead brown grass appear in spring and enlarge throughout the summer. Grass blades are cut off at the soil surface. At night, moths can be seen flying over the lawn in a zigzag manner.
Treatment: Apply insecticide in the evening when the insects are most active.

If grubs or other insects invade your lawn, an insecticide should help destroy them.

LAWN GRASSES

Grass	GT	L	MO	M	F	MH	P	WT
Agropyron species Wheatgrass	C	S	D	L–M	1–3	2″	S	H
Agrostis species Bent grass	C	S,LSh	M	H	1½–2	¼–¾″	S,P,So	L
Axonopus affinis Carpetgrass	W	S	M	L–M	1–2	1–2″	S,P	L
Buchloe dactyloides Buffalo grass	W	S	D	L	½–2½	½–1¼″	S,P	A
Cynodon Dactylon Bermuda grass	W	S	A	H	3	½–1″	S,P	H
Dichondra micrantha Dichondra	W	S,Sh	M	M–H	4	½–1″	S,P	L
Eremochloa ophiuroides Centipede grass	W	S,LSh	A	L	½–1½	1–2″	S,P	L
Festuca arundinacea Tall fescue	C	S,PSh	D	M	2½–6	1½–2¼″	S	H
Festuca duriuscola Hard fescue	C	S,PSh	D–A	M	1¼–3	1–2½″	S	H
Festuca rubra commutata Chewing fescue	C	S,PSh	D	M	1¼–3	1–2″	S	H
Festuca rubra rubra Creeping red fescue	C	S,PSh,Sh	D	M	1¼–3	1–2½″	S	A
Lolium multiflorum Italian ryegrass	C	S,LSh	M	M	2–6	1½–2″	S	A
Lolium perenne Perennial ryegrass	C	S,LSh	M	M	2–6	1½–2″	S,So	H
Paspalum notatum Bahia grass	W	S,PSh	A–D	L	½–2½	1½–2½″	S	A–H
Poa pratensis Kentucky bluegrass	C	S,LSh	M	M–H	2½–6	1–2″	S,So	A–H
Poa trivialis Rough bluegrass	C	PSh,Sh	M	M	2½–6	½–1″	S	L
Stenotaphrum secundatum Saint Augustine grass	W	S,Sh	A–D	L–M	3–6	1½–2½″	P,So	A
Zoysia species Zoysia	W	S,PSh	D	M	3–6	½–1″	P,So	H

Top: *A rubber plant* (Ficus elastica) *in the process of being air-layered.*

Middle: *Lime raises soil's pH.*

Right: *Gravel-flint chips are among the many mulch choices available today.*

LAYERING

Layering is a method of propagation that causes roots to form along a stem of a plant while the stem is still attached to the main plant. For specifics, see **Propagation.**

LEAF MOLD

Leaf mold is the product of shredding, and/or composting, fallen leaves. See **Soil** and **Mulching.**

LIME

Lime, or calcium carbonate, is an alkaline compound used to raise the pH of soil. See **Soil.**

MICROCLIMATE

This is a climate within a small area that differs from the prevailing climate in the overall area. A microclimate may be colder or warmer than the surrounding climate. See **Hardiness.**

MOWING

Mowing is the mechanical removal of the tops of blades of grass. See **Lawns.**

MULCHING

THE BENEFITS OF MULCH

A mulch is a layer of loose material that is placed on top of the soil. Mulch may be organic or inorganic; in either case, the benefits of mulch are many. Mulch reduces soil blowing and erosion. It keeps weeds from germinating and growing. It also keeps the soil cool, moist, and at an even temperature. If mulch is organic, it adds organic matter and some nutrients to the soil. Mulch also promotes root growth, and controls the spread of diseases. It keeps mud from splashing and adds beauty to the garden.

TYPES OF MULCH

The **Mulch Chart** outlines the most common materials used for mulch. Select one that is readily available, and will do the job for you.

Black plastic has become a common mulch, especially in vegetable gardens. In addition to the other benefits of mulch, it absorbs a lot of heat, which keeps the ground warm. Be sure to poke holes in black plastic mulch so that water can pass through. Other mulching material can be placed on the plastic to hide it and make the planting more attractive.

WHEN TO APPLY MULCH

The time to apply mulches depends on the benefit you want to derive from them. Mulch applied in early spring will keep the ground cool. It will help pansies grow into the summer months, but may not be good for tomatoes if it keeps the ground too cool. For plants requiring warm soil temperatures, do not apply mulch to the ground around them until the soil is warm in spring.

You can leave mulches in place, and add more as needed. You can also work mulches into the soil once each season and replace them, which improves the condition of the soil. Those mulches with a rapid decomposition rate will need to be replaced more often than those that decompose slowly.

You will often hear the expression "winter mulch." For more information on this, read about **Winter Protection.**

NITROGEN

Nitrogen is an element that is essential to plant growth. Nitrogen promotes plants' stem and leaf growth and their dark-green color. See **Fertilizing.**

OFFSHOOTS

Offshoots are small plants that develop at the base of the main plant. They can be removed and grown on their own. See **Propagation.**

MULCHES

MATERIAL	DEPTH	DECOMPOSITION RATE	COMMENTS	TYPE
Black plastic	1″	Slow	Excludes light; attracts heat	Inorg.
Buckwheat hulls	3–4″	Medium	Dark color	Org.
Cocoa hulls	3–4″	Medium	Supplies K	Org.
Compost	2–3″	Rapid	Good soil conditioner	Org.
Fir bark	2–3″	Slow	Good weed control	Org.
Grass clippings	2″	Rapid	Becomes too hot as it decomposes; can become slimy	Org.
Gravel	1″	None	Hides standing water	Inorg.
Hay or straw	3–4″	Rapid	Can carry weeds; may be flammable	Org.
Leaf mold	2–3″	Rapid	Easily accessible	Org.
Marble chips	1″	None	Attractive	Inorg.
Newspaper	1″	Rapid	Breaks down quickly	Org.
Peanut hulls	2–3″	Medium	Supplies N–P–K	Org.
Peat moss	2–3″	Medium	Not recommended; pulls moisture from the soil; difficult to moisten	Org.
Pine bark	2–3″	Slow	Good weed control	Org.
Pine needles	2–3″	Slow	Good insulator	Org.
Sawdust	1–2″	Slow	Add N–P–K if fresh	Org.
Sugarcane	1–2″	Slow	Retains water heavily	Org.
Wood chips	2″	Slow	Add N–P–K	Org.

RIGHT: *Ornamental grasses, with their varying shapes and colors, can add an interesting touch to the garden.*

BELOW: *This bountiful organic vegetable garden features a pair of lifelike scarecrows to help control damage caused by birds. A slatted ranch-style fence encloses the garden to keep out foraging animals, and the plot is fertilized with well-decomposed animal manure.*

ORGANIC GARDENING

Organic gardening is a method of gardening that uses only natural materials as soil amendments such as compost. Organic gardeners also do not use chemical fertilizers or pesticides, which are better for the environment. They are not, however, necessarily more effective gardening aids.

ORNAMENTAL GRASSES

When thinking of grass, a gardener should think beyond the green carpet of his lawn. A small but important part of the grass family is ornamental, and can play a valuable role in the landscape design. Not only are ornamental grasses striking, they are also quite easy to care for.

SELECTING ORNAMENTAL GRASSES

Ornamental grasses fall into both annual and perennial categories, and the type you choose involves the same considerations you would have for planting any other annual or perennial (see **Annuals** and **Perennials**). Annual grasses fit in perfectly as edgings for flower beds, in borders, or as attractive fillers. Perennial types hold a permanent place in any planting. They can be used, depending on their size, for just about anything. Tall varieties are effective as screens, bold accents, or as backgrounds for lower-growing plantings. Many ornamental grasses are effective for erosion control, tolerate poor soil, and withstand air pollution. The flowers and seed heads of ornamental grasses form interesting tufts or plumes that add an interesting touch to the garden. Some grasses are white, some are tinted pink, but most types are shaded in natural earth tones. Like all grasses, the foliage of ornamental grasses is long, flat, tapered, and often arching. Annual or

ORNAMENTAL GRASSES

	PH	PT	HZ
Agrostis nebulosa Cloud grass	8–20″	A	—
Arundo Donax Giant reed	12–20′	P	7–10
Avena sterilis Animated oats	3–4′	A	—
Briza maxima Quaking grass	2–3′	A	—
Coix Lacryma-Jobi Job's tears	2′	A	—
Cortaderia Selloana Pampas grass	14′	P	8–10
Erianthus ravennae Ravenna grass	14′	P	5–10
Festuca ovina glauca Blue fescue	12″	P	4–10
Hordeum jubatum Squirreltail grass	1½–2′	P	5–10
Lagurus ovatus Hare's-tail grass	1–2′	A	—
Miscanthus sinensis Eulalia	8–12′	P	5–10
Miscanthus sinensis zebrinus Zebra grass	4′	P	5–10
Panicum virgatum Switch grass	4–6′	P	5–10
Pennisetum setaceum Fountain grass	2–4′	P	5–9
Phalaris arundinacea picta Ribbon grass	3′	P	4–10
Setaria italica Foxtail millet	3′	A	—
Stipa gigantea Feather grass	6′	P	5–10
Tricholaepa rosea Ruby grass	4′	A	—

perennial, ornamental grasses are a perfect source of material for fresh or dried flower arrangements.

GROWING AND MAINTAINING ORNAMENTAL GRASSES

Propagating ornamental grasses is simple. Annual types are easily grown from seed sown outdoors, or they can be started inside. Read the section about growing plants from seeds under **Propagation.** Perennials may be grown from seeds or by division; read about division, also under **Propagation.** Plants usually need division every three to four years or when the center of the clump dies out. You can also buy both annual and perennial types.

Ornamental grasses are treated the same way as any other annual or perennial. Read the sections about **Soil** and **Planting.** Ornamental grasses grow best in full sun in neutral, well-drained soil. In early spring, cut stems of perennial types to 6 inches (15 cm) from the ground and apply fertilizer. Annual grasses should be fertilized at planting time, and need no further feeding during the year. Most grasses are quite drought-tolerant but benefit from deep watering during the heat of summer.

PEAT MOSS

Peat moss is an organic substance derived from the sphagnum moss plant, and is used to condition the soil. See **Soil** and **Mulching.**

PERENNIALS

Perennials are thought of as the backbones of the flower garden. While each plant may only bloom for a month or so, the choice of perennials is so vast that they can provide continuous color in the garden from early spring to late autumn. With the proper selection of plants, you will also be able to create different color schemes through the seasons.

A perennial is a plant whose tops usually die down during the winter, although the roots remain alive. Some perennials remain evergreen through the winter. Triggered by the warmth of spring, perennials regrow, year after year, dependably filling their beds with a vast array of flowers.

SELECTING PERENNIALS

There are several considerations when choosing perennials. After you choose a color scheme or schemes, you can make lists of those plants whose flowers fit those schemes. To enjoy the garden for the entire season, select plants with different bloom times so that you have continuous color. Hardiness must be considered to make sure the plants will have appropriate summer and winter climates (see **Perennial Chart**) as this is critical to their survival.

DESIGNING WITH PERENNIALS

Perennials can be used almost anywhere in the garden. They can be planted in

many ways. You can use one plant as a specimen, or plant them in clusters in a large bed or border. Perennials need not stand alone; they can be combined with annuals, bulbs, and roses in mixed beds and borders.

Edgings of low-growing perennials can line pathways and driveways, or be used in front of a shrub border. These same low-growing plants can be used as ground covers to unite different areas of tree and shrub plantings. Many perennials have a lovely fragrance to enhance their enjoyment, and others make good cut flowers.

Given the architecture of your house and the style of the rest of your garden, perennial plantings may be correspondingly formal or informal. In either case, it is always more effective to plant perennials in clumps of at least three in a bed or border so that the overall effect is not spotty.

You can also combine perennials of different heights, putting taller ones at the back of the border or the middle of the bed, descending to ground-hugging ones in the front. You can also combine perennials with different shapes, using spiked plants with those that have either

*Perennials such as Dame's rocket (*HESPERIS MATRONALIS*), BELOW, and polyanthus (*PRIMULA × POLYANTHA*), BOTTOM, can be mass-planted in one variety, or, BELOW RIGHT, different varieties can be planted together to create interesting shapes and textures.*

TOP: *Creeping phlox* (PHLOX STOLONIFERA).

ABOVE: *Autumn joy* (SEDUM SPECTABILE).

rounded or flat forms. Consider the texture and color of the foliage as well; you can combine rough- and fine-textured leaves as well as red-, bronze- or gray-leaved plants alongside those with green foliage.

For more information, read the sections on **Cutting Flowers, Drying Plants, Fragrance,** and **Landscape Design.**

GROWING AND MAINTAINING PERENNIALS

Perennials can be propagated by a variety of methods, including division, cuttings, offsets, and seeds. Read about these methods under **Propagation.** If you do not wish to propagate your own perennials, you can buy plants from your local garden center or from a variety of mail-order nurseries. Look for robust, healthy plants that are free of signs of insects and diseases.

PLANTING PERENNIALS

Perennials can be planted or transplanted as growth starts in spring, or in early autumn. Poppies, irises, and peonies must be planted or transplanted in autumn or they will not bloom the first year. Before planting, read **Soil** and **Planting.** Because perennials will remain in the same spot for many years, it is important that the soil be well pre-pared. Planting distances are given in the perennial chart.

FERTILIZING PERENNIALS

Most perennials benefit from the application of a balanced fertilizer such as 5-10-5 in spring when growth starts. Work the fertilizer into the soil and water it well. See **Fertilizing.**

WATERING PERENNIALS

Perennials vary in their water requirements (see **Perennial Chart**). Plants with average moisture requirements need 1 inch (25 mm) of water per week; others need either more or less. Water deeply and as infrequently as possible to encourage deep roots. Do not water plants subject to diseases or being grown for cut flowers overhead. See **Watering.**

PRUNING PERENNIALS

As soon as the flowers of perennials fade, they should be cut back. This will not only keep the plants tidy looking and prevent seedlings from sprouting from fallen seeds, it will generally encourage the plants to rebloom. Low-growing perennials can be headed back with a hedge clippers to remove faded flowers and keep the plants compact. Tall perennials will need to be staked.

When perennials become crowded, or cease to bloom properly, or the center of the plant dies out, they should be dug up and divided. Except for those perennials that must be planted in autumn, you can divide perennials either in spring or autumn. In autumn, after the tops have been killed by frost, the plants should be cut back almost to the soil line to keep the garden free of breeding sites for insects and diseases, and for a better visual appearance.

PROTECTING PERENNIALS

Perennial beds and borders benefit from summer mulch for appearance's sake as well as to keep the soil moist, cool, and weed-free. In winter, protection should be applied, especially where plants are grown close to their hardiness limits. Check several times during the winter to make sure small plants have not been heaved from the soil; if they have, gently push them back. See also **Diseases and Disease Control, Insects and Insect Control, Mulching, Staking and Tying, Weeds,** and **Winter Protection.**

PERENNIALS

	PH	FC	BT	L	MO	T	HZ	P	PD
Achillea species Yarrow	2–3'	YELLOW, PINK, WHITE	ESu,A	S	D	A–H	3–8	D,S	1–2'
Alcea rosea Hollyhock	4–10'	MIX	ESu	S	M	A	3–8	S	1½'
Aquilegia species Columbine	1–3'	MIX	LSp	S,LSh	A–M	C–A	3–8	S,D	1½'
Asclepias tuberosa Butterfly weed	2–3'	ORANGE	MSu	S	D	A–H	3–9	S,C	1–2'
Aster species Aster	2–8'	MIX	LSu,A	S	A	A	3–9	D,S	1–3'
Astilbe species Astilbe	1–3'	PINK	ESu	LSh	M	A	4–8	D	1–2'
Baptisia australis Blue false indigo	3–4'	BLUE	LSp	S	A–D	C–A	3–9	S,C,D	2–3'
Campanula species Bellflower	6"–5'	BLUE, WHITE	LSp–MSu	S,LSh	A–M	A	3–9	D	½–2'
Catanache caerulea Cupid's dart	1½'	BLUE	MSu	S	D	A	5–9	S,D	1'
Chelone Lyonii Turtlehead	3–4'	PINK	LSu,A	S,LSh	M	A	4–9	S,C	2'
Chrysanthemum species Chrysanthemum	6"–5'	MIX	LSu,A	S	A–M	A	3–10	S,C	½–2'
Coreopsis species Tickseed	1½–3'	YELLOW	ESu–LSu	S	A–M	A–H	4–10	S,D	1–1½'
Delphinium species Delphinium, Larkspur	1–6'	MIX	ESu	S	M	C	3–10	S,D	2'
Dicentra spectabilis Bleeding heart	2–3'	PINK	MSp	PSh	M	A	3–9	D,S	1½–2'
Dictamnus albus Gas plant	2–3'	WHITE	LSp	S	A	A	3–8	S	2–3'
Doronicum cordatum Leopard's bane	1–1½'	YELLOW	ESp	S,PSh	M	C–A	4–8	D	1–2'
Dracocephalum virginianum False dragonhead	2–5'	PINK	LSu	S	M	A	4–9	D,S	1½–2'
Echinacea purpurea Purple coneflower	2–4'	PURPLE	MSu	S,LSh	A–D	A	3–10	D,C	2'

PERENNIALS cont.

	PH	FC	BT	L	MO	T	HZ	P	PD
Echinops Ritro Small globe thistle	2–4'	PURPLE	MSu	S	D	A–H	3–9	D	1½–2'
Erigeron species Fleabane	1–2½'	MIX	MSu	S	A	A	4–10	S,D	1½'
Filipendula vulgaris Dropwort, Meadowsweet	1–3'	WHITE	MSu	S,LSh	A	A	3–9	D,S	1½–2'
Gaillardia × grandiflora Blanket flower	1–3'	RED, YELLOW	ESu–LSu	S	D	A–H	3–8	S,D	1½'
Geranium sanguineum Cranesbill	1'	PINK	LSp	S,LSh	M	A	3–10	S,D	1'
Geum Quellyon Avens	1½'	RED	LSp	S,LSh	M	A	6–10	D	1–1½'
Helleborus orientalis Lenten rose	6–12"	WHITE	ESp	PSh,Sh	M	C	3–10	S,D	1½–2'
Hemerocallis species Daylily	1–6'	MIX	ESu–LSu	PSh	A	A	3–10	D	1–3'
Heuchera sanguinea Coralbells	6–12"	RED, PINK	ESu	S,LSh	M	A	3–10	D	1'
Hosta species Plantain lily	6"–3'	WHITE, LAVENDER	MSu–LSu	PSh	M	A	3–9	D	1–2'
Iris × germanica Bearded iris	1–4'	MIX	ESu	S	M	A	3–10	D,S	1'
Kniphofia Uvaria Red-hot poker	2–3'	ORANGE	MSu	S	M	A	6–10	O,D	1–1½'
Lavandula angustifolia Lavender	2–3'	LAVENDER	MSu	S	M	A	5–10	D	1'
Liatris spicata Blazing star	3–6'	PURPLE	LSu	S,LSh	M	A	3–10	D,S	1–2'
Lobelia Cardinalis Cardinal flower	3'	RED	LSu	PSh	M	A	3–8	O,S,D	1–1½'
Lupinus hybrids Lupine	3–4'	MIX	LSp	S	M	C–A	3–9	S	2'
Lysimachia punctata Loosestrife	2–3'	YELLOW	ESu	S,LSh	M	A	5–7	D	2'
Lythrum Salicaria Purple loosestrife	3–4'	PURPLE	MSu	S,LSh	M	A	3–9	D,S	1½–2'
Mertensia virginica Virginia bluebells	1–2'	PINK, BLUE	MSp	PSh	M	A–C	4–8	S,D	1'
Myosotis scorpioides Forget-me-not	8–12"	BLUE	ESp	PSh	M	C	3–10	D,S	9–12"

PERENNIALS cont.

	PH	FC	BT	L	MO	T	HZ	P	PD
Nepeta Mussinii Catmint	1–1½'	BLUE	ESu	S	D	A	4–8	D,S	1–1½'
Oenothera fruticosa Sundrops	1–2'	YELLOW	ESu	S	D	A	4–9	D,S	1'
Paeonia officinalis Peony	2–4'	MIX	ESu	S	A	A	3–10	D	3'
Papaver orientalis Oriental poppy	3–4'	MIX	ESu	S	D	A–C	3–9	D,C	8–12"
Penstemon species Beard tongue, Penstemon	1–6'	MIX	ESu,MSu	S	M	C	4–10	S,D	1–2'
Phlox paniculata Perennial phlox	3–4'	MIX	MSu	S	D	A	3–10	D	2'
Platycodon grandiflorus Balloon flower	2–3'	BLUE, WHITE	MSu	S	M	A	3–9	D,S	1½'
Polemonium caeruleum Jacob's ladder	2–3'	BLUE	MSp	PSh	M	A	4–9	D,S	1½–2'
Polygonatum odoratum Solomon's-seal	2–3'	WHITE	MSp	PSh	M	A	4–9	S,D	2'
Primula species Primrose	6"–3'	MIX	ESp	PSh	M	C	4–10	S,D	½–1'
Rudbeckia hirta Black-eyed Susan	2–3'	YELLOW	MSu	S	D	A–H	4–9	S,D	1–1½'
Scabiosa caucasica Pincushion flower	2–2½'	BLUE, PINK	MSu	S	A	A–H	4–10	S,D	1–1½'
Sedum species Stonecrop	3"–2'	MIX	MSp,LSu	S	A–D	A–H	3–10	D,C	1–2'
Solidago species Goldenrod	2–5'	YELLOW	LSu	S	A–D	A–H	3–10	D,S	1½–2'
Stokesia laevis Stokes' aster	1–2'	BLUE	MSu	S,LSh	A–D	A	5–10	D,S	1'
Trillium grandiflorum White wake-robin	½–1½'	WHITE	MSp	PSh	M	A–C	3–8	D,S	1'
Trollius europaeus Globeflower	1½'	YELLOW	MSp	PSh	M	A–C	5–10	D,S	1'
Veronica spicata Speedwell	1–3'	BLUE	ESu	S	M	A	4–10	D	1'
Viola species Violet	½–1'	MIX	MSp	LSh,PSh	M	C–A	3–10	O,S,D	6"
Yucca filamentosa Adam's needle	3–8'	WHITE	ESu	S	D	A–H	3–10	O	3'

TOP: *Majestic giant pansies* (VIOLA × WITTROCKIANA) *bring wonderful color to the garden.*

MIDDLE: *Hyacinths* (HYACINTHUS spp.) *being forced.*

BOTTOM: *Spading the garden site.*

pH

pH measures the acidity or alkalinity of the soil. See **Soil.**

PHOSPHORUS

Phosphorus is an element necessary for stem and root growth, and photosynthesis. See **Fertilizing.**

It's a good idea to add a phosphorus source such as superphosphate to the soil when preparing it for woody plants to ensure good root growth, but do not add any other fertilizer. Plants that grow and die in one season, such as annuals, vegetables, and some herbs, should have complete fertilizer added at planting time.

Unless a plant is properly planted, it will probably not perform well. Its roots will be so confined that they will not grow, which means that the top of the plant cannot grow either.

PHOTOPERIODISM

Photoperiodism is a phenomenon that causes a plant's blooming cycle to depend upon day length. See **Forcing.**

PINCHING

Pinching is the removal of a plant's growing tip; this encourages side branching and bushiness. See **Pruning.**

PLANTING

Building a garden is no different than building a house in that neither endeavor will succeed without a good foundation. The garden's foundation is a combination of proper soil preparation and the correct placement of the plants into the soil. Before planting, read about **Soil.**

PLANTING WOODY PLANTS

When you buy a woody plant, be it a tree, shrub, rose bush, fruit tree, small fruit, ground cover, hedge, or vine, it will be either bare-root, containerized, or balled and burlapped (except for roses, which are rarely balled and burlapped). The techniques for planting plants bought in each manner vary somewhat, but in all cases, it is important to dig a hole large enough to allow for root growth; this hole should be about twice the size of the root ball or spread.

PLANTING BARE-ROOT PLANTS

Bare-root plants are dormant plants that have no soil around their roots. Plants purchased from mail-order nurseries will most often be bare-root. Garden centers also sell bare-root plants; the roots are often wrapped in a protective covering such as peat moss and enclosed in a plastic bag. Bare-root plants must be planted either in spring or autumn when they have no leaves or active growth.

If you cannot plant a bare-root plant immediately, keep the plant in a cool, dark place so it will not start to grow. Keep the roots moist by wrapping them in wet peat moss or newspaper. The day before you plant, soak the roots in a bucket of water to restore lost moisture. If one piece of root is much larger than the others, it should be pruned back. Any roots that are damaged or broken should be pruned away as well.

BELOW: *Planting a bare-root plant. 1: Dig hole slightly larger than root area of plant. Place cone of soil at bottom of hole that is high enough so that crown of plant will be at soil level after planting is complete. 2: Plant shrub slightly deeper than it grew before. Place a shovel across the hole to help determine planting depth.*

1

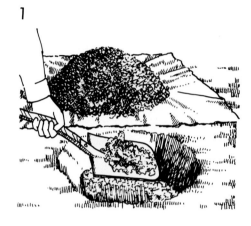

2

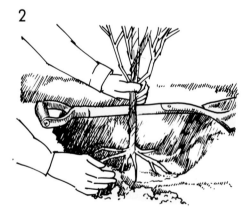

BELOW: *Planting a container plant. 1: Be sure hole is deep and wide enough. 2: Mix compost with soil from hole; break up soil at bottom. 3: Water well, remove container, and make sure plant has developed root system. 4: Cut off damaged or diseased roots. 5: Hold plant in position; fill in hole. 6: Tread soil and add more until it is level. Water thoroughly. 7: Prune stumps of old wood flush with stem. 8: Remove damaged and diseased wood; always cut just above a bud.*

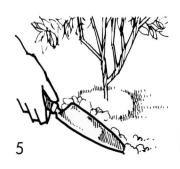

1

2

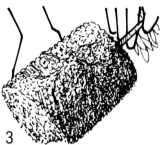

3

4

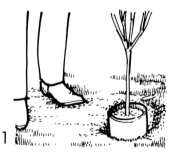

5

6

7

8

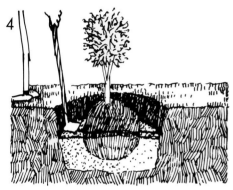

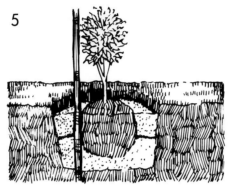

After digging the hole and preparing the soil, place a cone of improved soil in the bottom of the planting hole that is high enough so that the crown of the plant will be at soil level after planting is complete. Spread the roots out evenly over the soil mound and fill the planting hole about two-thirds full. Gently tamp down the soil with your hands and fill the hole with water. After the water has completely drained away, completely fill the hole with soil and water again.

Mounding soil over the base of the plant until growth starts will help to keep its branches or canes from drying out. Once growth has started, the soil can be washed away with a gentle stream of water.

PLANTING CONTAINERIZED PLANTS

Containerized plants are plants sold in plastic, metal, paper, or compressed peat pots. To plant, dig a planting hole twice the diameter of, and a little deeper than, the container. Place improved soil in the bottom of the planting hole until it is the right depth so that after planting, the plant will be at the level at which it grew before.

No matter what the container is made of, remove it before planting. Some plants are sold in "plantable" boxes, but it is still better to remove these boxes, as they will restrict root growth until they

disintegrate. Disturb the roots as little as possible while removing the container. Watering the soil before removing the container will help the medium hold together better. Turn the plant upside down and rap the bottom of the container until it easily pulls off. If a plant is too heavy to pick up, you can cut away its container with heavy shears.

Place the plant in the hole and rotate it until its best side is facing forward. Fill the hole halfway with soil and fill the hole with water. After the water has drained, completely fill the hole with soil and water again.

PLANTING BALLED AND BURLAPPED PLANTS

Balled and burlapped plants are field-grown plants that are dug and wrapped in burlap. Sometimes the burlap is covered with plastic to keep the root ball moist; if so, it must be removed before planting. The planting procedure is the same as for containerized stock, except that the burlap is not completely removed. Once the plant is in position in the hole, cut any strings that may be holding the burlap around the roots, and pull the burlap back, but do not remove it; it will quickly disintegrate anyway.

After a deciduous plant is planted, remove about one-third of the branches to help it adjust to the transplanting shock and possible root loss. Start by

ABOVE: *Planting balled and burlapped plants. 1: Carry balled and burlapped plant to planting site on tarp or piece of canvas. 2: Set root ball in hole twice the width of root ball and 6 inches (15 cm) deeper than its height. 3: Add soil, cut twine, peel burlap back, but do not remove. Scrape ball gently if it has crust on it. 4: Fill in soil, making sure to tamp it down when hole is half-full so root ball will not settle below ground after plant has been watered. 5: Drive stake so it rests solidly in ground and against (but does not injure) root ball. 6: Tie trunk to stake, but not too tightly. Flood hole several times to water plant deeply.*

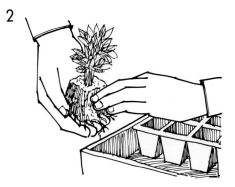

ABOVE: *Planting herbaceous plants.*
1: Carefully remove plants from
containers. 2: Separate or cut off matted
roots if necessary. 3: Dig a hole, and
place plant at level it grew before. Gently
firm soil around root ball with your
fingers. 4: Without damaging roots,
form watering basin around each plant.
Water gently so as not to disturb soil or
roots. 5: Spread a mulch to protect plant
from water evaporation, and to insulate
roots and prevent weeds. 6: Small plants
grow quickly; be sure to leave room for
spreading.

cutting out broken or weak branches,
then trim back the remaining branches
to give the plant a symmetrical form.

Consider the mature size of the plant
before deciding on its location so that it
will not grow to cover windows or into
other plants. Large shade trees should
be about 30 feet (9 m) from the house so
they will not grow into the roof, and 10
feet (3 m) from patios, driveways, and
sidewalks so they will not crack the
pavement. Smaller trees should be at
least 10 feet (3 m) from the house.

To prevent back injury, move large
trees and shrubs to their planting sites
with a wheelbarrow or dolly, or drag
them on a large piece of cloth.

PLANTING HERBACEOUS PLANTS

Herbaceous plants, perennials, annuals,
vegetables, and herbs, are usually sold
in flats or small individual pots. After
preparing and watering the soil and the
plants, remove the plants carefully from
their containers. You can do this by turning the containers upside down and
allowing the plants to fall out, by rap-
ping the bottom of the container, or by
squeezing the containers. Dig a hole
with a trowel and place the plant at the
level it grew before and then gently firm
the soil around the root ball with your
fingers.

When setting out small plants, handle
them only by their leaves to prevent
damage to the stems. If roots are compacted, loosen them slightly before
planting. Once all the plants are in
place, water them again, and keep
watering daily until new growth starts.

Occasionally you will have flats of
plants that are not in individual cells.
Gently pull or cut them apart with a
knife to minimize root disturbance. For
plants grown in peat pots, peel away as
much of the pot as possible before you
plant, making sure that the lip of the pot
does not extend above the soil surface;
if it does, it will act as a wick and take
moisture away from the root ball.

If plants cannot be set into the ground
right away, keep them in a lightly shaded
spot and water daily. If possible, plant
them in the afternoon or on a cloudy
day to reduce transplanting shock.

Some large perennials are sold in containers, and they should be planted like
woody plants in containers.

Refer to **Annuals, Perennials,
Herbs,** and **Vegetables** for specific
planting times.

PLANTING BULBS

Most spring-flowering bulbs are planted
in autumn, and most summer-flowering
bulbs are planted in spring. See **Bulbs.**
When planting a large number of bulbs

in autumn, start with the smallest ones and/or the earliest-flowering ones.

Bulbs can be planted in one of two ways. You can either dig individual holes with a trowel or bulb planter; or you can dig out an entire area, set the bulbs in place, and cover them with soil to the right depth. The latter is easier if you are planting a large area.

WHEN TO PLANT

Woody plants that are bare-root should be planted in spring or autumn when they are still dormant. Woody plants that are containerized or balled and burlapped can be planted any time the soil can be worked, although spring and autumn are best because the weather is cooler and the roots will put out more growth at that time. The exceptions to this rule are: goldenrain tree, tulip tree, magnolia, black gum, as well as red, scarlet, English, bur, willow, and white oaks, which should be planted in spring only.

Autumn planting is favorable for hardy biennials, most woody plants, and perennials for many reasons. Air and soil temperatures are cool, which is favorable for root growth. The plant is not in active growth or flower production, so all its energy can go to root development. Roots will continue to grow until the ground temperature drops below 40° F (4° C), so if you plant in autumn, the roots will be better developed than if you delay planting until the following spring.

In any area of the country where winter temperatures do not drop below 0° F (–18° C), autumn planting is recommended except for the noted exceptions.

Containerized as well as balled and burlapped plants may be planted in summer, but if you do this, be sure to water and protect them from the heat of the sun until they show no signs of heat stress.

AFTER-PLANTING CARE

Water is the most critical aspect of after-planting care. Water must be applied deeply and regularly until the plant is established and new growth is strong. To direct water to the roots, make a catch basin of soil around the plant that is about as wide as the planting hole was.

TREES
Newly planted trees are subject to sunscald. To prevent this, wrap the trunks in burlap or tree tape, and keep the wrapping in place until the tree has developed a mature, thick bark. Newly planted trees also need staking; read about **Staking and Tying.**

SMALL PLANTS
Small plants, particularly annuals, vegetables, and other bedding plants, may suffer damage from the heat of the sun until their roots are established. Keep these plants well watered; mist the foliage if it starts to droop; place a shingle or shade cloth next to the plants so that they are not in direct sun until they have recovered from transplanting.

Plants set out in autumn should have winter protection the first year, even if they do not require it after that.

BELOW: *Two methods of planting bulbs. 1: Here bulbs are planted individually. They are placed over chosen sites at regular intervals. Point uppermost, each bulb is planted in a hole at least twice its depth, then covered with soil. 2: Here bulbs are mass-planted in a large hole 9 to 12 inches (22.5 to 30 cm) deep. Soil is added until hole depth is appropriate for the particular bulbs planted.*

1

2

POLLARDING

Pollarding is a method of pruning in which woody plant tops are cut back every year. This encourages new shoots that grow in a circular ball. See **Pruning.**

POTASSIUM

Potassium is an element that contributes to a plant's metabolism, hardiness, and disease resistance. See **Fertilizing.**

POTPOURRI

Potpourri is a mixture of dried flowers, leaves, essential oils, spices, and a fixative that retains its fragrance for many years. See **Drying Plants.**

PROPAGATION

While buying plants from your local garden center or nursery is the easiest way to start your garden, and offers instant results, growing your own plants can be more satisfying and rewarding, and is sometimes a necessity.

There are many reasons to propagate your own plants. Each year, seed companies introduce a slew of new annual and vegetable varieties. These new varieties often have larger or more colorful flowers, produce mouth-watering fruit, and are more productive or disease-resistant. Often the only way to get these varieties is by buying seed. If your garden is a large one, it is also much more economical if you start your own plants.

You can propagate your own trees, shrubs and other woody plants to increase the number of plants in the garden, to grow a certain type of plant that you may not be able to easily purchase, or just for pleasure. Additionally, perennials, bulbs, and houseplants often outgrow their spaces or fail to produce flowers the way they should. When this happens, they need to be divided—an excellent way of increasing your stock.

PROPAGATION MATERIALS

CONTAINERS

Some types of propagation are better performed directly in the ground, while others can be done either directly in the ground, or inside in containers. You can purchase peat or plastic flats, or make your own from salvaged cans, milk cartons, aluminum baking dishes, frozen food dishes or wooden boxes. Compressed peat pellets covered with mesh that expand when they are soaked in water also make excellent containers for propagating seeds and cuttings.

Almost any container will suffice if it has drainage holes, can be cleaned, and is adequately deep. Containers for sowing seeds should be 3 to 3½ inches (75 to 87.5 mm) deep. Those for leaf and root cuttings can be shallower (2 inches or 5 cm), while those for stem cuttings should be an inch or two (25 or 50 mm) deeper than the cuttings that will be placed in it. Unless a container is new, wash it thoroughly, then rinse it in a solution of 10% household bleach in water to ensure that it is sterile. One word of caution—don't ever reuse peat or compressed-fiber flats. You will never be able to get them clean enough, which makes introducing diseases into your propagating material more likely.

ABOVE: *This example of pollarding shows how the lower branches of American hornbeams planted in a circle have been pruned away to expose the trunks, while the tops are sheared to a square "topknot" of foliage for a formal decorate effect.*

BELOW: *Jiffy-7s are individual containers made of compressed peat moss that can be used for rooting cuttings or sowing seeds.*

PROPAGATING MEDIUM

Be fussy about your propagating medium. Under no circumstances use garden soil, as it invites insects, diseases, weeds, and causes poor drainage and aeration. You can buy a packaged soilless mix, or make your own with equal parts (by volume) of milled sphagnum, peat moss, and perlite. You can use the same type of mix for growing container plants for propagating. Never reuse propagating medium, as it might not be free of disease organisms. You don't have to waste the medium, however, as you can use it later in potting mix or in the garden.

Moisten the medium before you place it into the flats. If you are using peat or compressed-fiber flats, water them first so they don't draw water from the medium. Fill the flats with premoistened medium to within 1/4 inch (6 mm) of the top before sowing or planting cuttings.

STARTING SEEDS INDOORS

☐

STARTING ANNUALS, VEGETABLES, AND BIENNIALS

You can sow some annuals and vegetables directly into the ground when planting time comes, so you don't have to worry about starting those plants indoors. Other annuals and vegetables must be given a head start inside, either because seeds are too small to be sown outdoors, or because the plants won't have time to grow to maturity outdoors, except in the Deep South and the Southwest. Cabbage and its relatives, cucumbers, eggplants, peppers, tomatoes, begonias, coleus, geraniums, impatiens, lobelia, pansies, petunias, salvia, snapdragons, and African marigolds are almost always placed into the garden as plants, not seeds.

Timing is critical. You don't want to start your seeds too early or too late. Some seeds, like begonias, coleus, geraniums, impatiens, lobelia, petunias, salvia, or snapdragons, must be started indoors ten to twelve weeks before they are planted outdoors. Other annuals, such as ageratum, sweet alyssum, flowering tobacco, portulaca, and verbena, need six to eight weeks indoors. Marigolds, calendula, celosia and zinnias need only four to six weeks. Most vege-

1
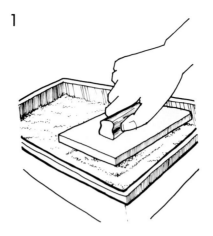

2
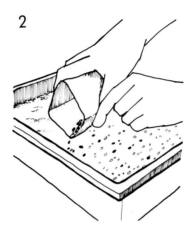

3
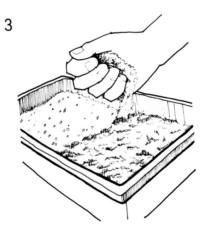

4
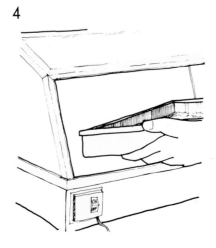

TOP: *Flowering tobacco (*NICOTIANA ALATA GRANDIFLORA*) is one of the many plants that require a head start indoors.*

ABOVE: *These herbs, which were started indoors, are almost ready to be transplanted to an outdoor garden.*

LEFT, TOP TO BOTTOM: *Starting seeds indoors. 1: Place moist medium in flat; level medium and press down gently. 2: Evenly spread seeds over medium. 3: Cover seeds with 1/4 inch (6 mm) of medium; fine seeds may not require covering. 4: Water flats and place them in propagator or cover with plastic.*

tables should be started indoors five to seven weeks before they are moved outside. The seed pack will have the information you need.

Biennials can be sown in summer or autumn, so they will germinate the same year, and bloom the following spring.

STARTING PERENNIALS, TREES, AND SHRUBS

Many perennial, tree, and shrub seeds need to be subjected to a cold treatment known as stratification before they will germinate. If the seeds are planted outdoors in autumn, nature will take care of breaking the dormancy. If the seeds are started indoors, place them in moistened peat moss in the refrigerator or freezer for three months before sowing them.

Some seeds have very hard seed coats or coverings. To hasten their germination, soak them in water for twenty-four hours, or nick the seed coat with a file or small scissors before sowing. This is known as scarification.

Seedlings often succumb to a disease known as damping off. Using a soilless mix will help to prevent it. For further insurance, drench the medium with a solution of 1 teaspoon of benomyl (Benlate) per gallon (5 ml per 3.8 l) of water before sowing. Let the flats stand for a few hours to drain off excess moisture.

PLANTING SEEDS

Except for fine seeds, which should be scattered evenly over the surface, it's easier to sow seeds in rows. Seeds should not be overcrowded, but spaced so they do not touch each other. Cover seeds with an amount of medium equal to their thickness, except for very fine seeds, which should not be covered at all. Merely press fine seeds into the medium so they are in contact with it.

You can plant several types of seeds in the same flat, but choose those that will germinate at the same time. Don't sow all your seeds. Save a few just in case something goes wrong and you have to start again. Label your flats, and mark each one with the variety planted and the date.

After the seeds are sown, place the flat in a clear plastic bag and secure it tightly. This creates a mini-greenhouse so you won't have to water until the seeds sprout, and prevents them from being dislodged. Bottom heat helps seeds to germinate. You can provide such heat with a heating cable, or by putting the seeds on top of the refrigerator. Until seeds germinate, place them in good light, but not full sun. When you see signs of life, remove the plastic bag and move the flats into full sun.

Fluorescent lights create an excellent environment in which to grow plants from seed. Seed flats should be 6 to 10 inches (15 to 25 cm) below the lights, which should be kept on constantly until germination, and twelve to fourteen hours a day after germination.

CARING FOR SEEDLINGS AFTER GERMINATION

After seeds have germinated, check them daily to see if they need watering. When watering, be careful not to dislodge or uproot young seedlings. Use a very fine mist or spray, or set the container in a tray of water and let it soak up water from the bottom. Once all the seedlings are growing, add a soluble fertilizer at one-quarter the recommended rate once a week to ensure steady growth.

TRANSPLANTING SEEDLINGS

The first leaves that appear on seedlings are cotyledons, which are the seed's food-storing cells. Once two sets of true leaves have fully developed, you should

BELOW: *To encourage germination and prevent containers from drying out too quickly, cover newly seeded trays with plastic domes. The clear plastic admits light but traps moisture, so that soil will not become dry due to evaporation. When the seeds are up, the domes are removed.*

BOTTOM: *Daphnes are sweet-smelling shrubs. This species,* DAPHNE × BURKWOODII, *blooms in spring.*

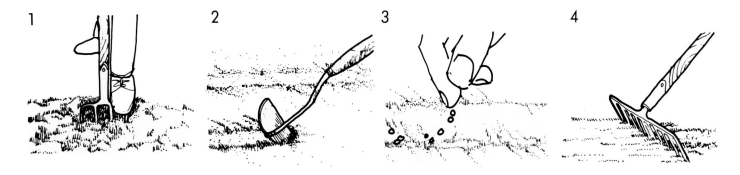

1   2   3   4

---

transplant your seedlings. Unless young plants are very thinly spaced in the container in which they were sown, they should be moved into individual pots of plastic or peat. If you use peat pots, make sure they are wet before filling them with medium.

Handle the seedlings carefully. The medium should be moist before you try to dig out the tiny plants. Disturb the roots as little as possible by gently lifting them with the help of a spoon handle.

Fill the pot into which you are transplanting the seedling with moistened medium, and make a hole in the center with a dibble or a pencil. Holding the seedling by its leaves, never by its stem, lower it into the pot and firm the medium gently around the roots. Continue to water and feed as before.

Before indoor-grown seedlings can be shifted to their outdoor home, they must get used to the change in environment. This process is called hardening off. Ten days before you put the plants in the garden, place the plants outdoors in a protected area during the day, and bring them back inside at night. Gradually work up to leaving them outside all the time.

When you're ready to plant, make sure the ground is well prepared. Unless it has rained, water the ground first. You will also need to water the seedlings. Remove the plants from their pots carefully to keep the roots as intact as possible. If the plants are in peat pots, peel away the pot as much as possible before planting so roots will not be confined. Read about **Planting.**

If your plants have become too tall indoors, you can pinch them back to make them bushy. If they have flower buds on them, you can pinch them off, as you want the plants to spend their energy growing roots for the first few weeks. Don't do this to African marigolds, however; they should be in bud or blooming when planted.

STARTING SEEDS OUTDOORS

Many vegetable, annual, perennial, herb, and other seeds can be started outdoors (refer to charts for specifics). In fact, many plants, especially those with deep tap roots, do not transplant well and are better started outside.

The time to sow seeds outside is generally the same as when you would set the same plants outdoors. Annuals and vegetables are planted any time from early spring to after the danger of frost has passed, but this depends upon the specific plant. Perennial seeds generally can be sown any time from mid-spring through midsummer. As they become available, seeds of trees, shrubs, and other woody plants are planted from midsummer through autumn, and usually germinate the following spring.

Before you plant, prepare the soil properly (see **Soil**), then rake it level before you sow. Make a slight depression in the soil with the side of a trowel or a ruler, and place the seeds into the depression so they will be covered with

1

2

3

ABOVE: *Dividing perennials. 1: Dig up and lift out plants. 2: Pull plants apart where they won't split easily; if they don't, use a knife or spading form. 3: Each division should contain a mass of healthy roots, the joining stem, and leaves.*

RIGHT: *Dividing bulbs. 1: When foliage yellows, dig up bulbs. 2: Gently separate small bulblets from base of main bulb.*

BELOW: *Iris divisions ready to be replanted.*

1
2

an amount of soil that is equal to their thickness. Lightly press the soil together with your hands and water the area with a fine spray. Water the area every day so the seedbed is never dry until the seeds germinate and are growing well. At that point, you can gradually cut back your watering to normal. Keep young seed-beds well weeded so the seedlings don't have to fight for water, light, and nutrients.

Follow packet directions for sowing distances and final thinning distances. Once the seedlings have developed two sets of leaves, you should thin them. Watering well first makes removing thinnings easier.

DIVISION

Most perennials and bulbous plants need regular dividing to keep the plants healthy, and to help them grow and flower at their peak. Some shrubs can also be divided.

DIVIDING BULBS

To divide bulbs, dig them up from the ground as soon as the flowers have faded and the foliage is starting to turn yellow. When the bulbs are dug up, you will see two or three large bulbs or a number of small bulblets around the base of the main bulb. Simply remove the bulbs and bulblets by pulling them apart with your hands, and replant them. It may take a year or two before a small bulb will flower.

Some tuberous plants have obvious growing eyes. When more than three eyes appear on a tuber, you should cut it into pieces with a sharp knife, but leave at least one eye per piece.

DIVIDING PERENNIALS

To divide perennials, dig them from the ground in spring when growth starts, or in early autumn. Wash the soil off the roots so you can better see the root system, and pull the plants apart where they will split easily. Sometimes perennial roots are tightly woven together, so you may need to pull them apart with a spading fork. Some root clumps will have no natural division; these can be cut in half with a knife or the handle of a spade.

DIVIDING SHRUBS

Shrubs that can be divided are handled in the same way as perennials.

STEM CUTTINGS

SOFTWOOD CUTTINGS

Many plants—shrubs, trees, perennials, houseplants, and others—are easily propagated by stem cuttings. To take a stem cutting, cut a piece of stem that has at least four leaves, to a length of about 4 to 6 inches (10 to 15 cm). If you are making a cutting from a flowering plant, the best time to do so is immediately after the flowers have faded. After you make your cutting, remove the bottom two leaves on the stem as well as all flowers and buds, and place the cutting into a container of propagating medium. The cutting should be inserted deeply enough into the medium so that the nodes where the two leaves were removed are covered.

Place the container in a plastic bag, then put it in good light, but not direct sun; you can also make indoor cuttings root faster if you give them bottom heat from a heating coil or the top of the refrigerator. Remove the plastic bag for a few minutes every day to provide good air circulation and prevent disease. In several weeks, test the cutting for rooting by tugging lightly at the stem. If it gives resistance, the cutting is rooted and you can permanently remove the plastic. If the cutting moves freely, replace the bag and try giving it a tug in several weeks.

Cuttings of hardy plants can also be rooted outdoors in beds of prepared soil that are not in full sun.

Place the cuttings in the soil in the same way you would place them in propagating medium. Mist the cuttings well every day, or cover them with plastic film or a glass jar until they are rooted. You can then transplant them into a protected spot, or place them in a cold-frame over winter. You can move them to their permanent garden position in spring.

Note that cuttings will root more quickly if their bases are dusted with rooting hormone before they are placed in the medium.

ABOVE: *Pelargonium stem cuttings.*

BELOW: *Taking a stem cutting. 1: Cut a piece of stem that has at least four leaves to a length of about 4 to 6 inches (10 to 15 cm). 2: Remove the bottom two leaves of the stem, as well as all flowers and buds, and place into container or propagating medium.*

1

2

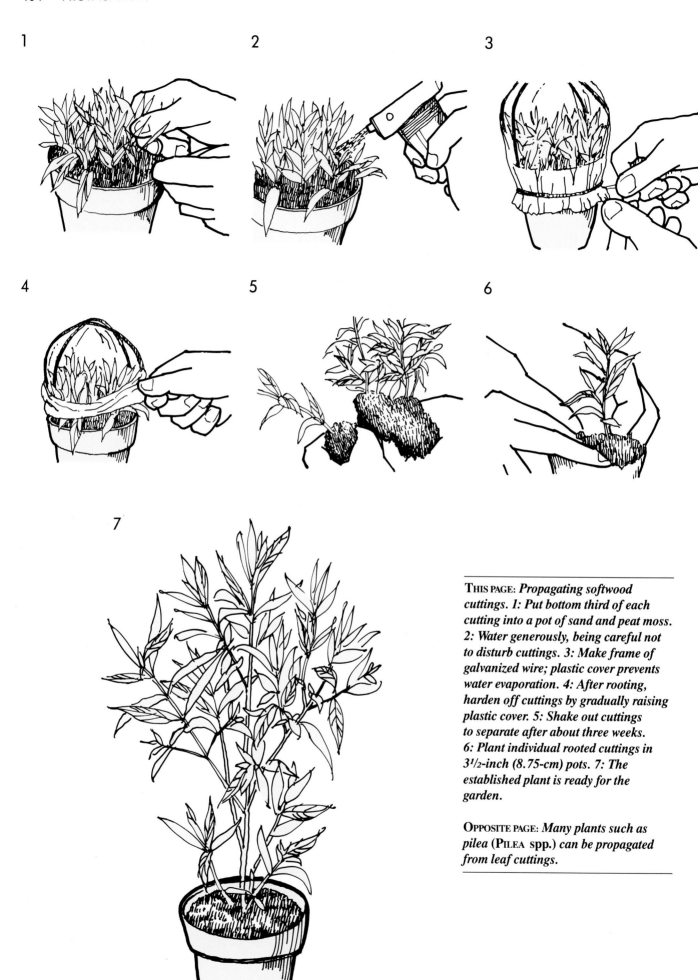

1

2

3

4

5

6

7

THIS PAGE: *Propagating softwood cuttings. 1: Put bottom third of each cutting into a pot of sand and peat moss. 2: Water generously, being careful not to disturb cuttings. 3: Make frame of galvanized wire; plastic cover prevents water evaporation. 4: After rooting, harden off cuttings by gradually raising plastic cover. 5: Shake out cuttings to separate after about three weeks. 6: Plant individual rooted cuttings in 3½-inch (8.75-cm) pots. 7: The established plant is ready for the garden.*

OPPOSITE PAGE: *Many plants such as pilea (PILEA spp.) can be propagated from leaf cuttings.*

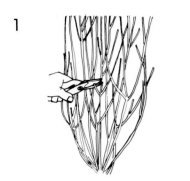

1

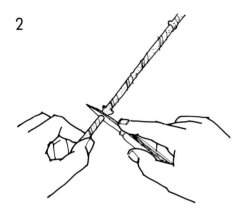

2

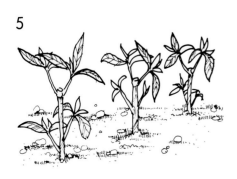

3

4

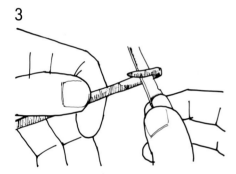

5

Hardwood Cuttings

A second method of propagating woody plants is known as hardwood cuttings. Take the cuttings in autumn as the leaves drop. You should remove any lower remaining leaves from the cutting, slice an inch (25 mm) of bark along its base, and dust the base with rooting hormone. Bury the entire cutting below the frost line, or place in a coldframe until spring. During the winter, callused tissue forms from which roots will later grow. In spring, dig the cuttings up, and plant them in a trench, leaving only 1 inch (25 mm) of the cutting above ground. The cuttings will be ready to move to their permanent home in a year.

LEAF AND ROOT CUTTINGS

☐

Leaf Cuttings

Many houseplants and succulents are propagated by leaf cuttings. There are two ways to take leaf cuttings. You can take an entire leaf with a piece of the leaf stalk left on it, and insert the leaf

LEFT, TOP TO BOTTOM: Propagating hardwood cuttings. 1: Take cuttings in autumn as leaves drop; cut them off close to the base. 2: Shorten each stem to 9 to 12 inches (22.5 to 30 cm). Cut below a bud at the base and just above the bud at the top. 3: Slice an inch (25 mm) of bark along the base, dust with rooting hormone, and bury below frost line. 4: In spring dig cuttings up, plant vertically in a trench, leaving 1 inch (25 mm) above ground. 5: The cuttings will be ready to transplant in a year or two.

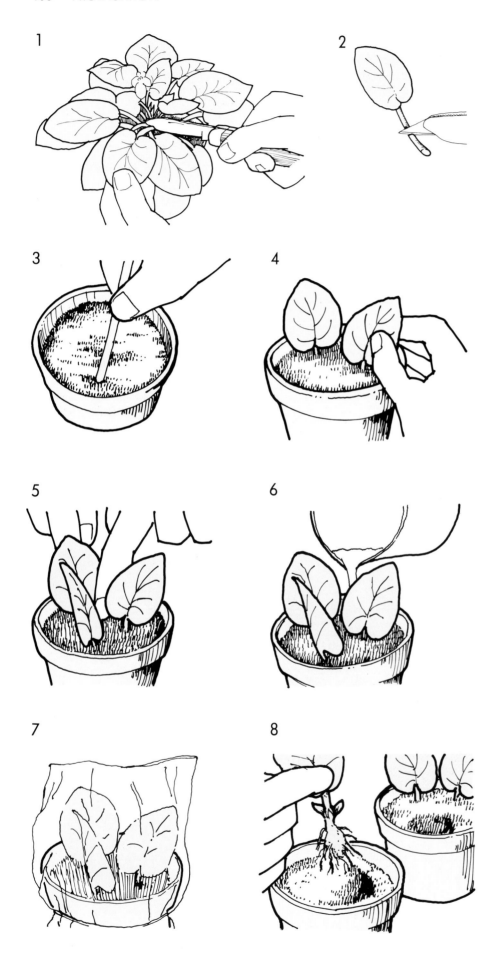

LEFT: *Propagating leaf cuttings. 1: Cut healthy leaves with stalks attached. 2: Trim stalks. 3: Using a stick, make a few holes in a pot of propagating medium. 4: Insert each cutting so that leaf is just above the medium. 5: Firm medium with your fingers, being careful not to injure stems. 6: Fill pot to top with water, then let drain. 7: Cover container with glass or plastic, make sure it's airtight, and place in good light. 8: When new growth is obvious, remove; repot after each cutting.*

RIGHT: *Propagating root cuttings. 1: Cut 1- to 3-inch (2.5- to 7.5-cm) pieces from base of plant. 2: Cut lower end of cutting at slant so top and bottom are easily distinguishable. 3: Slicing straight across, cut thin roots into 2-inch (5-cm) pieces. 4: Insert thick roots into medium, slanted side down; cover tops ¼ inch (6 mm). 5: Lay thin root cuttings on rooting medium, then cover with additional ½ inch (1.3 cm) of medium. 6: Cover with glass or plastic; when new growth appears, remove covering and repot.*

BELOW: *A collection of leaf cuttings of various succulents.*

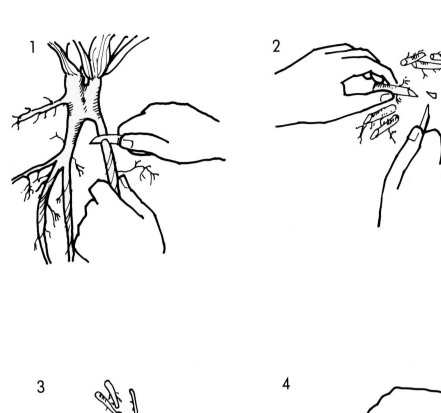

stalk into the propagating medium until the leaf is lying flat on the medium. You can also use a leaf without a stalk, or a piece of a leaf that contains a section of the main leaf vein. Lay the leaf on the medium, and secure it in place with a toothpick.

Whatever method you choose, cover the container with glass or plastic, and place it in good light, but not direct sun. When new growth is obvious, the covering can be removed.

ROOT CUTTINGS

Root cuttings involve digging up a plant in spring as growth starts, or in early autumn, and cutting its newest, most vigorous roots into pieces about 1 to 3 inches (25 to 75 mm) long. Place cuttings in a container of propagating medium. They should be spaced 2 inches (50 mm) apart and lie flat on the medium. Cover the cuttings with 1/2 inch (12.5 mm) of additional medium, then cover the container with glass or plastic and place it in good light, but not direct sun. When growth appears, the covering can be removed.

LAYERING

Layering is a method of propagation whereby roots are forced to grow along a stem while the stem is still attached to the main plant. Layering can be a slow process, but is often more successful than cuttings are because the stem is still attached to the mother plant during the rooting process and receives better nourishment. There are two types of layering: ground layering and air layering. The difference between ground and air layering is that air layering is done along the stem above ground.

GROUND LAYERING

Ground layering is done with vining plants or with plants whose branches are supple enough to be bent over to the ground. It is best to start ground layering in early spring, although you can successfully do it in summer. To ground-layer, take a piece of stem and make a small notch into its underside just below a leaf node. Dust the area around the notch with rooting hormone. Bury the notched section in 4 inches (10 cm) of soil, holding it in place with a wire loop if necessary. Allow the growing end of

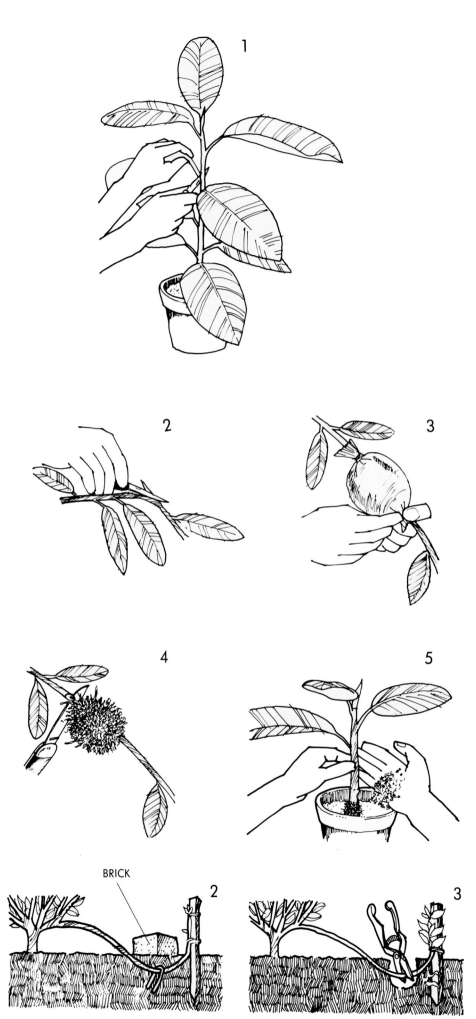

RIGHT: *Propagating plants by air layering. 1: To propagate a new plant from an overgrown one, cut off several leaves growing 6 to 9 inches (15 to 22.5 cm) from the top. This is where stem will be air-layered. Begin below a leaf node, and make a 1¹/₂-inch- (38-mm) long, upward-slanting cut. Gently prop open cut; dust with hormone rooting powder. 3: Wrap clear plastic around cut, and close at bottom with tape. Pack sphagnum peat moss into plastic opening; seal top shut. 4. When roots appear, sever stem just under them. 5: Pot new plant in container filled with potting medium.*

BELOW: *Propagating plants by ground layering. 1: Put a pebble into a notch cut halfway through a low, flexible branch the width of a pencil. Notch should be just below leaf node, 8 to 12 inches (20 to 30 cm) from branch tip. Dust cut with rooting hormone. 2: Bury notched section in 4 inches (10 cm) of soil, anchoring it in place with a wire loop; allow grounding end to stick out of soil. Water, stake growing end, put weight on soil surface. 3: When growing end puts out new shoots, rooting has occurred. Cut new plant away from mother plant, and transplant it.*

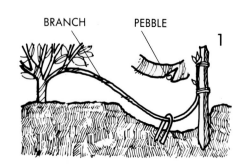

BRANCH   PEBBLE   BRICK

ABOVE: *An India rubber tree (*FICUS ELASTICA*) being propagated by air layering.*

BELOW: *Propagation by suckers. In autumn or winter, uncover the base of a sucker to see if roots have formed. If they have, cut off sucker near its point of origin, lift out, and transplant.*

the stem to extend out of the soil. When the growing end produces new shoots and leaves, it is a sign that the stem has rooted. You can then dig down into the soil where the new roots have formed, cut the new plant away from the mother plant, and transplant it.

Where winters are below 0° F (-18° C), or where new growth is sparse, wait until the following spring to cut away and transplant the newly formed plants.

AIR LAYERING

Air layering is usually done with houseplants that have single, thick stems, but you can also air-layer with woody plants that are difficult to root. To air-layer, make a slanted cut one-third of the way into the stem just below a leaf node. Insert a matchstick or toothpick into the cut to keep it open, and dust it with rooting hormone. Wrap moistened sphagnum peat moss around the cut, several inches (mm) above and below it, and cover the peat moss with clear plastic.

Fasten the plastic to the stem tightly with twist-ties used to secure garbage bags.

When you can see roots growing in the peat moss, cut the new plant off the main stem below the roots and transplant it. It is advisable to reduce the number of leaves on the new section by half to compensate for the smaller, developing root system.

RUNNERS AND OFFSHOOTS

Some plants, like strawberries and carpet bugle, naturally send out long stems, or runners, at the end of which new plants develop. To help the main plant root and develop new plants, pin runners to the ground with metal clips or wire loops. When new plants have formed and rooted at the ends of the runners, you can cut the new plants away and move them to a new location.

Offshoots are new plants that develop at the base of the main plant. You can pull them away from the main plant by hand or with a trowel, taking as much of the root system as possible, and transplant them.

GRAFTING AND BUDDING

Grafting and budding are similar propagation methods in that they involve the joining of one plant onto the roots of another. These methods are used for plants that are difficult to propagate by other methods, or with plants that need a more vigorous root system than their own to grow, flower, or fruit more successfully. The new plant will have all the characteristics of the main plant.

GRAFTING

Grafting is commonly done with fruit trees and many flowering shrubs and trees. This method is often used to produce trees with more than one variety of fruit, or that are self-pollinating. Grafting is best done in early spring, just before the growth buds start to swell. To graft, select a 2- to 3-inch (5- to 7.5-cm) piece of stem of the plant with at least one growth bud. This piece of stem is known as the scion. The plant onto which the scion will be grafted is known

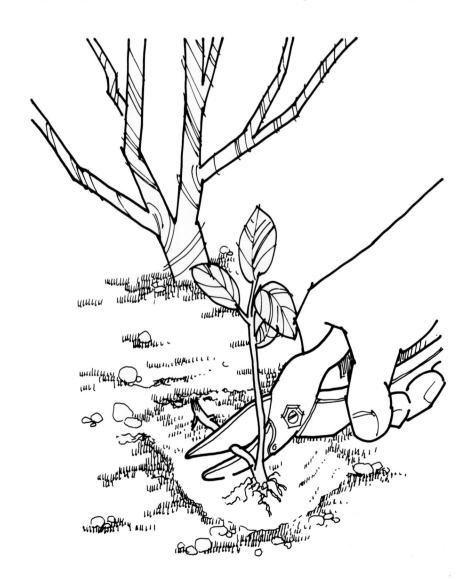

ABOVE: *Pruning a spindle tree.*

BELOW: *Grafting a bud onto an understock. 1: Cut out a piece of branch that has a strong bud (budwood); the cut should be made ¹/₂ inch (1.3 cm) below bud and 1 inch (2.5 cm) above it. 2: Peel and keep bark from budwood. 3: Growth bud will be a small bump on inside of budwood. 4: Slide the growth bud into T-cut of the understock. (See instructions for making a T-cut on OPPOSITE PAGE). 5: Carefully cut off end of growth bud and close bark. 6: Attach growth bud and stem with electrical tape, leaving bud exposed. 7: When bud starts to grow, remove tape and cut top growth of understock away; this allows plant to grow. 8: When new growth is several inches long, pinch back above second bud.*

as the understock. It is essential that the diameters of the scion and the understock are the same or the two plants will not grow together. The scion and the understock should also be close botanical relatives, preferably in the same genus, although you can sometimes use plants in the same family.

Cut the understock so that about 2 inches (50 mm) of stem remains above a growth bud, then make a diagonal cut at the top with a sharp knife. Select a piece of scion and make a diagonal cut into it; the cut should match the cut on the understock in exact length and angle. The growth bud on the scion should be just above the top of the cut. Fit the two pieces together, making sure they align exactly. Wrap both sticks together ¹/₂ inch (12.5 mm) above and below the ends of the cuts with electrical tape.

New growth on the scion tells you that the graft has taken place. Leave the tape in place for two to three years to ensure that the graft does not break apart in wind or storms.

BUDDING

Budding is the joining together of a bud and an understock. This method of propagation is commonly used with roses. Budding is done during the early summer. The bud will lie somewhat dormant during the first season, and will start to grow the following spring.

To prepare the understock, make a vertical cut 1 inch (25 mm) long into the bark of a branch at the bottom of the plant, cutting through to the wood. Then

make a horizontal cut at the top of the vertical cut about one-third of the way around the branch, so that the cut looks like a T. The bark should pull away easily; if it does not, it may be too early in the season. Try again in a few weeks.

To prepare the bud, take a branch of the plant to be budded and, with a sharp knife, cut out a piece of the branch that contains a strong bud. The cut should be made ¹/₂ inch (12.5 mm) below the bud and one inch (25 mm) above it, with the cut made into the wood. Then take the piece of stem with the bud and insert it into the opening made in the bark of the understock. Tie the two together with electrical tape or a rubber band, but leave the bud exposed. When the bud starts to grow, the tape can be removed and the top growth of the understock should be cut away, allowing only the new plant to grow.

In both grafting and budding, it often happens that shoots will develop from the understock below the graft or bud union. These shoots, known as suckers, must be removed as soon as they appear or the understock will eventually outgrow the desired plant that has been grafted or budded to it.

No matter what method of propagation you have used to increase your plants, treat the new plants with tender loving care while they are young. Their root systems are small, and are vulnerable to attack from the weather, insects, and diseases. You'll need to give them extra watering and light fertilizing, and keep an eye out for signs of other problems until they are well established.

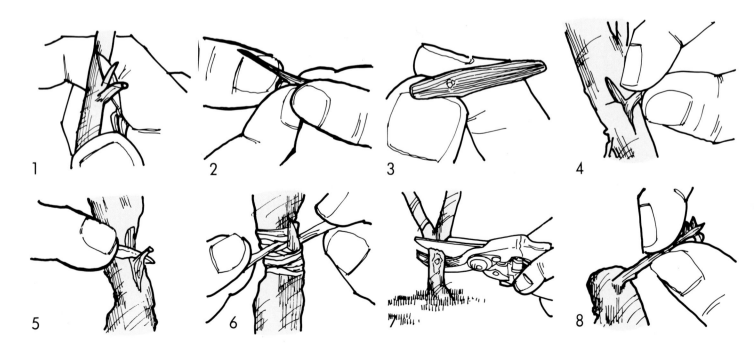

1 2 3 4

5 6 7 8

1

2

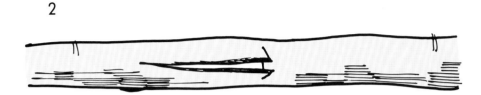

ABOVE: *Preparing the understock for grafting. 1: Make a vertical cut 1 inch (2.5 cm) long into bark of a branch at bottom of plant, cutting through to the wood. Make a horizontal cut at top of vertical cut about one-third of the way around the branch so that cut looks like a T. 2: Bark should pull open easily; if it doesn't, it's either too early or too late in the season. If it's too early, try again in a few weeks.*

BELOW: *This long-handled pruner, sometimes called a "lopper," is great for getting at those hard-to-reach spots that are in need of pruning.*

PRUNING

REASONS TO PRUNE

Pruning is the science of removing growth from a plant, and it is done to achieve many different goals. Pruning is used to control the size of a plant, or to improve its shape. With proper pruning, you can direct a plant's growth. Pruning also encourages new growth at the point at or below where pruning cuts are made. Pruning is necessary to remove dead, damaged, or diseased branches, and to correct overgrowth. Pruning can also increase flowering and fruit production.

Pruning plants, especially when they are young, is necessary to direct their shape and growth. You can eliminate multiple trunks and weak crotches. Multiple branches growing from the same point can be removed so that only the best one remains. If a tree is developing two leaders, one should be removed so the tree will retain its symmetry.

Pruning is also necessary to remove suckers that grow from the base of the plant. Often shrubs and trees are grafted or budded onto a different rootstock, so removing suckers is necessary to ensure that the rootstock does not grow so large as to overtake the top growth.

Pruning keeps hedges dense and growing evenly. Prune to remove branches that are growing into utility wires or onto the roof of the house to prevent damage.

Roots can be pruned as well. When a tree or shrub is planted or transplanted, broken or damaged roots should be pruned. You can compensate for root loss by removing about one-third of the top growth. Before transplanting a large tree or shrub, it is a good idea to prune the roots with a spade as much as a year in advance so that the root ball will be more compact and easier to move.

PRUNING TOOLS

Read the section about **Tools** so you know what kind of pruning tools to purchase and how to use them. Make sure your tools are kept sharp and clean, as diseases can be spread with contaminated shears. Alcohol is good for disinfecting pruning tools. When pruning, cut flush to the stem, and never leave a stub, as this can be the entry point for insects and diseases.

HOW TO PRUNE

Always prune to about 1/4 inch (6 mm) above a bud. Do this at a 45° angle that is slanted away from the bottom of the bud. A cut that is too close or too far away from the bud, or is too flat or too angled, can cause the bud to die. Pruning cuts should also be made above an outward-facing bud so that branches do not grow into the center of the plant. Prune deeply into a plant to prevent a large amount of small twiggy growth around its perimeter.

PRUNING SHRUBS

A good general rule for pruning shrubs is to prune spring-flowering shrubs after they bloom, and to prune summer-flowering shrubs in spring as growth starts. The reason for this is that most spring-flowering shrubs bloom on old wood, the branches that grew the previous summer; pruning before the plant blooms will result in a loss of flower buds. Most summer-flowering shrubs bloom on new wood.

Shrubs may or may not need annual pruning. If the plants are growing as desired, and there are no dead or damaged branches that need to be removed, you don't need to prune. If pruning is necessary, you can remove dead or damaged branches in late winter or early spring before the leaves are on the plants; it is also easier to see what needs to be done at these times. Pruning will not interfere with flowering as you will leave the best branches on the plant. This is also a good time to thin out weak or crowded growth.

You can rejuvenate an old, overgrown shrub by removing one-third of its branches to ground level every year for three years. An alternate way to do this is just to remove the oldest branches, thereby encouraging new growth at the bottom of the plant.

Always prune a deciduous shrub back to just above its buds, which is where new growth will appear. This will encourage denser growth and better flower production. When cutting, remember that you want to keep the plant looking as natural as possible, unless you are training plants into formal shapes.

Evergreens are pruned to maintain their desired shape and size. Even if you don't like a formal look, evergreens will often develop wayward shoots that should be removed so that the plant will not look awkward. It is almost impossible to make bottom branches of an evergreen regrow if they die, so be sure to check them at least once a year. Pines grow from an annual growth known as candles, which are elongated shoots. By cutting a candle in half as it appears, a pine will remain smaller and more dense.

PRUNING HEDGES

A hedge should be sheared so that its bottom is wider than its top. This allows the lower branches to receive the light and air they need. Deciduous hedges can be severely cut back if they become overgrown, and will regrow to their desired size within a few years. It is difficult to do this with evergreens, as new growth at the bottom of the plant is rarely produced if the lower branches die.

BELOW: *1: Pruning encourages denser growth and increases flower production. Always prune a deciduous shrub back to just above its buds. 2: You can rejuvenate an old, overgrown shrub by removing one-third of its branches to ground level every year.* BOTTOM RIGHT: *This shrub has been cut back to stimulate growth; notice how the stronger branches have been left.*

1

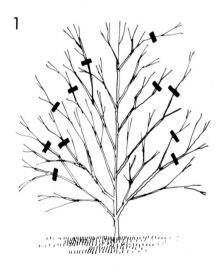

2

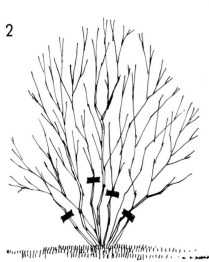

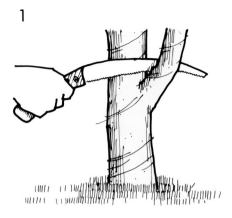

1

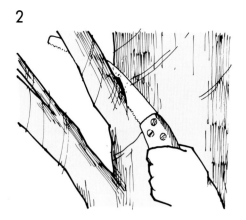

2

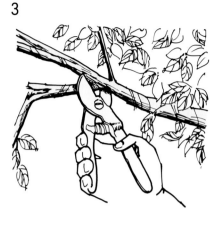

3

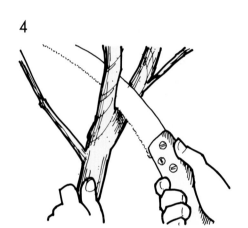

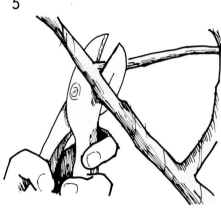

4

5

Depending on the formality or informality of the hedge, you may need to prune it only once a year, or several times a year.

PRUNING TREES

YOUNG TREES

Pruning a new deciduous shade tree is necessary to give it a healthy start, and to help it develop its ultimate shape, size, and strength. Remove any weak or dead wood, or branches that rub against or cross each other, or grow into the center of the plant. Remove shoots that are low on the trunk. You should also remove one branch if two branches are growing from the same point. Prune away any branches that interfere with the tree having a balanced distribution of branches around the trunk. Pruning this way when a tree is young will allow pruning cuts to heal faster.

As a tree grows, keep cutting off any branches that will be too low if you need to walk under the tree to mow the lawn. Cut back growing tips to encourage lateral branches. Also make sure the tree also has only one leader, or growing tip. If you wait too long to remove it, the tree will be misshapen.

Small ornamental trees can be allowed to develop multiple leaders and many branches. Prune them only to shape and outline the branches. Most ornamental trees should be pruned after they bloom.

Young evergreens need less pruning. Make sure only one leader is developing, and cut back lateral branches to ensure that the plant remains compact and full. Pine, fir, spruce, and hemlock should be pruned after new growth has started, while juniper, arborvitae, and yew are pruned before growth starts.

MATURE TREES

Mature trees need pruning to remove dead, damaged, or diseased limbs, to control the size of the tree, to allow more light to reach a lawn or garden, or to remove branches that are too low or growing into utility lines or the roof. Although trees can be pruned at almost any time of year, doing so in early spring before the leaves are present makes the job easier, and allows you to better see the outline of the branches. Cuts also heal faster at this time. The exceptions to this rule are the "bleeders"—maple, birch, and beech—which should be pruned in late spring.

Mature flowering trees that bloom in spring should be pruned after their flowers fade, while those that bloom in summer should be pruned in early spring as growth starts.

When a number of branches need to be removed, it is best to do this over a two- to three-year period to allow the bark to adjust to the increased sunlight and to prevent it from suffering from sunscald.

Follow this three-step procedure when removing large limbs. Make your first cut on the underside of the branch, about 15 inches (37.5 cm) from the

ABOVE: *Pruning young trees. 1: Low branches distort tree shape, make lawn mowing difficult, etc., so before they grow too large, cut them off close to trunk. Keep lowest limb at least 6 feet (1.8 m) from ground, and if tree has more than one low limb, only cut one per season. 2: Closely spaced branches can cause weak growth and uneven foliage cover. Cut off less attractive branch as close to main trunk as possible. Never leave a stub as this only encourages disease. 3: Remove broken, damaged, or diseased branches immediately. Cut close to parent limb to prevent further damage. 4: If young tree develops a secondary leader, remove it as soon as it appears; if you wait until the tree is mature, it will be misshapen, and may develop a weak crotch which can lead to splitting in high winds. 5: Remove any branches that rub against or cross each other, or grow into center of plant to prevent poor circulation or wounds that provide an entryway for diseases.*

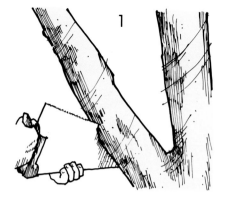

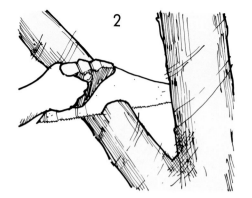

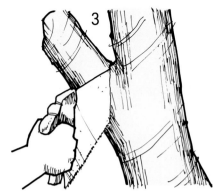

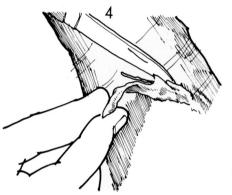

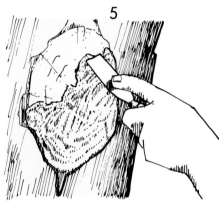

ABOVE: *Pruning mature trees. 1: Follow this three-step process when removing large limbs. Make a first cut on underside of branch, about 15 inches (37.5 cm) from trunk. This will keep branch from tearing when making the final cut. 2: Make second cut on top of branch, about 4 inches (10 cm) out from first cut. Saw all the way through the limb. When branch falls, bark will strip back to the first cut without damaging bark on main trunk. 3: Remove stub of branch, cutting flush with trunk. Support stump as you cut or its weight will tear bark from trunk. 4: Trim bark around cut with sharp knife so there are no loose pieces. Wound will heal more quickly if it's round or oval. 5: Paint surface of wound with tree-wound paint to prevent diseases and insects from entering and to keep out water until it heals. Reapply paint every spring until wound closes.*

trunk and about one-quarter of the way into the branch. This will keep the bark on the trunk from tearing when you make the final cut. Make your second cut on the top of the branch, about 4 inches (10 cm) out from the first cut; saw all the way through the limb. Finally, remove the stub, cutting flush with the trunk; support the branch to keep the bark from ripping.

Trim the bark around the cut with a sharp knife so there are no loose pieces. The wound will heal more quickly if it is round or oval. Paint the surface of the wound with tree-wound paint to prevent insects and diseases from entering, and to keep out water until the wound heals. If it takes several years for the wound to heal, reapply the paint every spring.

Very heavy branches should be tied with rope before they are cut and lowered to the ground to prevent injury to plants or the lawn.

PRUNING ROSES

Modern bush roses—hybrid teas, floribundas, grandifloras, and miniatures—need annual pruning to keep them shapely and vigorous, as well as to keep flower production high and of good quality. Pruning should be done in late winter or early spring when the buds start to swell and break, but before the

leaves fully open. This is generally about the time that forsythia blooms.

Start pruning bush roses by removing any dead or thin canes; cut them flush with the bud union. Next, remove canes growing into the center of the plant or those that crisscross each other. Then select three or four of the newest and healthiest remaining canes, and remove the rest. Canes of hybrid teas should be pruned to a height of 12 to 18 inches (30 to 45 cm), and those of floribundas and grandifloras should be pruned to a height of 18 to 24 inches (45 to 60 cm) so that they will be fuller plants. Prune miniatures to about half their summer height. Always prune to an outward-facing bud.

As for climbing roses, you can remove any canes that are dead, damaged, too long, or misshapen in early spring. Leave all other pruning until after the plants first flower, as climbers bloom on old wood. The oldest canes should be removed to the ground to leave room for new growth; dense growth should be thinned out. Climbers will bloom more heavily if they are trained horizontally along a fence or trellis. Removing flowers as soon as they fade encourages some climbers to repeat their bloom during the summer.

Old garden and species roses and polyanthas do not require severe pruning. In early spring, cut out weak, damaged, or dead wood, and prune only to shape the plant, or control its size.

Tree roses are pruned like modern bush roses; bear in mind, however, that tree roses must be symmetrical if they are to be attractive.

PRUNING FRUIT TREES

Fruit trees should be pruned in early spring. The pruning of a fruit tree in its early years is critical to developing a long-lasting tree that yields a large crop of high-quality fruit. Once a tree's shape is established, pruning is mainly done to remove weak or dead branches and watersprouts, which are thin stems that grow from the base of the plant, or along the main branches. If the tree is getting large and all fruit production is occurring at the ends of the branches, cut into the branches and remove two-thirds of the previous year's growth.

The ideal fruit tree is an open tree with horizontal branches. You can accomplish this either by removing branches that grow upright, or by wedging or tying branches so that they grow in a horizontal plane. Select the leader and six to ten of the strongest branches that are evenly spaced around the trunk, and remove the rest. Each spring, cut the ends of the branches back to remove about half of the previous year's growth and encourage new growth.

1A

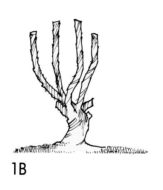

1B

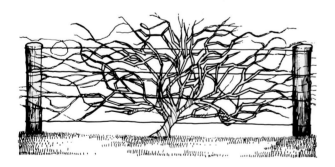

2A

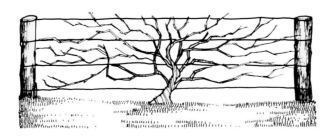

2B

TOP: *Pruning bush roses. 1A: In late winter or early spring, start pruning bush roses by cutting off any dead or thin canes, then remove weak, diseased, or damaged wood. Always prune to an outward-facing bud. 1B: Remove any canes growing into center of plant, and those that cross each other. Select three or four of the healthiest and newest remaining canes, and remove the rest. Don't leave any stubs.*

BOTTOM: *Pruning climbing roses. 2A: In early spring, remove dead and misshapen canes. Leave all other pruning until later in spring after plants first flower because climbers bloom on old wood; secure the flowers to a fence or trellis at this time. 2B: After a climber has bloomed, remove two or three of the oldest canes to leave room for new growth. Thin out dense growth, and shorten canes that have grown too large. Climbers will bloom more heavily if trained along a fence or trellis. Removing flowers as soon as they fade encourages some climbers to repeat their bloom during summer.*

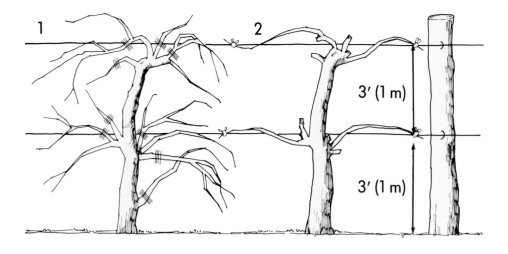

RIGHT: *Pruning grapes. 1: The "Kniffen system" is one good way to prune grapes. In the plant's second year, allow it to develop four arms—two east and west of the trunk, or one pair per wire. 2: Choose four canes, one from each of the main arms, and prune to two buds. The following spring, leave four canes and four spurs, and remove all other wood.*

PRUNING SMALL FRUIT

Bush-type small fruit, such as gooseberries, currants, and blueberries, are mostly pruned in the same manner as other shrubs. Each year, cut back into the previous year's growth to encourage new growth, heavy flowering, and fruiting. Old branches should be completely removed to allow new branches to develop. Any dead or damaged branches should be removed as they appear.

Cane fruit, raspberries and blackberries, must be pruned early every spring or after harvest to keep them productive and prevent them from becoming a tangled mass. The canes bear fruit for only one year, after which they should be removed. Leave five to eight of the strongest canes to produce fruit for the following year, and remove the rest. Shorten black raspberry canes to 6 inches (15 cm), red raspberry canes to 24 to 36 inches (60 to 90 cm), blackberry canes to 12 inches (30 cm). In midsummer, cut back the tips of trailing canes to encourage branching.

PRUNING GRAPES

Grapes are usually grown on trellises that have two parallel wires; the bottom wire is set 3 feet (1 m) from the ground, and the second wire is 3 feet (1 m) above the first. When a grape vine is first

RIGHT: *A grape vineyard in Glen Ellen, California.*

BELOW: *Pruning small fruit. At the end of summer, cut down canes that have borne fruit. Leave five to eight of the strongest canes to produce fruit for the next year, and remove the rest.*

planted, it should be pruned to a single stem with four buds, two on each side of the plant at different heights that match the configuration of the trellis on which the vine will be trained. Allow the stem to grow as high as the top wire of the trellis, and then cut it off to encourage side branches.

As the side buds grow, train them along the wires, placing one branch per wire in each direction from the trunk. Early each spring, prune away all old stems, shoots, and suckers, but leave four more buds that will grow into new branches. Keep removing old branches and allowing new ones to grow in their place for maximum fruit production.

When grape vines are grown for shade rather than fruit, pruning does not need to be as severe. Each year, remove the oldest canes and allow new ones to grow. The new canes will produce some fruit, but not as much as would be produced if the vines were grown for fruit production.

COMMON PRUNING TERMS

PINCHING

Pinching is a method of pruning in which the growing tip is "pinched" out with shears or with the fingers. The purpose of pinching is to temporarily halt top growth, but promote side or lateral growth. You can pinch a plant any time it grows too long or too tall, or if you wish to make it fuller.

DISBUDDING

Disbudding is the removal of a bud. While growth buds can be removed to stop growth at the point where the bud is, a technique useful in espalier, bonsai, and topiary, disbudding usually refers to the removal of flower buds. When a plant naturally blooms in clusters of flowers, disbudding all but one bud results in fewer but much larger flowers. Disbudding can be done with shears, but it is just as easy to rub out the buds with your fingers.

DEADHEADING

Deadheading refers to the removal of faded flowers. You can shorten stems and branches to their desired length once the flowers are removed. Always

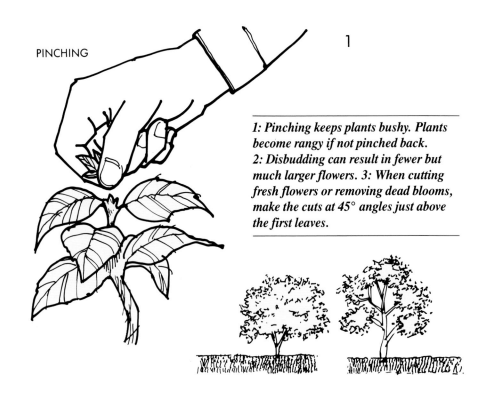

PINCHING

1: Pinching keeps plants bushy. Plants become rangy if not pinched back. 2: Disbudding can result in fewer but much larger flowers. 3: When cutting fresh flowers or removing dead blooms, make the cuts at 45° angles just above the first leaves.

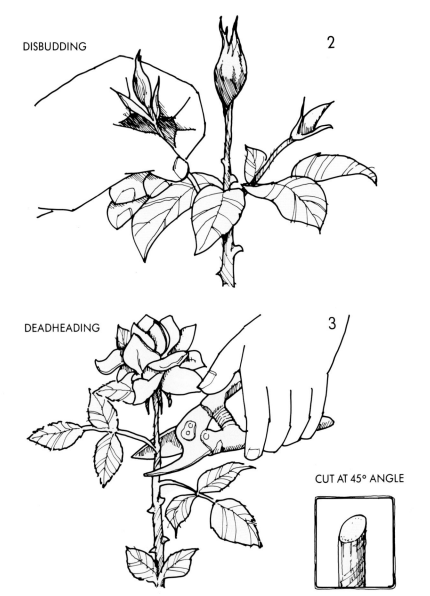

DISBUDDING

DEADHEADING

CUT AT 45° ANGLE

Making a Bonsai from a Nursery Specimen. 1: Choose a young dormant tree that suggests an interesting form. Observe it from all angles, and gently remove a little soil from the roots to evaluate their sculptural potential. 2: Prune tree for form. Eliminate opposite branches, and cut back long ones. Two lowest branches should face in opposite directions. Cut root ball back by one-third to one-half. 3: Plant tree. When new growth develops, wrap annealed copper wire in a spiral around trunk and main branches as you gently bend them to the desired shape. Do not wrap too tightly or you will scar bark. Rewire growth as girth increases. 4: In about a year, plant the tree in a shallow bonsai container. Place galvanized wire screening and layer of sifted drainage material on the bottom of the container, then cover with thin layer of peat moss and coarse potting soil. 5: A week before planting, prune back majority of top growth. Prepare container, and remove plant from its pot. Loosen soil, and cut roots back to main horizontal members and feeder roots; try to do this quickly so that the roots don't dry out. 6: Place plant in container and spread roots evenly; add soil if necessary. Pass insulated electrical wire over roots and through small holes in bottom of container to firmly secure plant. 7: Hold plant as you firm soil around roots with a chopstick. Add thin layer of fine soil, and top with moss. Saturate with water, then place the plant in a safe place where it will not be disturbed until new growth appears. 8: Make a sketch of how you ultimately envision your bonsai tree. This should help guide pruning as plant grows.

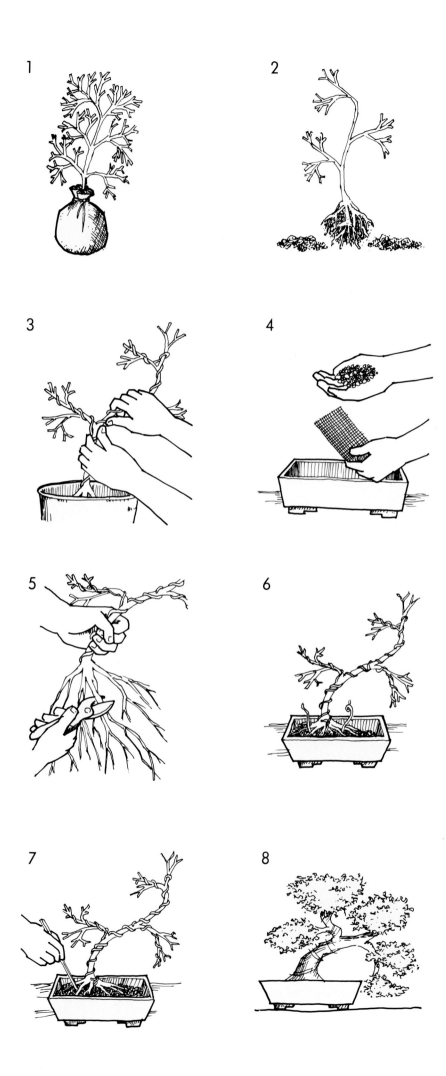

deadhead to just above a bud so as to not leave a stump; make your cut like any other pruning cut. Always remove flowers as soon as they fade so the plant's energy can be directed towards putting out new growth and sometimes flowers, instead of setting seed.

SPECIALTY PRUNING

BONSAI

Bonsai is the Asian art of dwarfing trees and shrubs. The objective of bonsai is to train plants in such a way that, although they are dwarfed, they have the same proportions as the same specimens in nature, and give the appearance of great age. This is accomplished by pruning both branches and roots, and growing the plants in a confined container to minimize development. The contorted and twisted branches usually found in bonsai are achieved by wiring them as they grow.

The most successful bonsai specimens are made with plants that have small leaves, as large leaves hide the contour of the branches and would not be in scale with the small plant. It is neces-sary to start with young plants, remove those branches that are not needed in the overall design, wire the remaining branches into the desired shape, and frequently prune the plants to keep them small.

Since bonsai specimens are made with woody plants, the humidity in most homes is too low for them; greenhouse culture is more satisfactory. Bonsai plants also need frequent watering as the containers are so small.

ESPALIER

Espaliered trees are trees that are pruned, trained, and tied to grow in a geometric pattern on a flat plane. Although many plants can be espaliered, this method of growing is done primar-ily with fruit trees.

To espalier, select a young tree and decide on the pattern in which you want it to grow. Select those buds that are positioned where they will be a part of the design, and remove all others. Allow the remaining buds to grow into branches, and remove all laterals that are not part of the design. The branches will need to be tied to a fence, trellis, or other support, which can be made of wood or wire. Early each spring, prune

BELOW: *An espaliered pear tree.*

LEFT: *This azalea (MACRANTHUM AZALEA-SATSUKI HYBRID) is a good example of a successful bonsai specimen.*

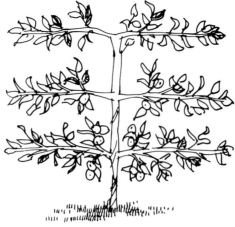

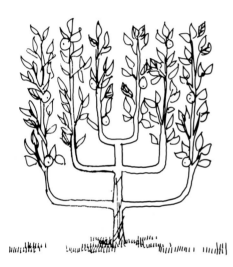

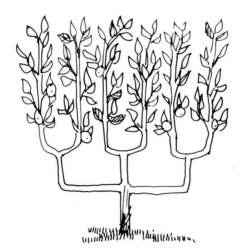

ABOVE: *Through espalier, many plants can be trained to grow in a variety of interesting geometric patterns.*

to shape, train, and tie growth as it appears during spring and summer. Prune out any secondary and unwanted growth as it appears.

POLLARDING

Pollarding is a popular technique in Europe, but is not often found in North America. To pollard, cut all of the branches back to the main trunk at a height of 5 to 6 feet (1.5 to 1.8 m) every year. A pollard puts out long, thin branches, which give the tree a rounded appearance. After being pollarded many times, the tree forms a thick trunk, and a large, gnarled crown forms where the branches were removed.

TOPIARY

Topiary is the art of shaping plants into various forms, such as animals and geometric shapes. Several different methods can be used to do this. The easiest way is to make a form from chicken wire, fill it with potting soil, and plant small plants into it. Then, all you need

to do is prune regularly to keep the topiary in its desired shape. The second method involves selectively pruning the plant into the desired shape, and pruning it regularly to maintain the shape. You may also find it necessary to wire some of the branches to direct them into the desired shape.

Woody or vining plants can be used for topiaries. Evergreens give the most pleasing results. Plants that have small leaves are the best to use because large-leaved plants can be distracting from the topiary's shape.

RAISED BEDS

The raised bed is one of the oldest tricks gardeners use to solve soil and watering problems. There are many ways to plant above ground level, and the results are almost always good.

Wherever soil is so poor that it does not support plant growth well or does

BELOW: *A raised bed of staked tomatoes and beans.*

BOTTOM: *Raised beds with walls can be made using a variety of materials, including the landscape timbers pictured below.*

not drain well, the raised bed is an excellent solution. The content and structure of the soil mixture within the bed is totally within the gardener's hands, and it is easier to control that mixture than it is to amend ground-level soil.

In areas where heavy rains are common, raised beds are an asset. Because water drains more quickly from a raised bed than it does from the ground, plant roots won't languish in waterlogged soil.

A raised bed both dries out and warms up more quickly in the spring than the soil does, which permits earlier planting, especially of cool-season annuals and vegetables. It is also easy to figure out fertilizer requirements for raised beds, because all you have to do is measure the area, and base your application on label recommendations per 100 or per 1,000 square feet (9 or 90 m²).

Gardening with raised beds is easier to do, especially for people with physical limitations because they can garden closer to hand's reach and do not have to stoop down or kneel on the ground. The tops of wooden, brick, or stone raised beds can also double as seating areas. Raised beds can be used as landscape features to bring height to the garden, break up monotony, or retain soil in sloped areas where gardening may be problematic.

Raised beds have other benefits as well. They make it easy to adjust soil pH, have no chance of compaction since you don't walk on them, are more easily protected from invasion from animals, and can be covered to shade plants or create a temporary "greenhouse" for propagation.

Many raised beds have walls, but they are not necessary. Improved soil can be mounded into a raised bed, a technique used often in vegetable gardens. Of course, this is limited by the height of the bed you build; a bed any higher than 12 to 18 inches (30 to 45 cm) would probably be unstable.

Raised beds with walls can be made with wood, brick, concrete blocks, logs, railroad ties, or stones. They can vary in height from 12 inches (30 cm) to several feet (m), depending on the visual look you want to create and the condition of the soil. A raised bed should be narrow enough so you can reach its center without walking on it. To keep it stable, a raised bed needs some type of support driven into the ground onto which it is attached. These supports can be made of wood, pipe, or steel rods.

If you're lucky, the soil in the bottom of a raised bed is good enough to accept the water that drains from the bed. If the soil doesn't accept the water, drainage holes need to be installed every 2 to 3 feet (60 to 90 cm), 2 to 3 inches (50 to 75 mm) up from the ground; drainage pipes may also need to be installed into the center of the bed. Filling a raised bed with 8 to 10 inches (20 to 25 cm) of gravel before adding the soil mixture will also improve the bed's drainage.

The soil mixture in a raised bed may be a soilless one of compost or peat moss mixed with perlite, vermiculite or coarse sand, or it can contain soil mixed with other components, like the soil you use in your garden. Read about **Soil.** If your soil is poor, heavy, or drains poorly, you will have better results with a primarily soilless or completely soilless mix. Water the soil before planting, allowing it to settle to within 2 to 3 inches (50 to 75 mm) of the top of the bed.

RHIZOMES

Rhizomes are thick, food-storing stems that grow along or just below the soil surface. See **Bulbs.**

ROCK GARDENS

A rock garden is a collection of rocks and plants that is designed so that each component complements and enhances the other's beauty. Originally, rock gardens were designed to create an ideal growing site for alpine plants, but the concept has been expanded to include many other types of low-growing plants that will grow to conform to the shape of the rocks. A rock garden is an ideal solution to landscaping a slope, but can be constructed on flat land as well.

DESIGNING A ROCK GARDEN

When designing a rock garden, remember that it is supposed to emulate nature. On high mountains, plants naturally grow under and around the protection of rocks found there. The plants are situated to receive the full benefit of the sun while the rocks protect them from the wind and rain.

ABOVE LEFT: *Rhizomes.* ABOVE: *Dragon's blood sedum* (SEDUM SPURIUM) *is one of the many sedum species suitable for a rock garden.*

BELOW: *The Betty Ford Rock Garden in Vail, Colorado, features an assortment of evergreen conifers and perennials among outcrops of rock designed to resemble the local environment. The yellow plants are different forms of Scotch broom. Bearberry, a durable evergreen ground cover, spills over the rocks on the left.*

BELOW LEFT: *This is a good example of what a rock garden should look like— natural, not formally arranged.*

Designing a rock garden may seem deceptively simple, but it is more than arranging rocks and plants in a random manner. Study photographs or, if possible, natural and man-made rock gardens to get ideas of how rocks are arranged in nature. The design will be better if it is based on a few large rocks rather than many small ones. A rock garden is also more natural-looking if weathered rocks are used rather than shiny, fancy, or colored ones. Don't try to build a mountain, but rather, a small section of a mountain landscape.

Selecting plants for a rock garden is no different than selecting plants for any other garden. Think of blooming time, flower color, foliage color, and texture, and autumn color or berries. Choose plants that are complementary and provide a long period of color and interest. Small bulbs can be used in a rock garden for early spring color, and annuals can be added for summer effect. In nature, most rock garden plants are perennials, but small shrubs can be used as well. It is essential that the plants be low-growing, except for larger plants that may be needed as a background.

BUILDING A ROCK GARDEN

Before putting the rocks in place, prepare the soil and make any modifications in the contour of the area that are necessary. Mounds of earth can be created to give height to flat areas. Start by placing the largest rock first and aligning the smaller rocks around it. Balance, not symmetry, is essential. For example, if a large rock is placed on one side of the garden, you might set two smaller rocks on the other side. Once the rocks are arranged, they should be buried to the original ground line, or until they are firmly secured.

Most rock garden plants require fast-draining soil. Heavy clay soil is difficult to amend and should be replaced. Other soils, unless naturally gravelly, should be mixed with an equal part of fine gravel or coarse sand to a depth of at least 6 inches (15 cm). Pieces of gravel or rock fragments placed around the base of the large rocks will look natural and provide very sharp drainage at the planting sites.

Place the plants into the garden in irregular groups to strengthen the

desired naturalistic effect. Plants should be placed in front of, or in the crevices of, rocks, where they would be found in nature. Specimen plants should be set by themselves in places where they will be noticed. Trailing plants should be placed where they will be able to grow over a part of the rocks.

MAINTAINING A ROCK GARDEN

Maintenance of a rock garden is similar to that of any other type of garden. Plants will benefit from light fertilizing once each year when growth starts; most rock garden plants have low fertilizer requirements. Because the soil in a rock garden is fast-draining, you may have more watering than normal during the heat of summer. This depends on the types of plants in the garden, but many rock-garden plants are naturally drought-resistant. Weeding must be done regularly; since it may be difficult to climb into and work a rock garden, pre-emergent herbicides that prevent weed seeds from germinating are useful. Plants will need regular division and/or pruning to keep them the right size in proportion to the rocks and overall size of the garden. Short-lived plants will need regular replacement.

In autumn, remove any leaves that may have fallen into the garden. During the winter, check to make sure that small plants have not been heaved from the ground; a winter mulch can help prevent this.

ABOVE: *Winter daphne (*DAPHNE ODORA*), with its white flowers, can be used to add interest to almost any rock garden.*

BELOW: *Beautiful "Barnhaven" primulas have dark red petals and bright yellow "eyes." They are planted here among round boulders and clumps of wild red columbine and blue bugle weed.*

ROCK GARDEN PLANTS

Latin Name	Common Name	Plant Type
Anemone Pulsatilla	Pasqueflower	Perennial
Antennaria dioica	Pussy-toes	Perennial
Arabis caucasica	Rock cress	Perennial
Arctostaphylos Uva-ursi	Bearberry	Shrub
Arenaria montana	Sandwort	Perennial
Armeria maritima	Thrift	Perennial
Aster alpinus	Mountain aster	Perennial
Aubrieta deltoidea	Aubrieta	Perennial
Aurinia saxatilis	Basket-of-gold	Perennial
Calluna vulgaris	Heather	Shrub
Campanula species	Bellflower	Perennial
Chamaecyparis species	False cypress	Shrub
Cyclamen hederifolium	Baby cyclamen	Perennial
Daphne species	Daphne	Shrub
Dianthus species	Pink	Perennial
Dryas octopetala	Mountain avens	Perennial
Erica carnea	Spring heath	Shrub
Geranium sanguineum	Geranium, Cranesbill	Perennial
Geum species	Avens	Perennial
Helianthemum nummularium	Sun rose	Shrub
Helleborus niger	Christmas rose	Perennial
Heuchera sanguinea	Coralbells	Perennial
Hypericum species	Saint John's wort	Shrub
Iberis sempervirens	Edging candytuft	Perennial
Iris cristata	Dwarf crested iris	Perennial
Lithodora diffusa	Gromwell	Shrub
Oenothera missourensis	Evening primrose	Perennial
Paxistima Canbyi	Cliff-green, Mountain-lover	Shrub
Penstemon species	Beard tongue	Perennial
Phlox stolonifera	Creeping phlox	Perennial
Phlox subulata	Mountain pink	Perennial
Picea Abies 'Nidiformis'	Bird's nest spruce	Shrub
Picea glauca 'Conica'	Dwarf Alberta spruce	Shrub
Potentilla species	Cinquefoil, Five-finger	Perennial
Primula species	Primrose	Perennial
Saxifraga species	Rockfoil	Perennial
Sedum species	Stonecrop	Perennial
Thymus praecox arcticus	Mother-of-thyme	Perennial

Rainbow pinks (Dianthus chinensis) *are among the perennials that can be grown successfully in a rock garden.*

RODENT AND ANIMAL CONTROL

Unfortunately, especially for people who live in rural areas, a number of animals and small rodents can be a menace to the garden. While no method is foolproof or completely effective, there are certain measures that will reduce the damage that these critters do.

SQUIRRELS

Squirrels, field mice, chipmunks, and other small animals often dig up bulb plantings. This problem can be reduced by planting the bulbs into a chicken wire cage and plunging the cage into the ground, or by laying a piece of chicken wire over the planting bed and securing it. Animals can be trapped and moved to another location, but they often return.

Once bulbs are up and growing, squirrels sometimes make a feast of flowers and leaves, especially tulips. To discourage them, dust the leaves with the fungicide thiram, which smells unpleasant to squirrels, or apply dried blood around the bulb plantings. Dried blood washes away with the first rain or watering and must be reapplied; it also contains nitrogen, so recalculate your fertilizer needs if you use it to prevent overfeeding.

RABBITS AND DEER

Rabbits are particularly troublesome in vegetable gardens. The best solution is a fine chicken-wire fence that is 2 feet (60 cm) high and extends 6 inches (15 cm) below ground. Check the fence often for signs that rabbits have started to burrow below the fence line.

Rabbits and deer gnaw on tree bark, especially in the winter. A metal fence around the trunks will help deter them. The fence should be 2 feet (60 cm) high to deter rabbits and 8 feet (2.4 m) high to deter deer. Deer can also be discouraged by an electric fence, or a fence that has an extension built out from it at an angled distance of 8 feet (2.4 m), which prevents them from jumping over the barrier. Dogs may keep deer away as well.

Feeding animals in the winter sometimes keeps them away from your trees and shrubs. Put out apples, corn, seeds, and nuts. Deer can be deterred by some plants, including juniper, Oregon grape holly, iris, daffodil, tulip, eucalyptus, fir, cedar, zinnia, poppy, and foxglove.

BURROWING RODENTS

Burrowing rodents such as moles, voles, and gophers must be stopped, as they eat roots and push plants out of the ground. For gophers, locate their main tunnels and set traps inside them. They can also be repelled by chemicals that are available at the garden center. Underground barriers around planting holes or beds are somewhat effective. A professional exterminator may be necessary in severe cases.

Moles dig tunnels, but do not live in them permanently. Step on a mole hill as soon as you see it to collapse the tunnel,

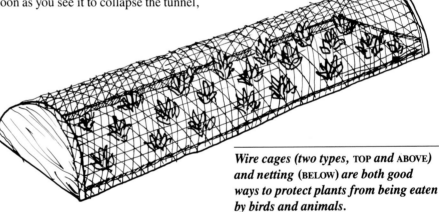

Wire cages (two types, TOP and ABOVE) and netting (BELOW) are both good ways to protect plants from being eaten by birds and animals.

ABOVE: *To stop gophers, use chemical repellents, or locate their main tunnels and set traps. This Macabee gopher trap can be set as follows: Dig through gopher mound to main tunnel; set trap and insert, business end first. String and tie wires, then fasten them to stake to facilitate retrieval and prevent loss.*

BELOW: *This beautiful rose garden is part of the Nixon Library, Yorba Linda, California. Featured in the foreground in a mass planting of Show Biz, a prolific flowering floribunda rose. In the background is the late president's birthplace.*

and return disturbed plants into contact with the soil. Traps and bait have very limited effectiveness. Moles eat insects, especially ants and grubs, so controlling the insects will somewhat control the moles as well.

Voles and field mice live in abandoned gopher and mole tunnels, and feed on the above-ground parts of plants. Cats can be a great help here, as can mouse and rat traps.

Commercial repellents and poisons are also available at garden centers. Some of these can not be used with food crops, so be sure to read the label before using them. You can also make your own repellents by soaking strips of heavy material in creosote or Tabasco™ sauce and hanging them near the garden.

You should also avoid laying winter protection on any type of plant until after the ground has frozen. This will minimize animals using the protection to set up winter housekeeping. Keeping beds clean of refuse will also help to keep small animals away.

Birds feast on many berries and on crops such as corn. If you want to attract birds to the garden, do nothing, but if you want to save your blueberry crop, cover the plants with netting or similar material. Birds also eat seeds and small seedlings, so protect planting beds with netting or cheesecloth until the plants are large enough so that the birds won't bother them.

ROSES

It is often said that the rose is the "Queen of the Flowers." No flower is as loved or steeped in history and lore. While roses require more care than most other garden plants, the beauty of their flowers and fragrance is well worth the effort.

SELECTING ROSES

Selecting roses for the garden depends on several factors. If you want flowers for cutting that have the classic rose form, choose hybrid teas and grandifloras. Polyanthas, floribundas, and shrub roses create the most effective color display. Fences and arbors can come alive with ramblers and climbers. Where space is limited, choose miniatures. Consider plant height and select roses in your favorite colors. For many months of color, choose varieties with good repeat bloom.

ROSE CLASSIFICATIONS

OLD GARDEN ROSES

Roses are divided into a number of different classifications. A rose that belongs to a classification that was in existence before the introduction of the Hybrid Tea in 1867 is an Old Garden Rose. These include the Alba, Bourbon, Centifolia, China, Damask, Gallica, Hybrid Foetida, Hybrid Perpetual, Hybrid Spinosissima, Moss, Noisette, Portland, Species, and Tea Roses.

SPECIES, SHRUB, AND HYBRID TEA ROSES

Species roses are often considered separately from each other. Species roses include the wild roses found in nature; these usually have single flowers. Shrub roses are usually large plants that are used in the same manner as other shrubs in the landscape. They include the Eglanteria, Hybrid Moyesi, Hybrid Rugosa, Kordesi, and Musk Roses. A hybrid tea rose usually has large, high-centered flowers of the classic rose form.

FLORIBUNDAS AND GRANDIFLORAS

Floribundas have clusters of flowers that are usually decorative; they are descendants of polyanthas that have clusters of very small flowers. Grandifloras are mostly large plants that have the clustering habit of floribundas and the flower form of hybrid tea roses.

CLIMBERS AND MINIATURES

Climbers, descendants of ramblers, have very long canes that can be supported on fences or arbors. Miniatures have smaller leaves, stems, and flowers, but otherwise resemble their larger cousins. Any rose can be grafted onto a trunk to make a tree rose.

HARDINESS

Hardiness is important when selecting roses. The hardiest roses are the old garden, species, and shrub roses, some of which are hardy to Zone 5 without protection, followed closely by polyanthas, climbers, and miniatures, which are hardy to Zone 6. The hardiness of hybrid teas, floribundas, and grandifloras varies; some resist very cold winters while others, especially those with yellow or pale pink flowers, are easily killed by frost. See the **Rose Chart** for hardiness information, and read the section on **Hardiness.**

DESIGNING WITH ROSES

Roses can be used anywhere in the garden where there is enough sun; they can be given their own garden or mixed with other shrubs, perennials, and annuals. Bulbs that bloom in early and mid-spring can be planted around roses to bring color before the rose canes come to life.

A formal rose garden is a thing of beauty. Lay it out in geometric patterns

BELOW LEFT: *Roses may require more care than most other garden plants, but their beauty and fragrance are well worth the effort.*

BELOW: *The grandiflora rose, Arizona.*

for a most interesting effect—circles, triangles, and squares. These gardens look best when planted with large blocks of the same variety or at least the same color. They can be edged with brick or a low growing hedge like boxwood.

Even where there is not room for a formal rose garden, roses have multiple uses. A dozen plants along the side of the house or garage will provide lots of color. Intermingle roses with other shrubs; many will bloom all summer, unlike most other shrubs. Instead of building a fence, why not plant a hedge of roses? Climbers can grace fences, walls and arbors. Miniatures can be used almost anywhere—as edgings, to accent the front door, in rock gardens, under the lamppost, and in containers dotting the patio. Some low-growing roses can be used as ground covers.

What would a cutting garden be without roses? Consider fragrance when designing with roses, and place them where you will enjoy their scent.

For more information, read **Cutting Flowers, Fragrance, Container Gardening,** and **Landscape Design.**

GROWING AND MAINTAINING ROSES

When you buy a rosebush, it will either be bare-root (dormant and without soil around the roots), or growing in a container. Bare-root roses are planted in early to mid-spring, or in autumn where winter temperatures do not drop below 0°F (–18°C). Container roses can be planted any time from spring through autumn. If you can't plant your roses right away, store them in a cool, dark place and make sure they are wrapped in plastic or other material so they will not dry out.

Roses purchased from mail-order companies will be bare-root, while some roses are sold in "plantable" containers. It is always better, however, to remove the container before planting so the roots are not confined until the container disintegrates.

PLANTING ROSES

Before planting, read the sections on **Soil** and **Planting.** Roses like a soil that is extremely rich in organic matter, so be generous with peat moss, compost, or whatever you use when preparing the soil. Be sure that the pH is between 6.0 and 7.0. Set hybrid teas and floribundas 24 inches (60 cm) apart; grandifloras, 30 inches (75 cm) apart; miniatures, 6 to 12 inches (15 to 30 cm) apart, depending on their ultimate size. Shrubs, old garden, and species roses need 3 to 6 feet (1 to 1.8 m) between plants, depending on size. If climbers are trained horizontally on a fence, allow about 8 feet (2.4 m) between plants. Place the roses where they will receive at least six hours of sun a day, perferably in the morning.

After planting, mound soil or mulch around the canes until new growth starts so the canes do not dry out.

FERTILIZING ROSES

Roses, being hungry plants, need to be fertilized often. Using a balanced fertilizer or rose food, feed roses as soon as they are pruned, after the first flush of bloom, and about two months before the first autumn frost. Those gardeners who

ABOVE: *A beautiful way to screen a patio is to use two old garden shrub roses: Rosa Mundi, a pink-and-white bicolor, and Will Scarlet, a brilliant red.*

BELOW: *Miss All-American Beauty.*

KEY

C   Classification
- CL   climber
- FL   floribunda
- GR   grandiflora
- HT   hybrid tea
- MN   miniature
- OG   old garden rose
- PL   polyantha
- SH   shrub
- SP   species

FC   Flower color
- AB   apricot blend
- DP   deep pink
- DR   deep red
- DY   deep yellow
- LP   light pink
- M   mauve
- MB   mauve blend
- MP   medium pink
- MR   medium red
- MY   medium yellow
- OB   orange blend
- OR   orange red
- PB   pink blend
- RB   red blend
- W   white
- YB   yellow blend

PH   Plant height
- L   low-growing
- M   medium-growing
- T   tall-growing

Heights are relative within specific classes and will vary with the climate and the length of the growing season.

Hardiness Zone (HZ) Zones within which the particular variety will not need winter protection.

ROSE CHART

VARIETY	C	FC	PH	HZ
America	CL	OB	M	7–10
Angel Face	FL	MB	L	6–10
Apricot Nectar	FL	AB	M	7–10
Aquarius	GR	PB	M	6–10
Austrian Copper	SP	RB	T	5–10
Beauty Secret	MN	MR	T	6–10
Belinda	SH	MP	T	5–10
Betty Prior	FL	MP	T	5–10
Blaze	CL	MR	T	6–10
Bonica	SH	MP	M	5–10
Cecile Brunner	PL	LP	L	6–10
Century Two	HT	MP	M	7–10
Cherish	FL	MP	L	7–10
Chicago Peace	HT	PB	M	7–10
China Doll	PL	MP	T	6–10
Chrysler Imperial	HT	DR	T	6–10
Color Magic	HT	PB	M	8–10
Crested Moss	OG	MP	M	6–10
Cupcake	MN	MP	M	6–10
Dainty Bess	HT	LP	M	7–10
Don Juan	CL	DR	M	7–10
Dortmund	SH	MR	T	5–10
Double Delight	HT	RB	M	7–10
Dreamglo	MN	RB	T	6–10
Duet	HT	MP	M	7–10
Electron	HT	DP	M	7–10
Europeana	FL	DR	T	6–10
Father Hugo's Rose	SP	MY	T	5–10
F.J. Grootendorst	SH	MR	T	5–10
First Edition	FL	OB	M	7–10
First Prize	HT	PB	M	8–10
Folklore	HT	OB	T	7–10
Fragrant Cloud	HT	OR	M	6–10
Frulingsgold	OG	MY	T	5–10
Frulingsmorgen	OG	PB	T	5–10
Garden Party	HT	W	M	6–10
Gene Boerner	FL	MP	M	7–10
Golden Wings	SH	MR	T	5–10
Granada	HT	RB	M	7–10
Holy Toledo	MN	AB	T	8–10

ROSES cont.

Variety	C	FC	PH	HZ
Iceberg	FL	W	T	6–10
Impatient	FL	OR	M	7–10
Ivory Fashion	FL	W	T	6–10
Jean Kenneally	MN	AB	T	7–10
Judy Fisher	MN	MP	M	6–10
Lady X	HT	M	T	7–10
Little Darling	FL	YB	M	6–10
Madame Hardy	OG	W	T	6–10
Magic Carousel	MN	RB	T	6–10
Mary Marshall	MN	OB	M	6–10
Miss All-American Beauty	HT	DP	M	7–10
Mister Lincoln	HT	DR	T	6–10
Olympiad	HT	MR	M	6–10
Over the Rainbow	MN	RB	T	6–10
Paradise	HT	MB	M	7–10
Party Girl	MN	YB	M	6–10
Pascali	HT	W	M	7–10
Peace	HT	YB	T	7–10
Peaches 'n' Cream	MN	PB	M	6–10
Pink Parfait	GR	PB	M	6–10
Playgirl	FL	MP	M	6–10
Precious Platinum	HT	MR	M	6–10
Pristine	HT	W	M	7–10
Queen Elizabeth	GR	MP	T	6–10
Rainbow's End	MN	YB	M	7–10
Regensberg	FL	PB	M	6–10
Royal Highness	HT	LP	M	8–10
Showbiz	FL	MR	L	6–10
Simplex	MN	W	T	7–10
Simplicity	FL	MP	T	6–10
Snow Bride	MN	W	M	6–10
Starina	MN	OR	T	6–10
Summer Fashion	FL	YB	M	7–10
Sunsprite	FL	DY	L	6–10
Swarthmore	HT	PB	M	7–10
The Fairy	PL	LP	T	6–10
Tiffany	HT	PB	M	7–10
Touch of Class	HT	PB	M	7–10
Tropicana	HT	OR	T	6–10
York and Lancaster	OG	PB	T	5–10

want exhibition-size roses can feed them once a month from early spring to late summer. Read also about **Fertilizing.**

WATERING ROSES

Roses are thirsty plants. Water them enough so they receive 1 inch (25 mm) of water per week. Watering overhead is acceptable if it is done in the morning, but if diseases are a problem, water them with soaker hoses or another irrigation method that allows the foliage to stay dry. See **Watering.**

PRUNING ROSES

Prune established rose bushes in spring, as soon as the leaf buds start to swell, unless they are species, old garden or shrub roses, or climbers. The first three need to be pruned only to remove dead canes, shape the plants, or control their size; in some years, they may need no pruning. Climbers are pruned after they have bloomed, unless there are dead or awkward-growing canes to be removed in early spring. For specific directions on pruning roses, read **Pruning.**

As soon as flowers fade, they should be removed; this is called deadheading. This will keep the plant productive and ensure continuous bloom. When deadheading or cutting flowers for bouquets, always make a cut just about a five-leaflet leaf, and always leave at least two leaves on a stem so the plant can produce food.

In autumn, cut tall plants back by about one-third to prevent them from wind damage, but do no other pruning at this time. Plants will endure the winter better if the last blooms are not removed, but allowed to set seed heads called "hips." Where necessary, apply winter protection.

See also **Diseases and Disease Control, Insects and Insect Control, Mulching, Weeds,** and **Winter Protection.**

RUNNERS

Runners are long stems that grow from the base of some plants. New plants grow at the ends of runners. See **Propagation.**

SEASHORE GARDENING

SELECTING PLANTS FOR A SEASHORE GARDEN

Seashore gardening holds special challenges. Plants must not only be drought-resistant, they must also be able to tolerate salt spray, strong winds, occasional flooding, and the heat caused by reflection from the sand. Even though the soil along beaches drains quickly and is not water-retentive, the air is often foggy and humid. This condition separates plants that grow well in dry deserts from those that thrive along coastlines. Many plants that grow well along the seashore are low-growing plants that naturally protect themselves from the wind. The wind causes some plants to take on beautiful although contorted shapes. In general, you can assume that plants with thick leathery foliage, or plants with hairy leaves will grow well by the sea. Very small or narrow leaves are another type of built-in protection plants have against wind damage. Plants that have flexible branches also do better by the sea than rigid-branched plants as they will bend with the wind.

DESIGNING A SEASHORE GARDEN

Gardening by the sea is rewarding. The colors seem more vibrant, particularly against the blues and greens of the water. Plants are a delight to watch as they sway in the breeze. The fragrance of the garden combined with the fragrance of the salt spray makes the air fresh and bracing.

When designing a seashore garden, remember that the sea itself is an integral part of the overall picture. While some windbreaks should be planted, do not plant them so heavily as to prevent the vista of the sea. Ornamental grasses are naturals to include in a seashore garden, as are silver- and gray-leaved plants. Not only are these plants naturally drought- and salt-tolerant, they are also quite attractive both in the sunshine and the fog.

TOP: *The salt-tolerant plants in this cliff-top planting near Carmel, California, include yellow tree lupine, orange gazania, blue Pride of Madeira echium, purple sea lavender, and silvery lavender cotton.*

ABOVE: *Plants that have flexible branches do better than rigid-branched plants because they bend with the wind.*

RIGHT: *Ornamental grasses are a good choice for a seashore garden because they are drought- and salt-tolerant.*

MAINTAINING AND GROWING A SEASHORE GARDEN

Several gardening techniques ease the challenge of gardening by the seashore. The soil should be prepared with extra organic matter to improve water retention. Planting should be done in the cool days of spring or autumn unless extra attention can be given to heavy watering. Heavy mulching will hold more moisture in the soil and prevent overheating due to reflection from the sand. Since sandy soil drains quickly, you will need to apply more fertilizer than normal. Applying soluble fertilizer when watering weekly will replace nutrients in the soil and ensure uniform growth.

Watering, too, will need to be increased. Automatic sprinkler systems make more frequent watering easier. After a very high tide, a flood, or a bad storm, if plants become drenched with salt water, hose down the foliage to remove the salt buildup and water heavily to leach the salt from the soil.

More frequent pruning may be necessary at the seashore than in an interior garden, as plants are more apt to suffer damage. Since many shrubs and trees develop windswept contours, prune to enhance these shapes instead of trying to force them into symmetrical forms.

PROTECTING A SEASHORE GARDEN

In winter, **Winter Protection** will keep the plants from being heaved from the soil and will protect them from the winds and strong sun. Antidesiccant sprays will keep evergreens from drying out and protect their foliage from salt.

To protect the garden from the wind and salt spray, fences, walls, or protective hedges can be installed on the windward side of the garden. Plants with heavy root systems, or plants that root as they grow along the ground, should be included to hold the soil in place and prevent it from blowing away. Snow fences installed in winter will help prevent erosion. Plant two fences 30 to 40 feet (9 to 12 m) apart at a right angle to the prevailing winds.

Read about **Diseases and Disease Control, Insects and Insect Control,** and **Weeds.**

PLANTS FOR THE SEASHORE

Latin Name	Common Name	Type of Plant
Akebia quinata	Five-leaf akebia	Vine
Ammophila arenaria	European beach grass	Perennial
Ammophila breviligulata	American beach grass	Perennial
Andromeda Polifolia	Bog rosemary	Shrub
Araucaria heterophylla	Norfolk Island pine	Tree
Arctostaphylos species	Bearberry, Manzanita	Ground cover
Arenaria verna	Sandwort	Ground cover
Armeria maritima	Thrift	Ground cover
Artemisia Schmidtiana	Sagebrush	Ground cover
Artemisia Stellerana	Beach wormwood	Ground cover
Calluna vulgaris	Heather	Shrub
Campsis radicans	Trumpet vine	Vine
Canna × *generalis*	Canna	Bulb
Catharanthus roseus	Vinca, Rose periwinkle	Annual
Celastrus scandens	American bittersweet	Vine
Chamaecyparis species	False cypress	Tree
Cotoneaster species	Cotoneaster	Shrub
Cupressus macrocarpa	Monterey cypress	Tree
Cytisus species	Broom	Shrub
Elaeagnus angustifolia	Russian olive	Tree, Shrub
Erica carnea	Spring heath	Shrub
Eryngium mentimum	Sea holly	Perennial
Eucalyptus species	Gum tree	Tree
Euonymus Fortunei radicans	Wintercreeper	Vine
Fagus species	Beech	Tree
Festuca ovina glauca	Blue fescue	Perennial
Gelsemium sempervirens	Evening trumpet flower	Vine
Gleditsia tricanthos	Honey locust	Tree
Hedera Helix	English ivy	Vine, Ground cover
Hemerocallis species	Daylily	Perennial
Hippophae rhamnoides	Sea buckthorn	Shrub
Hosta species	Plantain lily	Perennial
Hydrangea species	Hydrangea	Shrub

PLANTS FOR THE SEASHORE cont.

LATIN NAME	COMMON NAME	TYPE OF PLANT
Hypericum species	Saint John's wort	Shrub
Ilex species	Holly	Tree, Shrub
Ipomoea purpurea	Morning glory	Vine
Juniperus species	Juniper	Tree, Shrub
Lathyrus japonicus	Beach pea	Perennial
Leiophyllum buxifolium	Box sand myrtle	Ground cover
Limonium latifolium	Sea lavender	Perennial
Lobularia maritima	Sweet alyssum	Annual
Lonicera species	Honeysuckle	Shrub, Vine
Mahonia Aquifolium	Oregon grape holly	Shrub
Malus species	Crabapple	Tree
Myrica species	Bayberry	Shrub
Nepeta Mussini	Catmint	Perennial
Nerium Oleander	Oleander	Tree, Shrub
Olea europaea	Olive	Tree
Petunia × *hybrida*	Petunia	Annual
Phlox species	Phlox	Perennial, Annual
Pinus species	Pine	Tree, Shrub
Polygonum Aubertii	Silver lace vine	Vine
Portulaca grandiflora	Moss rose, Purslane	Annual
Potentilla species	Cinquefoil	Shrub
Prunus maritima	Beach plum	Shrub
Rhus species	Sumac	Shrub
Robinia Pseudoacacia	Black locust	Tree
Rosa species	Wild rose	Shrub
Rosmarinus officinalis	Rosemary	Herb
Schinus Molle	California pepper tree	Tree
Tagetes species	Marigold	Annual
Tamarix species	Tamarisk	Tree
Taxus species	Yew	Tree, Shrub
Tilia cordata	Littleleaf linden	Tree
Uniola paniculata	Sea oats	Perennial
Vaccinium species	Blueberry, Cranberry	Shrub

TOP: *Phlox* (PHLOX spp.) *are hearty perennials that can meet the various challenges of seashore gardening.*

ABOVE: *The house at left helps to shelter a colorful garden of annuals on the cliffs near Monterey. Salt-tolerant shrubs along the perimeter of the garden help to break the force of coastal winds. The seeded fescue lawn is also salt-tolerant.*

SHADE GARDENING

Surprisingly, gardening in the shade is not a difficult thing to do. This is fortunate, as many of our gardens are shaded by tall trees or nearby buildings. With the proper selection of plants, a colorful shade garden is possible, with interest in every season of the year.

If, however, you feel that your garden has a little too much shade, there are several things you can do. You can prune away the lower limbs of large trees, which will allow more light to enter. Another tactic is to thin out the branches of large trees so that more light passes through the foliage, the effect being a dappled light.

In most aspects of plant care, gardening in the shade requires the same maintenance as growing plants in the sun. Some gardeners feel they can compensate for lack of light by fertilizing more heavily than normal. In fact, the opposite is true. Plants being grown in reduced light usually need less fertilizer than those being grown in full sun. Most shade-tolerant plants are also moisture-loving plants, so extra watering and mulching will be of benefit. Many shade-loving plants are native to woodlands, and benefit from soil with additional organic matter.

SELECTING PLANTS FOR A SHADE GARDEN

Plants of all types will thrive in the shade. When the shade in the garden is created by deciduous trees, spring-flow-

Plants of all types thrive in a shade garden, including English ivy (HEDERA HELIX), ABOVE, many ornamental grasses, RIGHT, and primrose (PRIMULA spp.), OPPOSITE PAGE, TOP.

PLANTS FOR THE SHADE GARDEN

Latin Name	Common Name	Type of Plant
Acer japonicum	Japanese maple	Tree
Ajuga reptans	Carpet bugle	Ground cover
Amelanchier species	Shadbush	Tree
Aquilegia species	Columbine	Perennial
Arisaema triphyllum	Jack-in-the-pulpit	Perennial
Asarum species	Wild ginger	Perennial
Aucuba japonica	Japanese aucuba	Shrub
Begonia Semperflorens-Cultorum Hybrids	Wax begonia	Annual
Berberis species	Bayberry	Shrub
Bergenia species	Bergenia	Perennial
Caladium × *hortulanum*	Fancy-leaved caladium	Bulb
Cercis species	Redbud	Tree
Clethra alnifolia	Sweet pepperbush	Shrub
Coleus × *hybridus*	Coleus	Annual
Cornus species	Dogwood	Tree
Dicentra species	Bleeding heart	Perennial
Enkianthus campanulatus	Enkianthus	Shrub
Epimedium species	Epimedium	Perennial
Euonymus alata	Winged spindle tree	Shrub
Forsythia species	Forsythia	Shrub
Fothergilla species	Fothergilla	Shrub
Halesia carolina	Carolina silverbell	Tree
Hamamelis mollis	Chinese witch hazel	Tree
Hedera Helix	English ivy	Ground cover, Vine
Helleborus orientalis	Lenten rose	Perennial
Hosta species	Plantain lily	Perennial

ABOVE: *This narrow passageway between houses creates almost permanent shade, yet allows a colorful assortment of plants to thrive, including red-leaf caladiums, a variegated hosta, pink impatiens, and blue wishbone flowers.*

PLANTS FOR THE SHADE GARDEN cont.

LATIN NAME	COMMON NAME	TYPE OF PLANT
Hydrangea species	Hydrangea	Vine, Shrub
Iberis sempervirens	Edging candytuft	Perennial
Ilex species	Holly	Shrub, Tree
Impatiens Wallerana	Impatiens	Annual
Kalmia latifolia	Mountain laurel	Shrub
Kerria japonica	Japanese rose	Shrub
Lamiastrum Galeobdolon	Yellow archangel	Ground cover
Leucothoe Fontanesiana	Leucothoe	Shrub
Ligustrum species	Privet	Shrub
Lindera Benzoin	Spicebush	Shrub
Liriope species	Lilyturf	Perennial
Mertensia virginica	Virginia bluebells	Perennial
Mitchella repens	Partridgeberry	Ground cover
Pachysandra terminalis	Japanese spurge	Ground cover
Pieris species	Andromeda	Shrub
Polygonatum odoratum	Solomon's-seal	Perennial
Primula species	Primrose	Perennial
Pyracantha species	Fire thorn	Shrub
Rhododendron species	Rhododendron	Shrub
Salvia splendens	Scarlet sage	Annual
Skimmia japonica	Japanese skimmia	Shrub
Styrax species	Snowbell	Tree
Tiarella cordifolia	Foamflower	Perennial
Trillium species	Wake-robin	Perennial
Vinca minor	Periwinkle, Myrtle	Ground cover
Viola species	Violet	Perennial
Many genera	Ferns	Perennial

ering bulbs, even if they prefer to be grown in the sun, can be successfully grown, because the leaves are not on the trees at the time most bulbs bloom.

Sometimes the garden simply has too much sun. Some shade is essential both for your sake and the garden's. You can create necessary shade with trees, but since trees take time to grow, you'll need to take temporary measures. Quick-growing shrubs can be planted to cast shade. Overhead lathes and trellises can be built and covered with vines. Shade cloth can be stretched over wooden frames.

If you have a choice, it's best to plan a garden that receives morning sun and afternoon shade. Plants grow better out of the afternoon's heat, and the garden will be more enjoyable for your relaxation as well. Before you plant any large trees or shrubs that will cast shade, study the path of the sun during the day to determine the best location for them.

SHRUBS

Shrubs have a wide variety of uses in the garden. They are planted around homes to hide the foundation and enhance the architecture. They frame windows and soften corners. They can line the pathway to the front door. Shrubs can be used as "living fences" instead of manufactured barriers. Hedges mark property lines, separate different areas of the garden, or provide privacy. When the branches are thorny, the barrier will be even more impenetrable. Specimen shrubs can be highlighted, standing alone in the center of the lawn.

Depending on the type, flowering shrubs provide color from early spring to late autumn. Some shrubs have spectacular autumn foliage or colorful berries, while others have interesting winter silhouettes or bark.

SELECTING SHRUBS

There are a few considerations to bear in mind when selecting shrubs. Think about flower color and bloom time to make sure the color will complement your home and the rest of the plants in the landscape. Shrubs with colorful autumn foliage or berries can extend your gardening season, too. Also consider what the shrub will look like when it is not in bloom or touting autumn's colors, and select those with foliage, bark, or overall form that pleases you.

Shrubs may be deciduous or evergreen. Those that are on display all year, such as those in the front of the house, will be more satisfying if they are evergreen. Among evergreens, shrubs may be coniferous, with needlelike leaves, or broad-leaved. For the best effect, plant a combination of both types, as the size and texture of the needle-leaved and broad-leaved evergreens complement each other nicely.

Consider a shrub's mature height so it won't outgrow its setting or cover a window.

Shrubs also have specific needs regarding light and soil; this information is outlined in the **Shrub Chart** and should be studied before you decide what to plant. Also ensure that the shrubs you want to plant are hardy in your area. All shrubs have minimum winter temperatures that they will endure; some types must have cold

weather during the winter or they will not bloom. See also **Hardiness.**

Read about **Hedges** if you will be using shrubs in this way. Also read the sections on **Cutting Flowers, Container Gardening, Fragrance,** and **Landscape Design** to help you make final selections. Refer to the section on **Drought Resistance** if water supplies are short, and to **Shade Gardening** if large trees or buildings limit the light on the shrub plantings.

GROWING AND MAINTAINING SHRUBS

☐ PLANTING SHRUBS

Shrubs purchased at the garden center or through the mail are either bare-root, containerized, or balled and burlapped. Read the section about **Planting** for an explanation of each of these three different packing types and for directions on how to plant each one. The section also

ABOVE: *Lilac* (BUDDLEIA DAVIDII) *adds delightful fragrance to the garden.*

LEFT: *Shrubs, such as the Forsythia* (FORSYTHIA × INTERMEDIA) *pictured here, can be used as "living fences" in place of manufactured barriers.*

BELOW: *A beautiful assortment of evergreen shrubs combines effectively with Japanese maples. Prostrate juniper cascades down the retaining wall, while the tightly knit needles of a cone-shaped Alberta spruce are contrasted with the cascading branches of an evergreen leucothoe.*

Shrubs can be used to divide the garden or property, BELOW RIGHT, *or as edging to line walkways,* BOTTOM.

outlines the proper times for planting. Read the section on **Soil** before planting.

PROPAGATING SHRUBS

When you are purchasing shrubs for a new house or a renovated landscape, you will probably want to buy large shrubs so the effect is immediate. It is also fun to propagate your own shrubs, and place them in small areas of the garden or in specialty gardens where they can take the necessary time to mature. The **Shrub Chart** outlines the various methods of propagation for shrubs. Read the **Propagation** section for further information.

FERTILIZING SHRUBS

Shrubs are usually not high-maintenance plants, but they do need some annual care to keep them in top shape. They benefit from a yearly application of a balanced fertilizer such as 5-10-5, which can be applied in early to mid-spring as growth starts, or in late autumn after the plants become dormant. If the leaves of broad-leaved evergreens become yellow, fertilize them

with a fertilizer for acid-loving plants (most broad-leaved evergreens prefer acidic soil). See **Fertilizing.**

WATERING SHRUBS

Shrubs vary in their needs for water; this is outlined in the **Shrub Chart.** Plants with average water requirements need 1 inch (25 mm) of water per week from rain or irrigation; others need more or less water, and the amount given should be adjusted as necessary. Water deeply and as infrequently as possible to encourage deep roots, which will aid in making shrubs more resistant to drought, wind, and storm damage. See **Watering.**

PRUNING SHRUBS

Many shrubs will not need annual pruning, but all should be inspected yearly to see if they do. The small flowers of plants such as azaleas fall cleanly from the plant as they fade and do not need to be removed. Shrubs with large clusters of flowers, such as lilacs, should be deadheaded as soon as the flowers die. Read the section on **Pruning.**

MULCHING SHRUBS

A summer mulch will conserve moisture while it keeps the soil cooler and suppresses weeds. Mulch will also protect the roots of shallow-rooted shrubs such as azaleas and many broad-leaved evergreens. Avoid placing mulch against the branches to prevent both stem rot and spots for small animals to nest over the winter.

PROTECTING SHRUBS

When shrubs are grown near the low end of their hardiness limits, they will need winter protection. Mulch them after the ground has frozen with wood chips, shredded leaves, or evergreen boughs. If it has not rained, evergreens should be watered in late autumn to help them through the drying winds and sun of winter. Evergreens will also benefit from an antidesiccant spray. Tender shrubs can be wrapped in burlap, but this is not very attractive, especially at the front of the house. Snow and ice should be removed from weak-wooded shrubs as soon as possible to prevent breakage or disfigurement.

Refer also to **Diseases and Disease Control** and **Insects and Insect Control.**

SHRUBS

	PT	PH	FC	BT	L	MO	HZ	P	AI
Abelia × *grandiflora* Glossy abelia	E	2–6'	PINK	ASu	S,PSh	M	6–10	SC	C
Acanthopanax Sieboldianus Five-leaf aralia	D	5–9'	WHITE	MSp	S–Sh	A–D	5–9	RC,S	B
Amelanchier × *grandiflora* Serviceberry	D	9–30"	WHITE	ESp	S,PSh	M	4–8	D,L	B
Andromeda polifolia Bog rosemary	E	1'	WHITE	MSp	S,LSh	M	2–7	SC,S	—
Arctostaphylos Uva-ursi Bearberry	E	1'	PINK, WHITE	MSp	S,LSh	D	2–8	SC,S	B
Aronia arbutifolia Chokeberry	D	4–8'	PINK, WHITE	MSp	S,LSh	A	3–9	SC,L,D,S	B,C
Aucuba japonica Japanese aucuba	E	6–8'	PURPLE	MSp	PSh,Sh	M	7–10	SC,S,G	B
Berberis species Barberry	E,D	2–8'	YELLOW	MSp	S,PSh	M	3–8	SC,S	B,C
Buddleia Davidii Butterfly bush, Summer lilac	D	6–15"	LILAC	LSu	S	A	5–10	SC,S	—
Buxus species Boxwood	E	2–20'	—	—	S,PSh	M	4–9	SC,D	—
Callicarpa dichotoma Beautyberry	D	2–4'	PINK	ESu	S	A	5–8	SC,L,S	B,C
Calluna vulgaris Heather	E	1–2'	PINK, WHITE, LAVENDER	A	S	M	4–7	SC	C
Calycanthus floridus Carolina allspice	D	5–10'	BROWN	MSp	S,LSh	M	5–9	L,D,S	C
Camellia species Camellia	E	5–15'	WHITE, PINK, RED	ESp	PSh	M	7–10	SC,G	—
Caryopteris × *clandonensis* Bluebeard	D	2–3'	BLUE	LSu	S	M	3–10	S,SC	—
Chamaecyparis species False cypress	E	1–10'	—	—	S	A–M	3–9	SC	—
Clethra alnifolia Summer-sweet	D	4–20'	WHITE, PINK	MSu	S,LSh	M	5–9	S,SC,L,D	—
Cornus species Dogwood	D	6–20'	WHITE, YELLOW	ESp,MSp	S,PSh	A	2–9	SC,L,G	B,S

SHRUBS cont.

	PT	PH	FC	BT	L	MO	HZ	P	AI
Corylopsis species Winter hazel	D	6–8′	YELLOW	ESp	S,PSh	M	5–8	S,SC,L,D	—
Cotoneaster species Cotoneaster	E,D	1–8′	WHITE, PINK	LSp	S,PSh	D	3–9	SC,S	B
Cryptomeria japonica Japanese cedar	E	1–15′	—	—	S,LSh	M	5–9	SC,S	—
Cytisus, Genista species Broom	E,D	1–15′	YELLOW, RED	MSp	S	D	5–10	SC	—
Daphne species Daphne	E	1–4′	WHITE, PINK	ESp,LSp	S,LSh	D–A	4–9	SC,S,G	B
Deutzia gracilis Deutzia	D	2–6′	WHITE, PINK	LSp	S,LSh	A	4–8	SC,S,D,L	C
Elaeagnus species Elaeagnus	E,D	9–15′	—	—	S,PSh	A–D	2–10	SC,S	—
Enkianthus campanulatus Redvein enkianthus	D	6–12′	YELLOW	MSp	S,PSh	M	5–9	S,SC,L	C
Erica carnea Spring heath	E	½–2′	MIX	ESp	S,PSh	A	3–9	SC	—
Euonymus species Euonymus	E,D	1–15′	—	—	S,Sh	A	3–10	SC,L,S	C
Exochorda × *macrantha* Pearlbush	D	9–15′	WHITE	MSp	S,LSh	A	5–8	S,L,SC	B
Forsythia species Forsythia	D	5–12′	YELLOW	ESp	S,PSh	A	5–9	SC,S	—
Fothergilla species Fothergilla	D	3–10′	WHITE	ESp	S	M	5–8	S,L,SC,D	C
Gardenia jasminoides Gardenia	E	2–5′	WHITE	MSp	S	M	8–10	SC	—
Hippophae rhamnoides Sea buckthorn	D	9–30′	YELLOW	ESp	S	D	3–7	L,D,SC,S	B
Hydrangea species Hydrangea	D	3–8′	WHITE, PINK, BLUE	MSu	S,Sh	M	4–9	SC,S	—
Hypericum species Saint John's wort	E	1–6′	YELLOW	MSu	S,PSh	A	7–10	SC,S,L	—

SHRUBS cont.

	PT	PH	FC	BT	L	MO	HZ	P	AI
Ilex species Holly	E,D	4–20'	WHITE	ESp	S,PSh	M	3–10	SC,S,G	B
Jasminum nudiflorum Winter jasmine	D	3–5'	YELLOW	ESp	S,PSh	A	6–9	SC,L,S	B
Juniperus species Juniper	E	1–15'	—	—	S	D	2–10	SC,S	B
Kalmia latifolia Mountain laurel	E	6–12'	PINK	LSp	S,PSh	M	5–8	SC,S	—
Kerria japonica Japanese rose	D	5–8'	YELLOW	MSp	S,PSh	A–M	5–9	L,D,SC	C
Kolkwitzia amabilis Beauty bush	D	7–15'	PINK	LSp	S,LSh	A	5–8	S,SC	—
Leucothoe species Fetterbush	E	3–6'	WHITE	ESp	PSh,Sh	M	5–9	SC,S,D	C
Ligustrum species Privet	E,D	6–15'	WHITE	LSp	S,PSh	A	5–10	SC,S	B
Lindera Benzoin Spicebush	D	6–15'	YELLOW	ESp	PSh	M	4–9	S,L,SC	B,C
Lonicera species Honeysuckle	E,D	3–10'	PINK, WHITE	LSp	S,PSh	A	4–10	SC,S,L	B
Mahonia Aquifolium Oregon grape holly	E	3–6'	YELLOW	ESp	PSh,Sh	M	5–9	SC,S	C,B
Microbiota decussata Russian cypress	E	1–2'	—	—	S,Sh	D	2–10	SG,S	—
Myrica pensylvanica Bayberry	D	3–9'	WHITE	MSp	S	D	5–9	L,D,S	B
Nandina domestica Heavenly bamboo	E	6–8'	WHITE	ESu	S,PSh	D	7–10	S	C,B
Osmanthus species Devilweed	E	3–10'	WHITE, YELLOW, ORANGE	MSp,A	S,PSh	M	7–10	SC	—
Paxistima Canbyi Cliff-green, Mountain-lover, Paxistima	E	1'	WHITE	LSp	S,PSh	M	4–10	SC,S,D	C
Philadelphus species Mock orange	D	4–9'	WHITE	LSp	S,LSh	A	4–9	S,L,SC	—
Pieris species Andromeda	E	3–10'	WHITE	ESp	S,PSh	M	4–9	SC,S	C

SHRUBS cont.

	PT	PH	FC	BT	L	MO	HZ	P	AI
Platycladus orientalis Oriental arborvitae	E	3–12'	—	—	S,LSh	M	6–10	SC	—
Potentilla fruticosa Shrubby cinquefoil	D	1–4'	YELLOW	ESu	S,LSh	M	2–9	S,D,SC	—
Pyracantha species Fire thorn	E	3–15'	WHITE	LSp	S	A	6–10	SC,S	B
Rhododendron species Azalea	E,D	3–8'	MIX	ESp–LSp	S,PSh	M	6–10	SC	—
Rhododendron species Rhododendron	E,D	3–20'	MIX	ESp–LSp	PSh,Sh	M	4–9	SC	—
Rhodotypos scandens Jetbead	D	3–6'	WHITE	MSp	S,Sh	A	5–10	SC	B
Rhus species Sumac	E,D	5–10'	PINK, WHITE	MSp	S	A	2–10	RC,S	C,B
Sarcococca Hookerana Sweet box	E	2–6'	WHITE	ESp	PSh,Sh	M	6–9	SC,S	B
Skimmia japonica Japanese skimmia	E	2–4'	WHITE	MSp	PSh,Sh	M	7–9	SC,S	B
Spiraea species Spirea	D	1–8'	WHITE, PINK	LSp	S,PSh	M	5–10	SC	—
Styrax japonica Snowbell	D	5–30'	WHITE	LSp	S,PSh	M	5–10	L,SC	C
Symphoricarpos × *Chenaultii* Snowberry	D	3–6'	PINK	MSp	S,PSh	A	3–10	SC	B
Syringa species Lilac	D	6–20'	LILAC	LSp	S	M	2–8	SC,L	—
Taxus species Yew	E	1–20'	—	—	S,PSh	M	3–8	SC,S	B
Thuja occidentalis American arborvitae	E	1–20'	—	—	S	M	5–9	SC,S	—
Tsuga canadensis Canada hemlock	E	6–12'	—	—	S,LSh	M	3–8	SC	—
Virburnum species Arrowwood, Virburnum	D,E,	4–15'	WHITE	MSp	PSh,Sh	M	2–10	SC	B
Vitex Agnus-castus Chaste tree	D	9–20'	PURPLE	LSu	S,PSh	A	6–9	SC,L	—
Weigela florida Weigela	D	6–10'	PINK	ESu	S,PSh	A	5–8	SC,L	—

SOIL

If you want your garden to grow to be large and healthy and give you beautiful flowers and fruit, it must have a good foundation. The garden's foundation is the soil.

To treat soil properly requires an understanding of what soil is. Soil is composed of varying amounts of particles. The size of these particles is referred to as the soil's texture, while the arrangement of these particles is referred to as its structure.

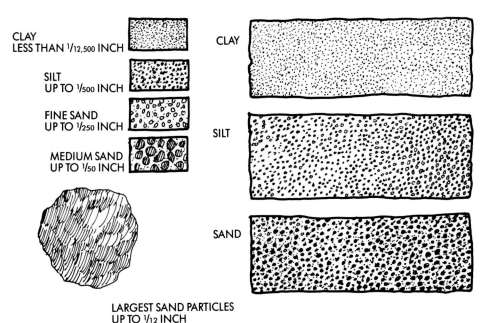

CLAY
LESS THAN 1/12,500 INCH

SILT
UP TO 1/500 INCH

FINE SAND
UP TO 1/250 INCH

MEDIUM SAND
UP TO 1/50 INCH

LARGEST SAND PARTICLES
UP TO 1/12 INCH

CLAY

SILT

SAND

THE ELEMENTS OF SOIL

The mineral particles that make up soil are known as sand, silt, and clay. Almost no soil is composed of exclusively one size particle; soils are made up of some of each of these materials plus organic matter, air, and water.

Sand is the largest soil particle. Consequently, sandy soils drain well and have excellent aeration, but they dry out quickly, and do not retain nutrients for long because of the leaching or washing away of fertilizers by rain or watering. Sandy soils have a coarse texture and a loose structure. Silt soils are composed of particles that are smaller than sand but larger than clay. Silt soils are very similar to clay soils, with fine texture and dense structure. Clay soils are composed of the smallest soil particles; these tend to stick together. Clay soils have poor drainage and aeration because the particles are so tightly packed together, and they hold excessive water. They have fine texture and dense structure.

The ideal garden soil is called loam and is a mixture of sand, silt, and clay. Loam drains well, but not too quickly, and has water- and nutrient-holding capacities that encourage good plant growth. Loam has a medium texture and a crumbly structure.

In some areas of the United States, there are "muck" soils, which are almost all organic matter with little or no clay or sand. They have tremendous water-holding capacity and are good for crops like celery and onions. They are hard to work, especially when dry.

The solution to improving any type of soil to give it the texture of loam is to add organic matter. Organic matter acts like clay in sandy soil and like sand in clay soil. In sandy soil organic matter increases water retention and nutrient-holding capacity. In clay or silt soil, organic matter congeals the tiny particles, improving water infiltration, drainage, and root growth.

Humus is another term used to refer to organic matter in the soil. It can be added in many forms, such as sphagnum peat moss, leaf mold, dried manure, bark, sawdust, mulch, or compost. Add enough so that the soil is approximately 25% organic matter after it has been improved. You will notice that when your soil has enough organic matter plants will grow larger and be healthier.

The content of the rest of the soil, if it is ideal, is 25% air, 25% water, and 25% mineral particles. If these proportions are achieved, the soil will have enough air spaces (aeration) to hold enough water to provide moisture to the roots without drowning them or depriving them (drainage). Aerated soil also provides the roots with oxygen and enables them to grow.

Clay soils can be improved with gypsum, which is calcium sulfate. This compound improves the structure and supplies calcium, essential for plant growth, but does not change the pH.

pH

Soil pH is the measure of the acidity or alkalinity of the soil. pH is measured on a scale of 1 to 14; 7.0 is neutral. Any

ABOVE: *All soil contains sand, silt, and clay; it is the size and form of these mineral particles that characterizes soil types.*

BELOW: *Potatoes are tubers, meaning that they actually grow under the soil.*

reading under 7.0 indicates an acidic soil, while a reading above 7.0 indicates an alkaline, or basic soil.

The ideal soil pH for most plants is between 5.0 and 7.0. At this level, nutrients in the soil are the most readily available for absorption by the roots. Broad-leaved evergreens and blueberries are notable exceptions to this rule, as they prefer a pH around 5.0. In general, soils east of the Mississippi and in the Northwest are acidic, while those in high or low desert areas, like the Southwest, are alkaline.

It is necessary to change the pH of the soil if it does not fall within the right boundaries. To lower soil pH, use sulfur; to raise soil pH, use limestone—follow package directions carefully for the right amount to use. When raising pH, dolomitic limestone is the best type of limestone to use, because it is slow acting and contains magnesium, an element essential for plant growth. If dolomitic limestone is not available, use ground agricultural limestone, but stay away from hydrated lime which can burn plant roots. In addition, fertilizers are acidic in nature and will also lower the soil pH somewhat.

Since it is impossible to guess what is in soil just by looking at it, it is advisable to have it tested. You can buy soil test kits at the garden center, or your county extension agent can test the soil for you. Most of these tests determine pH only. A commercial soil analysis can determine the soil's organic matter content and present nutrient level so that you determine exactly how to make improvements.

When taking a soil sample, collect a quart (.95 l) of soil from three or four different spots in the garden. Be careful not to include mulch, thatch, roots, or other foreign matter that would throw off the test results.

Soil fertility is essential for good plant growth. Read about **Fertilizing.**

IMPROVING THE SOIL

Soil is rarely so good that it could not be improved. However, no soil should be improved before its time, or its structure will be ruined. When soil is improved when it is still wet from spring rains and melting snow, it will become too compacted. Therefore, to test for readiness, take a ball of soil and squeeze it tightly. If it stays intact, it is too wet. Wait a few days and try again. The soil is ready if it crumbles in your hand. If, on the other hand, the soil is so dry that it is fine and dusty, water it well and test it again in a few days. Where very large areas need to be improved, it is easier to buy or rent a Rototiller™ to save many hours of hand labor.

The soil should be improved to the depths that the roots will eventually reach. This equals 8 to 12 inches (20 to 30 cm) for annuals, bulbs, perennials, vegetables, and herbs, and 24 inches (60 cm) for trees and shrubs. Dig out the planting area and add enough organic matter so that it comprises 25% of the total soil. Mix the organic matter well and proceed with planting.

If you're planting immediately, add no fertilizer except one that is high in phos-

BELOW: *The ideal soil pH for most plants is between 5.0 to 7.0, but blueberries* (Vaccinium corybosum) *are an exception—they prefer a soil pH of about 5.0.*

1

2

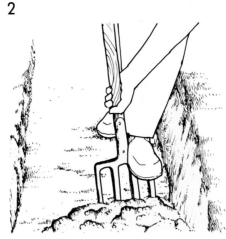

3

4

ABOVE: *Double digging. 1: Dig out soil to the depth of one spade. 2: Use a fork to break up the soil at bottom of hole, and work in some humus. 3: Dig out second hole, turning the soil upside down into the first hole. 4: Use pile of soil from first hole to fill in second hole.*

phorus, such as bone meal or super-phosphate, to ensure good root growth. If the soil can be prepared at least one month in advance of planting, a balanced fertilizer such as 5-10-5 can be added. If both pH adjustment and fertilizing are necessary, adjust the pH at least one month before fertilizing.

Where good topsoil and poor subsoil co-exist, a technique known as double digging is recommended. This puts the good soil in the bottom of the hole where the roots are, to help them grow better. To double-dig, dig out the soil to a depth of one spade and place the soil to the side. Then dig out more soil to another spade depth. Place the good soil in the bottom of the hole and the soil that was on the bottom on top.

OTHER SOIL PROBLEMS

It is sometimes necessary to treat problems in the soil. Chlorosis is a condition caused by the plant's inability to absorb iron from the soil. It can be diag-

nosed by yellow areas between the leaf veins or, in severe cases, by entire leaves turning yellow. It is particularly problematic with broad-leaved evergreens. The condition can be treated by adjusting the pH or by adding iron or iron sulfate to the soil.

An excess of salts in the soil is a problem in arid areas, particularly those found in the southwest United States. Excess salt can stunt growth, burn foliage, or kill plants. This problem can be detected by white deposits of salt found on the soil surface. The solution is deep, slow watering; this will help to wash the salt out of the root zone.

Hard pan is an impervious layer of soil at or near the soil surface. Roots and water simply can not penetrate through it. Sometimes power equipment can break up hard pan. Improving the soil with generous amounts of organic matter will make it workable. If this can not be done, you will need to install a drainage system or revert to raised beds.

Garden soil should not be used in containers; read the section on **Container Gardening** for directions on mixing soilless media for containers.

SPRAYING

The spraying of chemical formulations, whether they be insecticides, fungicides, herbicides, or fertilizers, is an essential part of keeping the garden healthy.

TYPES OF SPRAYERS

There are several different types of sprayers. The compression sprayer is a sprayer that is pumped after the liquid is placed into it to achieve the necessary pressure to deliver a spray. Both metal and plastic types are available; the plastic ones are lighter and easier to keep clean as they are corrosion-resistant. Small sprayers with rechargeable batteries eliminate pumping and are convenient to use. Some sprayers have hand-driven plungers, but these do not deliver as even a spray as the compression or battery-driven types.

While you are spraying with a compression sprayer, it will be necessary to repump it once or twice to keep the pressure high enough. If the sprayer contains powdered material, the tank should also be shaken several times to keep the material evenly dispersed in the water. It also helps to put a small amount of liquid detergent in the sprayer if powdered material is being used to help it to better adhere to the plants' leaves.

Other sprayers are placed on the end of a garden hose. The concentrated solution in the spray bottle is diluted with water as it comes from the hose. This is the least convenient sprayer to use as you not only have to drag the hose around, but there is also often an uneven distribution of the concentrated material from the spray bottle.

Some sprayers have long tubular or sliding attachments called trombones that make it easy to spray tall trees and shrubs. Tank sprayers that roll on wheels are available and convenient for use in very large gardens; some of these are motor-powered.

Dusters are available for application of dry material, but they have given way to sprayers as spraying is a more even and effective way to apply materials.

PRECAUTIONS

Before you use a sprayer for the first time, read the instruction book for operating directions and information on capacity. Also read the label on the product you will be spraying and mix it exactly as directed. Make sure that dry material has fully dissolved or is in suspension before starting to spray. Never reuse a spray solution; mix only what you need for one application, and if there is any left over, dispose of it properly.

When spraying a toxic chemical, wear a mask, gloves, and protective clothing, and change your clothes when you have finished the job.

If you are going to be spraying herbicides as well as other chemicals, it is wise to have a separate sprayer for use only with herbicides to prevent any possible contamination and plant injury.

Make sure plants are well-watered before you spray, as damage is more likely to occur on dry leaves than on wet ones. Never spray on a windy day, as too much of your spray will be lost. Spray both the upper and lower leaf surfaces until the spray starts to run off the leaf. Nozzles can be adjusted to produce different droplet sizes; the finer the spray,

the more even the coverage. Coarse sprays are good for tall trees, shrubs, and lawns.

CLEANING, MAINTENANCE, AND STORAGE

Do not buy more product than you will use in a year or two as chemicals can lose their effectiveness. Always store product in the original container in a safe place where children will not be able to reach it; if possible, keep it under lock and key. Keep it out of the sun and heat as well.

Regular cleaning and maintenance will be necessary to keep your sprayer in good working order. Spray nozzles are small and clog very easily, so fill the sprayer with clean water after every use and spray it through the nozzle to make sure no solid material remains inside. If a nozzle becomes clogged, it can be cleaned with a thin wire. It may be necessary to apply a light oil to the pump cylinder of a compression sprayer to keep it in good working order from time to time.

*Bushy plants like peonies (*Paeonia *spp.) require three or four stakes placed around them to keep them growing erect.*

STAKING AND TYING

Some plants, especially taller ones, need to be staked to keep them growing erect. Some plants have naturally weak stems and some, although their stems are strong, need a little extra support to keep them from being damaged by strong winds or rain.

The type of staking done for annuals, biennials, perennials, herbs, or bulbs depends on the individual plant. Plants with one main stem require only one stake per plant; the stake should be close enough to the plant to keep it erect. You can also tie two plants to the same stake. Be sure the stake is as tall as the ultimate height of the plant; as the plant grows, tie it to the stake as necessary.

Bushy plants such as tickseed, peonies, and bellflowers require three or four stakes set around them. String should be tied around the stakes to encircle and contain the plant. When plants are grown in a row, as in a cutting garden, stakes and strings can be set along both sides of the row.

You can also purchase wire cages that hold plants upright. These cages are also used for tomatoes and other vining vegetables, although vegetables and other vining plants can also be tied to trellises, arbors, and A-frames.

It is best to set stakes at planting time so that roots are not accidentally damaged later. Since stakes are not especially attractive, you might want to place them where plant growth will later hide them.

Newly planted trees need staking to prevent them from moving and loosening the soil. Two stakes are recommended for trees with less than a 3-inch (75-mm) caliber (diameter); use three stakes or guy wires for larger trees. Set stakes beyond the edge of, and drive them below, the bottom of the roots; they can be attached with rope or wire run through a hose. However, make sure the trunk does not become girdled. Stakes can be removed after a year.

Stakes can be made of wood, bamboo, plastic, or metal. At the end of the growing season, remove the stakes from the flower garden, wash them, and store them indoors over winter to lengthen their life span.

Tie plants loosely to a stake with soft string or twine, rubber, or plastic tape. Wire can be used, but it can damage stems and become too hot in the sun; insulated or coated wire is a better choice. Wire covered with a piece of hose is best for tying trees. Twist-ties covered with paper or plastic coatings make good ties, but if they are made with a paper coating they do not last long.

THATCH

Thatch is a dense layer of undecomposed organic matter that lies on the soil surface at the base of grass plants. See **Lawns.**

TOOLS

Choosing the right tool for the job is among the best gardening advice you can follow. Proper tools make gardening easier and more enjoyable. When you shop for tools, remember that the best price may not be the best buy. However, it's a good idea to pay a little more for a good tool since it will serve you for many more years than a less well-made alternative.

Before you buy a tool, pick it up and hold it in your hand to make sure that it's the right size for you and that it's comfortable to handle.

As with any tool, it is important to keep gardening tools in top condition. Keep them clean, and remove any rust that forms. Keep cutting tools sharp, and oil them at least once a year.

There are a number of different tools that are essential for gardening, and there are others that would be nice to have although they are not necessary. The most common gardening tools include:

Asparagus Knife—Also called a dandelion weeder, the asparagus knife is used to harvest asparagus, but it can also remove deep-rooted weeds.

Bulb Planter—A bulb planter is a

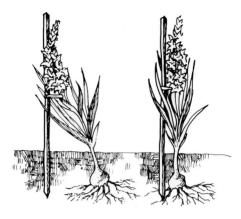

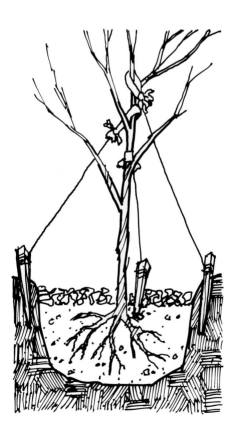

Top left: *Plants with one main stem, such as gladiolus or dahlias, need only one stake to keep them growing erect.*

Middle left: *Sprawling plants benefit from the support of stakes and wire or twine.*

Bottom left: *Hose-covered wire is best for tying trees, and helps them to grow correctly. All stakes should be planted as close to the plant as possible.*

Below: *An assortment of essential gardening and landscaping tools.*

WEEDER

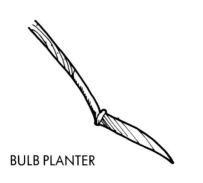

BULB PLANTER

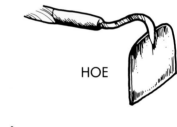

HOE

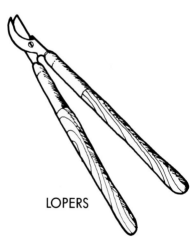

LOPERS

PRUNING SHEARS

cyclindrical tool with a sharp bottom edge and a handle at the top. It is used to dig holes for planting bulbs and other small plants. Bulb planters are available with both short and long handles. Bulbs can also be planted with narrow trowels.

Grass Shears—Grass shears are a type of spring-operated scissors that are used to trim the edges of the lawn where the lawn mower can not reach.

Hedge Clippers—Hedge clippers are a type of long-bladed shears that work somewhat like a scissors. They are used to trim hedges and soft-stemmed plants, but should not be used to cut through thick stems or branches. Some hedge clippers have extra-long handles for trimming tall shrubs. Electric hedge clippers are also available.

Hoe—A hoe is a tool with either a flat blade, or flat or curved "fingers." A hoe is used to loosen soil and remove weeds. Hoes are available with short or long handles. To weed a large area, a hoe with a long handle will be easier to use as you won't have to stoop or kneel down. To use a hoe, pull the cutting edge toward you, taking up weeds at the same time. It is important to keep the blades or tines on a hoe sharpened with a file or a grinding wheel, as dull hoes will not cut weeds.

Lawn Mowers—Lawn mowers are used for cutting grass. A hand-operated mower is fine for a small lawn, but a power mower is almost essential for large areas. Both gasoline and electric mowers are available; electric mowers are not practical for lawns of more than 10,000 square feet (900 m²), or for areas that an extension cord can not reach. Electric mowers are also harder to use as you must constantly work around the cord. For large, unobstructed lawns, you'll save time and energy if you use a riding mower.

Always clean a lawn mower after each use to keep grass off the blades and to prevent the spread of disease. It is also essential to keep the blades sharpened so the grass is not bruised when it is cut.

Lopers—A loper is a type of pruning shears that has a longer handle and a larger blade than normal pruning shears. A loper is used for cutting branches thicker than a pencil and for reaching high branches.

Pruning Shears—Pruning shears are used to cut stems up to the thickness of a pencil and to remove faded flowers. There are two different types of pruning

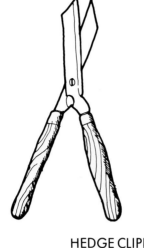

HEDGE CLIPPERS

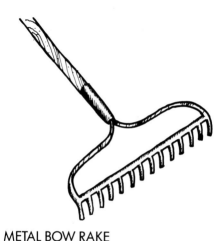

METAL BOW RAKE

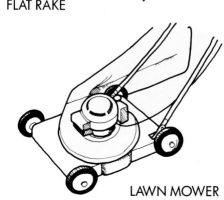

FLAT RAKE

LAWN MOWER

shears. The hook-and-blade type has two cutting surfaces; the anvil type has one cutting blade that pushes against a rigid surface. Anvil shears can crush softer stems, such as rose canes, so it is not the best tool for pruning a plant of that type. When using hook-and-blade shears, place the blade, not the hook, closest to the plant, or you will leave a small stub behind.

Pruning Saw—A pruning saw is used to remove thick branches. Its teeth form a more open pattern than those of a cross-cut saw used in carpentry, which makes the pruning saw easier to use. Power chain saws that are electric or gasoline-operated make pruning large branches or removing large trees easier and faster than if you used a pruning saw.

Rakes—There are two different types of rakes. Rakes with rigid, flat, or curved tines are used to smooth the soil in seedbeds and other planting areas. Rakes with flexible tines are used to rake leaves. Large rakes will make any job you do go faster, but small (or adjustable) rakes allow you to get into small places and under shrubbery. You can also buy a specific rake to thatch the lawn.

Shovel—A shovel has a rounded, usually pointed blade. A shovel is used for lifting and moving soil and other materials. Shovels are available with different-length handles, so you should be able to find one that is easy for you to use.

Spade—A spade is a type of shovel with a flat blade. The end of a spade may be either round, pointed, or flat. Spades are used for digging and mixing soil, working in fertilizer and soil amendments, root pruning, and edging.

When using a spade or a shovel, push it down into the soil with your foot, push back on the handle, then lift up or roll the soil to the side.

Spading Fork—A spading fork is shaped like a spade, but has rigid tines instead of a blade. Spading forks are used for digging up large clumps of perennials, tubers, or bulbs that you want to divide. A spading fork can also be used, as can a spade, to dig up a shrub for transplanting, but will loosen the soil around the roots without doing as much damage as a spade will. The tines of a spading fork will also break up large clumps of soil easier than a spade will.

Spreader—A spreader is a device for distributing dried materials to the soil such as fertilizers and herbicides. The

TROWEL

SHOVEL

SPADE

SPADING FORK

SPREADER

material is placed in a hopper through which it is released as the spreader is pushed. The openings at the bottom of the hopper are adjustable to the size of the particles you want to distribute and the rate at which you want to apply them. Some spreaders drop the material straight down, while others scatter it in a circular pattern. Older spreaders were made of metal and rusted easily; look for one of the newer kinds that are made of plastic.

String Trimmers—String trimmers are power tools used instead of grass shears to trim grass and/or weeds at the edge of the lawn, along fences, or in hard-to-reach places. They operate by a spinning piece of monofilament plastic that cuts the grass or weeds off at the desired height.

Trowel—Trowels are hand-held tools used for planting small plants such as annuals, perennials, vegetables, bulbs, and herbs. Long, narrow trowels work best for digging in small areas, or for digging narrow holes. Invest in a trowel with a strong handle so it will not bend.

TOPIARY

Topiary is a method of pruning that converts plants into geometric shapes or figures such as animals and characters. See **Pruning**.

TRANSPLANTING

Transplanting is the moving of a plant from one area of the garden to another. There are many reasons to transplant. A plant may have overgrown its space and may need to be given a roomier spot or the color of its flowers may look better in a different area. Plants may need more or less light, or different moisture conditions, and need to be moved to an appropriate location. If you are adding a patio or deck to your landscape, some plants might be in the way of construction.

WHEN TO TRANSPLANT

There are several general rules about the proper time to transplant. Most perennials should be transplanted in spring as growth starts, or in early autumn. The main exceptions to this rule are peonies, poppies, and irises, which should only be moved in autumn. Evergreens should be moved in early to mid-spring, or in early autumn. Deciduous trees, shrubs (including roses), and vines should be transplanted when they are dormant and without leaves; this can be done either in early spring or, where winter temperatures do not drop below 0° F (-18°C), in mid- to late autumn. Bulbs are best transplanted after they flower; their foliage starts to turn brown, making this the easiest time to locate them.

TRANSPLANTING TECHNIQUES

It is important when transplanting to leave as many of the roots as possible intact. When digging perennials, bulbs, and small woody plants, dig around the roots to the width of the plant and lift the roots carefully from the soil. If the plant is dormant, it is not necessary to move the roots with soil around them, although it will do no harm. When transplanting large trees and shrubs, root-prune the plants up to a year in advance of moving them.

With a sharp spade, dig into the soil up to 2 feet (60 cm) from the base of the plant in a circle around it. This will allow new feeder roots to form around the plant base and cause less damage when you move it.

When moving a plant with a ball of soil around the roots, place a piece of burlap or other material around the root ball to keep it intact until the plant is set into its new home. Always water any plant well before transplanting it.

Plants, especially perennials and bulbs, often need to be divided when being transplanted. See **Propagation.**

Once a plant is dug from the ground, follow the procedures outlined under **Planting** to set it into its new location. After transplanting, care for the plant as you would any other newly planted plant.

TREES

If you were to visualize your house and garden as a beautiful oil painting, the

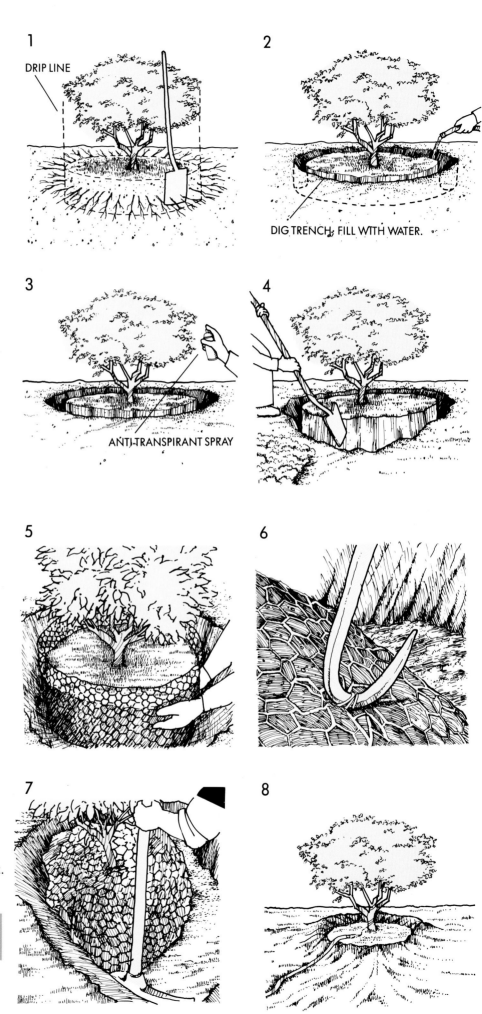

ABOVE: *A weeping Higan cherry* (PRUNUS SUBHIRTELLA). *The color of a tree's flowers can greatly enhance the overall design of your landscape.*

OPPOSITE PAGE: *Transplanting a shrub or small tree. 1: Up to a year before moving shrub, root-prune it by digging into soil up to 2 feet (60 cm) from base of plant in circle around it. This causes plant to form fresh feeder roots, and helps reduce damage when moved. 2: Soak roots as shown two or three days prior to moving plant; extra water will make root ball easier to handle. 3: Coat foliage with anti-transpirant spray to slow water loss. 4: Cut down shrub with spade or back of shovel. Root ball should be as large as you can manage. 5: Wrap root ball with chicken wire, and secure loose ends. 6: Slip hay hook or similar tool through wire and twist tightly; repeat four or five times in different places. 7: Cut under root ball with shovel or mattock. Sliding chicken wire underneath can help to keep root ball intact if earth crumbles. 8: Place plant at new site; mound a ridge of soil around the hole to make a basin that is same diameter as foliage. Water well.*

trees would be their picture frame. Trees frame the view to and from the house, providing a welcoming overhead canopy. Trees can be used at either side of the entrance to the driveway, or set off from the corners of the house. Shade trees provide relief from the heat of the sun and a place to hang your swing or hammock. Trees can be used for camouflage, or to enhance the landscape year-round. Ornamental trees add seasonal color from their flowers and berries, and can be used as accents or lawn specimens.

SELECTING TREES

A tree, since it endures many years, is a permanent addition to your home. Because it is permanent, select both the tree and its location with care. Check the ultimate height and spread of a shade tree before planting it to be sure it will be in scale with the rest of your property when it is mature. Do not plant it so close to your home that it will eventually grow onto the roof or against the walls.

While most trees have green leaves, some have yellow, red, or bronze leaves, and this difference in color might be an asset to the overall design of your landscape. Many trees have magnificent autumn color, which will extend their season of interest, while others have berries or seedpods that may remain to provide color against a snowy background. Many trees have unusual silhouettes, or colored or patterned bark that brightens the winter landscape. Trees that bear berries or nuts are attractive to birds during the winter.

Some shade trees provide color from

flowers, as do most ornamental trees. Check a tree's flower color and blooming time to make sure it fits with the other plants in the landscape. Many trees bloom in the spring, but many also bloom in summer when little other color is available from large plants. You can use columnar trees in tall hedges, and small trees as landscape accents or plants for the center of flower beds. Trees may be deciduous or evergreen; evergreens work best for screens or windbreaks.

Trees have certain requirements for light and soil moisture, and this is outlined in the **Tree Chart.** They also have specific hardiness limits; checking this first is a must (refer to the **Tree Chart**).

Read about **Landscape Design** before selecting and placing trees.

GROWING AND MAINTAINING TREES

PLANTING TREES

Trees purchased at the garden center or through a mail-order catalog are either bare-root, containerized, or balled and burlapped. Read the section about **Planting** for an explanation of each of these types and directions on how to plant them. This section also outlines the proper times for planting. Read the **Soil** section before planting. Since trees are permanent, proper soil preparation is essential. Young trees will need support; read about **Staking and Tying.**

If the level of soil needs to be changed at the point where the tree is to be placed, do so before planting. Changing the soil level after a tree is established, either raising it or lowering it, usually kills the tree.

Young trees are susceptible to sunscald, which causes their thin bark to burn and split open. Sunscald occurs most often in winter when the sun warms the bark during the day, thus thawing the water in the bark's cells; the water freezes again at night when the temperature drops. To prevent this, wrap tree trunks in burlap or tree tape until the tree develops a thick bark.

At a new house or in a newly renovated landscape, large trees will have an immediate effect. It is also fun to propagate your own trees and place them in areas of the garden where you can afford to give

RIGHT: *The blooms of an American linden* (TILIA AMERICANA).

BELOW: *Sargent's crabapple* (MALUS SARGENTII).

BOTTOM: *Planting of trees like these often requires regular mulching.*

them the time to mature. The **Tree Chart** outlines the various methods of propagation for trees. See **Propagation.**

FERTILIZING TREES

Trees are not usually high-maintenance plants, but they do need some annual care to keep them in prime condition. The fertilizer applied to the lawn around the base of trees will usually meet their fertilizer needs, but when trees show signs of needing additional food, be sure to apply fertilizer so that it covers the entire root area. Apply fertilizer to the ground 2 to 3 feet (60 to 90 cm) beyond the branch spread of the tree. Special fertilizer pellets that are probed into the soil work well, as do tree-root fertilizers, which place the fertilizer deep into the soil closer to the tree's roots. When root-feeding trees, start 2 feet (60 cm) from the base of the trunk. Trees can be fertilized either in early to mid-spring, or in late autumn after the plants are dormant.

WATERING TREES

Trees vary in their needs for water. (See **Tree Chart.**) Plants with average water requirements need 1 inch (25 mm) of water per week from rain or irrigation; of course, some trees need more or less than this. Trees should be watered as necessary. Water deeply and as infrequently as possible to encourage deep roots, which will aid in making the trees more resistant to drought, wind, and storm damage. If it does not rain, water evergreens deeply in late autumn to lessen winter injury from drying winds and sun. See **Watering.**

PRUNING TREES

Some trees will not need any pruning at all, but all should be inspected yearly to see if they do. The majority of tree-pruning is done when they are young to establish their shape and branch contour, but mature trees sometimes need pruning to remove branches that are dead, diseased, damaged, or are growing into the house or utility lines. Read the section on **Pruning.**

MULCHING TREES

A summer mulch will conserve moisture while it keeps the soil cool and suppresses weeds. It will also protect the roots of shallow-rooted trees and provide an attractive alternative to a lawn.

If a tree's bark is damaged by the lawn mower, nail it back before it dries out, or remove the bark and paint the area with tree-wound paint.

Refer also to **Diseases and Disease Control** and **Insects and Insect Control.**

TREES

	PT	PH	FC	BT	L	MO	H	P	AI
Abies species Fir	E	100'	—	—	S,PSh	M	2–8	S,SC	—
Acacia species Acacia	E	90'	YELLOW	ESp	S	A	8–10	S	—
Acer species Maple	D	75'	—	—	S,PSh	M	2–9	S,G,SC	C
Aesculus hippocastanum Horse chestnut	D	40'	WHITE	LSp	S	M	4–8	S	N
Ailanthus altissima Tree of heaven	D	60'	YELLOW	MSu	S,PSh	A	4–9	S,RC	SP
Albizia Julibrissin Mimosa	D	40'	PINK	MSu	S	D	6–10	S,RC	SP
Betula species Birch	D	100'	BROWN	ESp	S	M	4–9	S	BK
Carpinus species Hornbeam	D	60'	BROWN	MSp	S,Sh	M	3–9	S	N,C
Carya species Hickory	D	100'	BROWN	MSp	S	M	4–9	S	C,N
Castanea mollissima Chinese chestnut	D	100'	BROWN	MSu	S	D	4–8	S	C,N
Catalpa species Catawba	D	90'	WHITE	ESu	S	D	4–9	S,SC	S
Cedrus species Cedar	E	60'	—	—	S	A–D	5–9	S,G	—
Celtis occidentalis Hackberry	D	80'	—	—	S	A–M	4–8	S,G,SC	C,B
Cercidiphyllum japonicum Katsura tree	D	60'	WHITE	ESp	S	M	5–9	S,SC	C,SP
Cercis species Redbud	D	40'	PINK	ESp	S,PSh	A	5–9	S,SC	—
Chamaecyparis species False cypress	E	100'	—	—	S	M	5–9	S,SC	—
Cladrastis lutea Yellowwood	D	50'	WHITE	ESu	S	D	4–8	S,RC	C,S
Cornus species Dogwood	D	40'	WHITE, PINK	LSp	PSh	A	3–8	S,G,SC	C,B
Corylus species Filbert, Hazelnut	D	120'	BROWN	ESp	S,PSh	A–D	4–8	S,G	N

TREES cont.

	PT	PH	FC	BT	L	MO	H	P	AI
Cotinus obovatus American smoke tree	D	30′	PURPLE	LSp	S,LSh	A	5–8	SC	C
Crataegus species Hawthorn	D	30′	WHITE	LSp	S	A	4–9	S	B
Cryptomeria japonica Japanese cedar	E	60′	—	—	S,PSh	M	6–9	S,SC	—
Cupressus species Cypress	E	90′	—	—	S	A	6–9	S,G	—
Elaeagnus angustifolia Russian olive	D	20′	SILVER	MSp	S	A–D	2–7	S,SC	—
Eucalyptus species Gum tree	E	100′	MIX	LSp	S	D	9–10	S	—
Fagus species Beech	D	100′	—	—	S	M	3–9	S,G	C,N
Franklinia Alatamaha Franklin tree	D	30′	WHITE	LSu	S	M	6–8	SC,S	C
Fraxinus species Ash	D	80′	—	—	S	A	2–9	S	C
Ginkgo biloba Ginkgo, Maidenhair tree	D	80′	—	—	S,PSh	M	4–8	S,SC	C
Gleditsia tricanthos Honey locust	D	70′	GREEN	LSp	S	A–M	3–9	S,SC	C,SP
Juglans species Walnut	D	70′	BROWN	ESp	S,PSh	M	3–8	S	N
Koelreuteria species Golden-rain tree	D	60′	YELLOW	MSu	S,PSh	A	5–9	S,SC	SP
Laburnum × *Watereri* Golden-chain tree	D	30′	YELLOW	LSp	S,PSh	A	4–7	S,G	SP
Lagerstroemia indica Crape myrtle	D	60′	WHITE, PINK, RED	MSu	S	A	7–10	SC	C
Larix decidua European larch	D	75′	—	—	S	M	2–7	S,SC	C
Liquidambar Styracifluap Sweet gum	D	80′	—	—	S,PSh	M	5–9	S,SC	C,SP
Liriodendron Tulipiferap Tulip tree	D	100′	CREAM	ESu	S	M	5–9	S,SC	C
Magnolia species Magnolia	D	25′	WHITE, PINK	ESp	S,PSh	M	4–9	S,G,SC	—

TREES cont.

	PT	PH	FC	BT	L	MO	H	P	AI
Malus species Flowering crabapple	D	25'	PINK, WHITE	MSp	S	M	2–6	S,G	B
Metasequoia glyptostroboides Dawn redwood	D	80'	—	—	S	M	5–8	S,SC	C
Nyssa sylvatica Black gum	D	75'	—	—	S,PSh	M	5–9	S	C
Oxydendron arboreum Sorrel tree	D	75'	WHITE	A	S,PSh	M	6–9	S	C
Phellodendron amurense Amur cork tree	D	60'	—	—	S	A	3–7	S,SC	C,B
Picea species Spruce	E	100'	—	—	S	M	1–7	S,G	—
Populus species Poplar, Aspen, Cottonwood	D	100'	BROWN	ESp	S	D	1–9	S,SC	C
Prunus species Flowering Cherry, Peach, Plum	D	60'	PINK, WHITE	MSp	S,PSh	A	2–9	G,SC	—
Pseudotsuga Menziesii Douglas fir	E	100'	—	—	S	M	3–7	S,SC	—
Pyrus species Flowering pear	D	50'	WHITE	MSp	S,LSh	A	4–10	S,G	C
Quercus species Oak	D	100'	—	—	S	M	2–10	S,G	C
Robinia Pseudoacacia Black locust	D	75'	WHITE	LSp	S	A	3–8	S	SP
Salix species Willow	D	75'	BROWN	ESp	S,PSh	M	2–9	SC,S	C
Sophora japonica Japanese pagoda tree	D	50'	WHITE	MSu	S	A	5–8	S,G,SC	SP
Sorbus aucuparia European mountain ash	D	40'	WHITE	MSp	S	A	3–7	S	B
Stewartia koreana Korean stewartia	D	30'	WHITE	MSu	PSh	M	5–8	S,SC	C,BK
Tilia cordata Littleleaf linden	D	80'	YELLOW	ESu	S	M	2–8	S	—
Ulmus species Elm	D	90'	—	—	S	M	2–9	S,SC	C
Zelkova serrata Japanese zelkova	D	50'	—	—	S	M	5–9	S,G	C

TRELLISES AND ARBORS

Trellises and arbors are structures used in the landscape to provide privacy, accent, or shade, or to support a vine. A trellis is technically a frame of lattice work which may be arranged in square, rectangular, diagonal, horizontal, or vertical configurations. A trellis is usually placed vertically in the garden and is usually covered with a vining plant. When a trellis is placed on supports so that it lies horizontally overhead, it is called an arbor.

Trellises are often made of wood; pressure-treated pine, redwood, cypress, or cedar are the most durable. Do not use creosote as a preservative for lumber that you use in your landscape as it is toxic to plants. A wooden trellis can be left to age naturally, or it can be painted. Remember, once a trellis is painted, it may need repainting some time, which can be difficult if it is heavily covered with a vine.

Trellises can also be made of PVC pipe, metal pipe, dowels, strings mounted within a frame, or wire. However, metal and wire can become quite hot in the sun and may burn tender growth. Insulated wire works well, and pipes can be painted white to reflect rather than absorb heat. Whatever the material, be sure it is strong enough to hold the plant that will cling to it. Mature ivy weighs a lot more than a planting of annual sweet peas.

Trellises must be anchored into the ground with 2×4s to a depth of at least 2 feet (60 cm) to prevent them from tipping over. Allow 3 to 4 feet (1 to 1.2 m) between the posts; this depends on the weight of the vine. When a trellis is to be placed against the wall of a house, it should be hinged at the bottom and set several inches (mm) from the wall. This will provide good air circulation and enable the trellis to be swung away for painting and cleaning.

Trellises are used to support decorative vines, climbing roses, espaliers, and vining vegetables. Trellises in an A-frame configuration work well for many vegetables, like pole beans, peas, tomatoes, and cucumbers. If the trellises are hinged at the top, they can easily be folded up and stored for the winter. Small trellises can be placed in containers to support pot-grown vining plants.

A trellis, once installed, needs little maintenance. Pruning woody and perennial vines of excess growth each year will reduce the weight on the trellis and help it last longer.

When installing an arbor, make it high enough so that there will be sufficient head clearance after the plant growing on it is mature. For example, if you are covering an arbor with wisteria, the arbor should be at least 7½ feet (2.3 m) to accommodate the hanging flowers. An arbor should also be wide enough so that you can walk under it without brushing against the plants, especially thorny plants like roses.

Also read about **Vines.**

Cherry tomatoes (LYCOPERSICON LYCOPERSICUM).

TUBEROUS ROOTS

Tuberous roots are roots with thick, fleshy, food-storing structures that resemble tubers. See **Bulbs.**

TUBERS

Tubers are thick, underground, food-storing stems. See **Bulbs.**

VEGETABLES

Vegetable growing is one of the most rewarding types of gardening. Harvesting and eating fresh vegetables from your own garden brings enormous satisfaction. Vegetables let you, your family, and your neighbors enjoy the pleasurable and nutritious bounty of a home garden within a few months of its planting.

Vegetables are usually herbaceous (not woody) plants grown for food. Depending on the crop, either the leaves, leafstalks, fruits, roots, or flower buds may be eaten. Vegetables are easy to distinguish from the fruit that grows on trees and bushes, but there is an overlap between fruit such as melons and other vegetables. Most books, including this one, include melons with vegetables rather than fruit, because the techniques of growing these fruit is the same as for growing vegetables.

Vegetables are classified as annuals, biennials, or perennials, depending on their life cycle. Most vegetables are annuals, or are grown as annuals. These plants grow, flower, set their fruit, and die within one growing year. Annuals may be further classified as tender, half-hardy, or hardy. Tender annuals will not tolerate frost and are planted in late spring after the danger of frost has passed. Half-hardy vegetables will grow when weather is cool, but will not tolerate frost. Hardy vegetables will tolerate frost and can be planted in the garden in early spring, or for an autumn crop.

Vegetables are also referred to as

Top: *A row of shallots* (**Allium cepa**).

Above: **Early summer harvest of turnips, lettuce, peas, broccoli, and onions in a well-designed food garden where shredded leaves are used between rows as a weed-suffocating mulch.**

either warm-season or cool-season. Warm-season vegetables are the tender vegetables that grow best during the heat of summer. Cool-season vegetables are the half-hardy or hardy vegetables that grow best during the cooler days of spring and autumn, and in mild areas in winter. These differences are outlined on the **Vegetable Chart.**

Biennials are vegetables that grow during their first year, then flower and set fruit the second year before they die. Biennial vegetables that are grown for their leaves or roots are usually grown as annuals because they become tough or unpalatable the second year. There are a few vegetables that are true perennials; they grow each spring, are harvested each year, then die to the ground in autumn. Some tender perennials can be grown as annuals in areas that are not frost-free.

PLANNING THE VEGETABLE GARDEN

No matter what climate you live in, selecting the site for a successful vegetable garden involves both common sense and a few facts.

Sunlight and Air Circulation

Almost without exception, vegetables must be grown in full sun, which is equal to at least six hours of direct sun each day. The areas of your garden that receive the most sun are where you will want to grow early spring vegetables and warm-season crops. Garden sites that don't enjoy as much sun can still produce some good vegetables, however. Leafy vegetables grow well in a little less sun and are fine for areas that receive shade in the afternoon. If the climate is very hot, vegetables benefit from some shading in the hottest part of the day. The days are longer in the northern climates during summer than they are in southern areas; vegetables grow faster and larger with the extra light.

Besides considering sunlight, locate a vegetable garden where the air circulation is good, where the soil drains well, and away from large trees and shrubs whose roots will compete for water and food.

Making a Garden Plan

Planning your vegetable garden on paper helps you to grow the largest possible amount of vegetables in the available space with the least amount of maintenance. If you're a beginner, start with a garden about 15 × 20 feet (4.5 × 6 m). Lay the garden out on paper first, so you'll know how many plants to buy, and to help you plan for a succession of crops.

It is easiest to plan and maintain your garden if you plant in rows or in blocks. In northern gardens, lay the plants out so that the taller plants are on the east side. This prevents them from shading smaller plants.

One of the easiest ways to plan your garden is to make a list of the vegetables you'd like to grow, and then label each as a "spring," "summer," or "autumn" vegetable. This label is determined by whether the vegetable is a cool- or warm-season vegetable, and the number of days it needs to mature. This information is given in the **Vegetable Chart,** and is also found on seed packets and plant labels. The label also indicates how much growing time a plant will need before harvesting. You'll need approximately two-thirds of your space for warm-weather crops. After you harvest your spring crops, you can plant a late warm-season crop, or hold the space open for an autumn crop.

Planting Methods

The planting distances in the **Vegetable Chart** are based on the traditional method of growing vegetables in rows. However, to save space, vegetables can be grown by a method known as intensive gardening. To accomplish this, set plants close together, and plant them in blocks instead of rows. Prepare the soil properly and use raised beds. Wherever possible, train the garden to grow in a way that makes most use of the ground space. Harvest crops promptly and practice succession planting.

Succession planting is the method of planning the vegetable garden so that, as soon as a crop is harvested, it is replaced with more of the same crop or another crop. Sowing seeds of plants with relatively short maturity every two weeks will ensure a continuous harvest instead of having all of your plants mature at once.

Interplanting is another method of making the most use of space. To do this, plant two crops together that mature for harvesting at different times, such as lettuce and tomatoes. For example, by the time lettuce is ready to be picked, tomato plants will be growing large enough to take over the entire space.

Container gardening is an excellent way to grow vegetables, especially where space is at a premium. Select a container that has drainage holes, and is in proportion to what you will be growing in it. Plant the vegetables in a soilless medium of peat moss with perlite or vermiculite, and keep it evenly moist. This may require daily watering, depending on the temperature and the wind. Rotate the containers if they do not receive even sunlight. Fertilizers leach quickly from containers, so fertilize container plants frequently with soluble plant food.

From the size of your garden plan, and from the information given in the **Vegetable Chart** about spacing, you can easily determine how many plants to grow or buy. Make notes to help you adjust the garden for following years.

You may also need to buy a few specific items for your vegetable garden, such as tomato cages, trellises for vining plants, and stakes for large, nonvining plants. Read about **Staking and Tying.**

SELECTING VEGETABLES

Choosing the right varieties to match your environmental conditions is probably more important for vegetable gardening than it is for any other type of gardening. There can be differences in growing success based on climate, soil, or the length of the growing season. Your county agent may have a list of the varieties that do best in your climate. Seed catalogs often give this information as well.

HYBRID AND NON-HYBRID VARIETIES

With many vegetables, both hybrid and non-hybrid (open-pollinated) varieties are available. The hybrid varieties are more expensive, but have better vigor, increased yield, and increased disease resistance. When buying vegetables, especially tomatoes, look for initials after the variety name that indicate resistance to one or more diseases. New varieties come onto the market every year, and are fun to experiment with.

SEEDS

Seeds are available from mail-order catalogs and in racks at garden centers and hardware stores. Of course, how you choose to purchase seed is up to you, but mail-order buying will allow you to order specific varieties that may not be available in racks. Order or buy seeds early and store them in a cool, dry place.

TRANSPLANTS

If you decide to buy plants rather than start plants from seeds, look for healthy, green transplants that have no signs of insects or diseases and have obviously been watered and well cared for. If you can't plant transplants right away, keep them in a protected spot and check them every day to see if they need to be watered.

GROWING AND MAINTAINING VEGETABLES

There is more to preparing a new site than incorporating soil amendments and raking the soil smooth. After choosing the site for a new garden, skim off the top 1 to 2 inches (25 to 50 mm) of soil or grass to remove everything that is growing there. The material you remove can be composted and used later on. If the

TOP: *Summer squash* (CUCURBITA PEPO).

BELOW: *Bell peppers* (CAPSICUM ANNUUM).

RIGHT: *Spinach 'Melody Hybrid'* (SPINACIA OLERACEA).

plot contains deep-rooted grasses or weeds, use an herbicide to kill them before preparing the soil. Read about **Weeds.**

PREPARING SOIL

When preparing the soil in an existing garden, add about 1 inch (25 mm) of organic matter (unless the garden did not grow well the previous year, in which case you should add more than you did before), fertilizer, and any other soil amendments as needed. Some gardeners plant a "green manure," which is a combination of grasses or legumes which grow over winter and are incorporated into the soil the following spring. Test your soil every year or two to be sure of what it needs.

Vegetables grow best in healthy soil that drains moderately fast, retains nutrients, contains a generous amount of organic matter, and has a pH between 6.0 and 7.0. Regardless of its present condition, the soil will probably require some modification to bring its productivity to a level where vegetables will thrive. It is possible to prepare soil in autumn if you plan on planting early the next spring. See **Soil.**

PLANTING TIMES

When to add plants and seeds to the garden is determined by the weather and the type of plant you are growing. Refer first to the **Frost Date Maps** (see p. 178) to determine the last frost date for your area. Tender annuals can not be planted until late spring, after the last frost date and when the soil is warm. Half-hardy annuals can be planted in mid-spring, two to four weeks before the last spring frost. Hardy annuals can be planted in early spring one to two months before the last spring frost.

For an autumn crop, determine the number of days to maturity for the vegetable you will be planting. Subtract that number from the total number of days in the growing season to determine when in the summer or autumn the vegetable must be planted.

Biennials and perennials are usually added to the garden in spring.

PROPAGATING VEGETABLES

Depending on the crop, some vegetables are directly seeded into the garden. Other vegetables must be grown from plants that can be bought or started indoors because they take too long to mature from seeds sown outdoors. Seeds are usually started indoors six to eight weeks before the outdoor planting date. Specific planting guidelines are given in the **Vegetable Chart.**

Read the sections on starting seeds both indoors and outdoors in the **Propagation** section.

PLANTING VEGETABLE TRANSPLANTS

Whether you buy vegetable plants or start your own indoors from seeds, the method of planting them is the same (see **Planting**). Plant vegetable plants at the same level they grew before, except tomatoes, which should be planted deeper. Water well after planting, and on a daily basis if it does not rain, until you see new growth. To reduce transplanting shock, plant on a cloudy day or in the afternoon.

Until they are large and strong, young seedlings may be subject to some potentially devastating natural effects. If a late frost threatens, and you have already planted your warm-season vegetables, cover them with plastic film, plastic milk jugs with their bottoms cut out, or cloches. It doesn't matter what you use, as long as the plants are kept from frost damage. When it warms up, remove the protection. Read also about **Extending the Season.**

FERTILIZING VEGETABLES

Vegetables need to be grown in fertile soil, and managing plant food can be tricky. If there is too little fertilizer, plants will turn yellow and not grow. Too much fertilizer will cause fruiting vegetables to produce many leaves but little to eat. As a guideline, use a fertilizer high in nitrogen for leafy vegetables, and high in phosphorus for others. Apply according to the label directions.

Top: *A slicing tomato* (Lycopersicon lycopersicum). Bottom: *'Dusky' eggplant* (Solanum Melongena esculentum).

Make adjustments if you see your plants are not growing as they should. Fertilize at planting time and at least once more during the growing season. Read about **Fertilizing.**

WATERING VEGETABLES

Water vegetables deeply but infrequently to encourage strong root systems that will tolerate summer heat and adverse conditions. Frequent watering encourages shallow roots which cannot combat heat, drought, and winds. If it does not rain, applying 1 to 2 inches (25 to 50 mm) of water once a week should be enough unless it is very hot or windy—then you will need to water more often.

Keep foliage as dry as possible during watering by using soaker hoses or drip irrigation, which also use less water. If you must water overhead, water in the morning so the foliage is dry before nightfall. Read about **Watering.**

MULCHING VEGETABLES

Mulching around vegetables will keep weeds from germinating, conserve moisture, and keep the soil at an even temperature. If you are growing cool-season vegetables, apply the mulch early to keep the soil cool.

If you are growing warm-season vegetables, do not apply mulch until the soil is warm and the plants are growing; the mulch will keep the soil too cool and deter growth if you put it down too early.

Organic mulches, such as peat moss, bark chips, dried grass clippings, and straw, are usually used because they break down into humus and will enrich the soil. Plastic mulch is a favorite in vegetable gardens; be sure to cut holes in the plastic so water and nutrients can pass through to your plants. Clear mulches trap more heat than black mulches and are better for warm-season vegetables in the North. A newer mulch is a woven fabric known as landscape cloth; it holds down weeds but allows water to pass through easily to the plants. You can cover non-organic mulches with an organic mulch for appearance's sake.

WEEDS

Weeds compete with vegetables for space, food, and water, and harbor insects and diseases. Even if you mulch, a few weeds will get through, and should be removed as soon as they appear. Removal is easiest after a rain or watering. In large gardens, weeding can be a little easier if you use a hoe. It is safe to use pre-emergent herbicides around vegetables, but not post-emergent herbicides. Read about **Weeds.**

PROTECTING VEGETABLES AGAINST DAMAGE AND DISEASE

Be on the lookout for snails and slugs and apply bait to stop them. Cutworms often eat off young vegetable plants at soil level; place a protective collar around the plants to keep the insects outside of them. Proper watering and air circulation can help prevent many diseases. Insecticides and fungicides are available, and many are organic. Be sure to select a preparation that is safe for vegetables and be sure to read the label to see how many days after spraying you must wait to harvest. In autumn, remove all plants from the garden to reduce the spots where insects and diseases can overwinter. Read about **Insects and Insect Control** and **Diseases and Disease Control.**

You may have to plan on a fence or other protective device to ward off wildlife. Read about **Rodent and Animal Control.**

HARVESTING AND STORING VEGETABLES

The harvesting time for individual vegetables is given in the **Vegetable Chart.** It is important to harvest vegetables as soon as they are ready to keep the plants producing fruit or to keep them at their peak of flavor.

Most vegetables should be harvested in the early morning when they are still cool; beans are an exception to this rule; they should be harvested at midday, as diseases spread easily if the plants are wet. When you harvest, bring a bucket of cold water with you, and plunge the vegetables in it as soon as you pick them. This treatment helps many vegetables stay sweeter.

Although storage methods depend upon the individual vegetable, you can generally store vegetables in a refrigerator, cool root cellar, or at room temperature. They can also be canned, frozen, or dehydrated—preserving vegetables allows you to enjoy the fruits of your labor year-round.

VEGETABLES

	PT	SP	DH	SI	SO	PO	PD	DR	Storage	Preservation
Abelmoschus esculentus Okra	A	W	55–70	—	ESu	—	18″	3′	R	F,D,C
Allium Cepa Onion	B/A	W	75–100	ESp	MSp	MSp	2–5″	1′	R,RC	F,D,P,C
Apium graveolens Celery	A	W	90–110	LW	—	LSp	6″	3′	R	D
Armoracia rusticana Horseradish	P/A	W	120–150	—	—	MSp	12″	2′	R	D,P
Asparagus officinalis Asparagus	P	W	2 yrs	ESp	MSp	MSp	1–2″	20″	R	F,D,C
Beta vulgaris Beet	B/A	C	50–70	—	MSp– MSu	—	2″	15″	R,RC	F,D,C
Beta vulgaris Swiss chard	B/A	W	55–65	—	MSp– MSu	—	8″	1¹⁄₂′	R	F
Brassica Napus Rutabaga	A	C	90–120	—	ESu	—	6–8″	2′	R,RC	F
Brassica oleracea Broccoli	A	C	70–95	ESp	MSp	MSp	18″	2–3′	R	F,D
Brassica oleracea Brussels sprouts	A	C	90–120	MSp	LSp	ESu	2′	3′	R	F,D
Brassica oleracea Cabbage	A	C	70–80	LW	ESp	ESp	1′	2¹⁄₂′	R	F,D,P,C
Brassica oleracea Cauliflower	A	C	50–70	ESp	MSp	MSp– ESu	2′	3′	R	F,D,P
Brassica oleracea Collards	A	C	80–90	ESu	MSu	MSu	15″	2′	R	F
Brassica oleracea Kale	P/A	C	60–70	LW	ESp	ESp	9–12″	2′	R	F
Brassica oleracea Kohlrabi	A	C	50–60	LW	ESp	ESp	6″	1¹⁄₂′	R	F
Brassica Rapa Chinese cabbage	A	C	60	—	MSp	—	1¹⁄₂′	2′	R	F
Brassica Rapa Turnip	B/A	C	70	—	MSu	—	2–3″	1¹⁄₂′	R,RC	F
Capsicum annuum Pepper	A	W	60–80	MSp	LSp	LSp	1¹⁄₂′	2¹⁄₂′	R	F,D,P,C
Cichorium Endivia Endive, Escarole	A	C	80–100	LSp	MSu	MSu	8–12″	1¹⁄₂′	R	—

VEGETABLES cont.

	PT	SP	DH	SI	SO	PO	PD	DR	Storage	Preservation
Citrullus lanatus Watermelon	A	W	75–95	MSp	LSp	LSp	4'	8'	R	P (Rind)
Cucumis Melo Melon	A	W	65–90	MSp	LSp	LSp	2–3'	6'	R	—
Cucumis sativus Cucumber	A	W	50–75	MSp	LSp	LSp	1–2'	5–6'	R	P,C
Cucurbita pepo Summer squash	A	W	50–55	MSp	LSp	LSp	3–4'	3–4'	R	F,D,C
Cucurbita species Winter squash	A	W	75–120	MSp	LSp	LSp	6–8'	6–8'	RT,RC	F,D
Cucurbita species Pumpkin	A	W	90–120	MSp	LSp	LSp	3–4'	6–10'	RT,RC	F,C
Daucus carota Carrot	B/A	C	50–70	—	ESp–ESu	—	1–2"	1–2'	R,RC	F,D,C
Lactuca sativa Lettuce	A	C	45–75	ESp	MSp	MSp	6–12"	1½'	R	—
Lycopersicon Lycopersicum Tomato	A	W	60–80	MSp	—	LSp	2–3'	4–5'	R	D,P,C
Pastinaca sativa Parsnip	B/A	W	120–150	—	MSp	—	2"	2'	R,RC	D
Phaseolus limensis Lima bean	A	W	60–80	—	LSp	—	8–10"	2–3'	R,RT (Dried)	F,D,C
Phaseolus vulgaris Bush green bean	A	W	50–70	—	LSp–MSu	—	2"	2–3'	R,RT (Dried)	F,D,P,C
Phaseolus vulgaris Pole green bean	A	W	60–90	—	LSp	—	3'	3'	R,RT (Dried)	F,D,P,C
Pisum sativum Pea	A	C	55–70	—	ESp	—	1"	2–3'	R,RT (Dried)	F,D,C
Raphanus sativus Radish	A	C	21–35	—	ESp	—	1"	1'	R	—
Solanum Melongena Eggplant	A	W	60–80	MSp	LSp	LSp	2'	3'	R	F,D,C
Solanum tuberosum Potato	A	W	90–120	—	—	MSp	12"	3'	R,RC	D,C
Spinacia oleracea Spinach	B/A	C	45–55	—	ESp	—	3–6"	1'	R	F,D,C
Tetragonia tetragonoides New Zealand spinach	A	W	60–90	—	LSp	—	1½'	3'	R	—
Zea Mays Corn	A	W	60–90	—	LSp	—	1'	3'	R	F,D,P,C

VINES

A vine is a plant with long, sprawling stems that can either grow up on trellises, arbors, walls, fences, strings, wires, tree trunks, or along the ground. Some vines are annuals, while others are perennials. Most perennial vines are woody in nature; some are deciduous, and others are evergreen.

Vines attach themselves to their supports by various methods. Some, such as clematis, bittersweet, honeysuckle, and nasturtium, have twining stems that wrap around anything that will hold them in place. They attach themselves readily to poles, arbors, and trellises. Others, such as sweet peas, attach themselves by tendrils, which are modified leaves that reach out and wrap around string, wire, stakes, lath, or other plants. Ivy, trumpet vine, and winter-creeper attach themselves by rootlike holdfasts that emerge along the stems. They can be aggressive growers, and can pull siding and paint off a house or grow into mortar and loosen it. They sometimes are difficult to attach to flat, smooth walls, but masonry hooks can help you do this.

Some vines find it difficult to cling, and will need to be tied to their supports with string or twist-ties. Climbing roses, while technically not vines, are a good example.

Vines are adaptable landscape plants that can be used in many ways. Allowed to grow up, they provide decoration, privacy, shade, and can screen wind and noise. Use them as a background for a flower garden or to soften strong architectural lines along the house or porch. Evergreen vines grown on the north side of a house will insulate the house in winter; deciduous vines on the south side of a house will insulate the house in summer, but will let the sun's heat through in winter. Grown on the ground, vines make excellent ground covers and can be used for erosion control. They can also be used to hide old tree stumps or construction pillars.

SELECTING VINES

Before you select a vine, find out what its ultimate size and growth rate will be so you will not choose something that will soon outgrow its space. The vine's flower color and bloom time should also be compatible with the rest of the landscape. Many flowering vines have fragrance, which is an added bonus when using them near the house or outdoor living areas. Some vines, like ivy, do not bloom, so they can provide a carpet of green for your landscape. You can add spot color with spring blooms or annuals.

Where vines are being used as a year-round feature, choose an evergreen rather than a deciduous vine. Small-growing vines of any type may also be used in hanging baskets.

Match vines to your landscape's climatic conditions. Perennial vines have certain hardiness limits in which they will survive; this is noted in the **Vine Chart.** Annual vines also have cli-

ABOVE: Clematis 'Ernest Markham' is a vigorous, free-flowering vine suitable for breaking up the monotony of a wall or a fence.

BELOW: Vines attach themselves to supports in different ways. 1: Some have tendrils, modified leaves that reach out and wrap around string, wire, stakes, lath, and other surfaces. 2: Others have twining stems that wrap around anything that will hold them in place. 3: Some vines attach themselves by rootlike holdfasts that emerge along the stems.

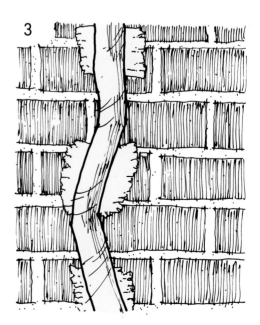

VINES

	PH	PT	FC	BT	MA	L	T	MO	HZ	P
Ampelopsis breviduriculata Porcelain vine	25′	D	BLUE (Berries)	A	Te	S	A–H	A	5–10	SC,L
Aristolochia durior Dutchman's pipe	30′	D	YELLOW	ESu	Tw	S,Sh	A	M	5–10	SC,L
Bougainvillea species Bougainvillea	25′	E	MIX	EB	Tie	S	A–H	D	10	SC,S
Campsis radicans Trumpet vine	40′	D	ORANGE	LSu	Te	S,PSh	H	A	5–9	SC,L
Celastrus orbiculatus Oriental bittersweet	40′	D	ORANGE (Berries)	A	Tw	S,Sh	A	A	5–8	SC
Clematis × Jackmanii Clematis	12′	D	MIX	ESu	Tw	S	C–A	M	4–10	SC,L
Clematis paniculata Sweet autumn clematis	30′	D	WHITE	A	Tw	S	C–A	M	6–10	SC,L
Euonymus Fortunei radicans Wintercreeper	25′	E	PINK, ORANGE (Berries)	A	H	S,Sh	A	A	3–10	SC,L D
Hedera Helix English ivy	30′	E	—	—	H	S,Sh	A	M	6–10	SC
Hydrangea anomala petiolaris Climbing hydrangea	75′	D	WHITE	ESu	H	S,Sh	A	M	4–9	SC,S
Ipomoea species Morning glory	10′	D	MIX	ASu	Tw	S	A–H	D–A	A	S
Lathyrus odoratus Sweet pea	6′	D	MIX	MSp,LSp	Te	S	C	M	A	S
Lonicera japonica Japanese honeysuckle	8′	D	YELLOW	ESu	Tw	S,PSh	A	A	5–10	SC,L
Parthenocissus quinquefolia Virginia creeper	50′	D	—	—	H	S,PSh	A	D–M	5–8	L,SC S
Parthenocissus tricuspidata Boston ivy	60′	D	—	—	H	S,PSh	A	D–M	5–8	L,SC S
Phaseolus coccineus Scarlet runner bean	12′	D	RED	ASu	Tw	S	A	M	A	S
Polygonum Aubertii Silver lace vine	30′	D	WHITE	LSu	Tw	S	A	A–D	4–7	SD,D S
Thunbergia alata Black-eyed Susan vine	6′	D	YELLOW, ORANGE	ASu	Tw	S,LSh	A–H	M	A	S
Tropaeolum majus Nasturtium	8′	D	MIX	ASu	Tw	S,LSh	C	D	A	S
Wisteria species Wisteria	15′	D	MIX	LSp	Tw	S,LSh	A	M	5–10	L,SC

matic preferences; these are outlined in the chart, as are moisture and light requirements.

GROWING AND MAINTAINING VINES

The care and maintenance of a vine depends to a large extent on whether it is an annual or perennial.

ANNUAL VINES

Annual vines can be grown from seed or from purchased seedlings, and are treated like an annual plant. Refer to the section on **Annuals** for directions on planting, fertilizing, watering, and other care. Annual vines are not heavy and need only lightweight supports. They need little if any pruning, and require little training to cover their support uniformly.

PERENNIAL VINES

Like shrubs, perennial vines are either bare-root, containerized, or balled and burlapped when purchased and, consequently, are treated like shrubs regarding planting, fertilizing, watering, and other care. Refer to **Shrubs** for specifics. The major difference between shrubs and vines is pruning. Although the timing of vine-pruning will not vary from that of other woody plants, it is essential to prune vines annually to remove dead wood, and control their size and growth direction. If dead wood is not removed, a tangled mass of branches will develop under the growing stems; this will make the vine too heavy for the support, and eventual restoration of the vine difficult.

PROPAGATING VINES

It is also possible to propagate your own vines, and the method of propagation is spelled out in the **Vine Chart.**

PRUNING VINES

Vines grown as ground covers will, in time, grow into the lawn, walkways or nearby plants. A metal or brick barrier will help to control growth into the lawn or walkway; however, you may need to prune every six months or yearly to keep them in check and prevent them from smothering any small shrubs and perennials that are interplanted with them.

Read also about **Staking and Tying.**

WATER GARDENING

It is often said, and it is true, that there is nothing more tranquil and charming than the sight and sound of water in the garden. No matter what the size of your garden, you can add some sort of water feature. If the size of the property allows it, you can construct a garden pond, or waterfall. If your property is small, you may be able to have one or two small containers for water plants. In addition to the beauty and diversity of its flowers and pool, a water garden can also be used to attract birds that will use it for drinking and bathing.

GARDEN POOLS

PREFORMED POOLS

You can purchase preformed pools of fiberglass in various sizes. These pools are sunk into the ground. On terraced property, you can install two or more small pools, and allow the water to cascade from one to another. With the aid of a small submersible pump, the water can be recirculated continually. This pump can also be used to circulate water to a waterfall. Synthetic rocks are available that are lightweight and make it easy to build a waterfall. You can also place rocks along the edges of the pool to give it a natural effect.

To install a preformed pool, dig a hole that conforms to the pool's shape, but is several inches (mm) wider and 1 inch (25 mm) deeper. Cover the bottom of the hole with 1 inch (25 mm) of sand, put the pool in place, and fill in around the edges with soil.

HOME-MADE POOLS

If you wish to make your own pool rather than buy a premade one, select a sunny spot in your yard, then mark the outline of the pool with string. Of course, the shape is determined only by your imagination and the pool's relationship with the rest of the landscape. Formal gardens usually call for square or symmetrical pools, while informal gardens look best with free-form pools.

Dig out the pool area to a depth of about 3 feet (1 m) if you will be including water lilies; shallower pools will

TOP: *Water gardens add tranquility to almost any landscape.*

ABOVE: *This small-space waterlily pool beside the back door of a suburban home features a collection of water plants displaying contrasting foliage. Featured plants include lotus (with parasol-shaped leaves), tropical water-lily (with floating, heart-shaped leaves), and spear-shaped water cannas.*

suffice for shallow-rooted plants (see **Water Plant Chart**). Make sure the pool is level; if not, raise up one side of the pool as needed.

After you dig the pool, place 1 inch (25 mm) of sand in the bottom of the hole. Spread a piece of 20-mil PVC liner over the hole, using a piece that is 7 feet (2 m) longer and wider than the largest surface dimensions of the pool. Situate the liner so that no less than 6 inches (15 cm) of the liner rests on the ground at any point around the pool, and weight it down with rocks or bricks. Fill the pool slowly with water, allowing the liner to conform to the shape of the pool. Make pleats or tucks in the liner to shape it to the edges. Once the pool is filled, the weight of the water will hold the liner in place. Remove the weights and trim the liner so that about 6 inches (15 cm) remains on the ground around the pool. You can cover the remaining liner on the ground with bricks, stones, or paving blocks so that no part of it is exposed.

It is also a good idea to create a ledge that is 3 to 6 inches (7.5 to 15 cm) deep around the edge of the pool into which shallow-rooted plants such as cattails, pickerel rush, and water chestnuts can be planted.

CONCRETE POOLS

Concrete pools without liners are rarely used because they settle and develop cracks, and eventually leak. Older concrete pools can be repaired by lining them in the manner described in **Homemade Pools.**

BELOW: *This medium-size pool features a collection of mostly hardy waterlilies decorating the surface of the water, while bog-loving plants—such as red astilbe, variegated flag irises, and arrowhead plants—enliven the pond margin.*

BOTTOM: *Goldfish enhance the informal beauty of this Japanese water garden.*

SELECTING WATER PLANTS

Water plants are available from mail-order and specialty nurseries. When selecting plants, you'll need to consider: their ultimate size and spread in relationship to the size of the pool; their flower color, size, and shape of the foliage; and hardiness. Include some oxygenating plants (anacharis, cabomba, curled pondweed, eelgrass, sagittaria, or water milfoil) to provide oxygen for fish and animal life, as well as to keep the water clear.

GROWING AND MAINTAINING A WATER GARDEN

PLANTING WATER PLANTS

It is best to plant water plants into containers and submerge the containers into the pool. This allows you to remove the plants easily when division is needed, and prevents the buildup of organic matter on the bottom of the pool, which causes the water to become murky.

Planting time depends on the hardiness of the specific plant and the climate in which you live. Plants that are hardy in your area are generally planted in mid- to late spring. Plants that are not hardy in your area can be grown as annuals, and should be planted when the water temperature is 70° F (21° C) or higher.

Fill the pool with water one to two weeks before planting to dissipate chlorine gas from the water; there are chemicals available which will help remove chlorine. Use special water-plant containers, or laundry baskets with mesh sides for planting, and garden soil without additional organic matter. Place the water plants into the container. After planting, place a layer of gravel on top of the container to keep the soil in place, and to prevent fish from disturbing the roots, then lower the container into the pool.

Planting depth is given in the **Water Plant Chart;** this figure is equal to the depth from the surface of the water to the top of the container. When a plant needs a shallower planting depth than the depth of the pool, you can rest the container on a stack of bricks or stones. In natural pools without liners, shallow-rooted plants can be planted along the edges of the pool.

Some water plants, such as water lettuce and duckweed, float on the water and are planted merely by placing them into the pool.

FERTILIZING WATER PLANTS

Water plants need fertilizing once each year in the spring. Special fertilizers are available for water plants, usually come in tablet form, and are inserted into the soil in the plants' containers.

PRUNING WATER PLANTS

Water gardens need full-to-partial sunlight if they are supporting flowering plants. As plants grow, selectively remove enough so that no more than one-half to two-thirds of the water surface is covered by foliage. Water plants can be divided in the same manner as other plants. See **Propagation.** Open areas of water are also necessary to reflect the sunlight and allow you to view the fish.

KEEPING YOUR POOL CLEAN

The presence of algae in the water will cause the water to become clouded and foul-smelling. To prevent this, keep the pool free of fallen and dead leaves and other debris, and grow oxygenating plants that rob the algae of the mineral salts they need to survive. Fish, snails, and tadpoles also eat algae and a certain amount of waste organic material, and thus help to keep the pool clean; they also keep under control the insect population that water attracts.

It is also advisable to remove water, fish, and plants once a year in spring or autumn to clean the pool.

There are chemicals that clarify water; read the label carefully, as not all types can be used with fish. The pH of the water in a pool should be neutral to slightly acidic; there are also chemicals available to test and adjust the water pH. Do not use insecticides in any pools that contain fish or animals.

FISH

The best fish to use in a water garden are common goldfish, comets, shubunkins, Japanese fantails, calicoes, and orandas.

WATER PLANTS

	FC	PDe	HZ	SZ
Cabomba caroliniana Cabomba	—	6–30″	6–10	submerged
Cyperus alternifolius Umbrella palm	—	6″	9–10	5′ × 3′
Eichhornia crassipes Water hyacinth	BLUE	floats	9–10	6″ × 4′
Eleocharis species Chinese water chestnut	BROWN	2″	7–10	3″ × 1′
Elodea canadensis Anacharis	—	6–30″	5–10	submerged
Hydrocleys nymphoides Water poppy	YELLOW	4–12″	9–10	2″ × 2′
Iris species Water iris	MIX	6″	4–10	2′ × 2′
Lemna minor Duckweed	—	floats	6–10	1″ × 3′
Myriophyllum species Water milfoil	—	12″	4–10	3″ × 2′
Nelumbo nucifera Lotus	MIX	2′	4–10	2′ × 5′
Nymphaea varieties Hardy water lilies	MIX	2′	3–10	6″ × 4′
Nymphaea varieties Tropical water lilies	MIX	1′	10	6″ × 4′
Pistia stratiotes Water lettuce	—	floats	9–10	2″ × 6″
Pontederia cordata Pickerel rush	PINK, WHITE	6″	3–9	2½′ × 3′
Potamogeton crispus Curled pondweed	GREEN	12″	6–10	3″ × 2′
Sagittaria species Arrowhead	WHITE	6″	5–10	2′ × 2′
Trapa natans Water chestnut	WHITE	3″/floats	6–10	3″ × 3′
Typha species Cattails	BROWN	6″	2–10	6–48″ × 1–4′
Vallisneria spiralis Eelgrass	—	6–12″	6–10	1–2′ × 2′

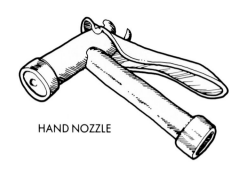

HAND NOZZLE

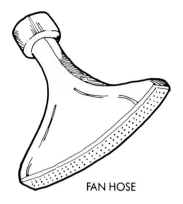

FAN HOSE

SOAKER HOSE

WINTER PROTECTION

In winter, fish and hardy plants will usually survive if the pool does not freeze solid. Even if the surface freezes, fish and plants can often live in the water below. In autumn, remove all frost-killed growth. Prevent leaves from falling into the pool by covering it with mesh or screening. In areas of severe cold, cover the pool with alternate layers of burlap and leaves. Float a large rubber ball or piece of wood on the surface of the water to prevent potential damage to the pool that alternate freezing and thawing causes.

WATERING

Watering, or irrigation, supplies plants with necessary moisture if natural moisture in the form of rain, dew, or underground sources is insufficient. Sometimes there is not enough rain. Extreme heat and wind also make soil moisture evaporate quickly, which causes leaves to transpire excessive amounts of water. In both cases, you will need to replenish the water supply more often.

FACTORS IMPACTING A GARDEN'S WATERING NEEDS

Watering frequency depends on general factors, the first being the type of soil you have in the garden. Sandy soil dries out more quickly than clay soil, and needs watering more often. If the soil is heavy, apply water slowly so that it is absorbed and does not run off. Properly prepared soil can help make the most efficient use of the water applied to it.

HEAT AND WIND

Watering frequency also depends on the heat and wind. Soil dries out more quickly during hot weather or where winds are high. There isn't much you can do about heat, except to install structures to provide shade. You can install a windbreak to lessen the wind's impact on the garden.

LARGE TREES

Roots of large trees can rob moisture from nearby grass or flowering plants, so more water in these areas may be needed. Catch basins that extend as far as the drip line, the imaginary line from the furthest extension of the foliage to the ground, will help collect water for the tree without depriving other nearby plants. Additional water may also be needed for trees planted along sidewalks, and installing catch basins around the trees here is also helpful. If trees' leaves start to droop or become dull or blue-colored, it is a sign that they need watering.

WEEDS

Weeds rob moisture from plants, so keep the garden well weeded and apply a mulch to reduce weeds. Mulching also holds moisture in the soil by preventing its evaporation and keeps the soil cooler.

WATERING TECHNIQUES

It is important to water deeply but as infrequently as possible to encourage deep roots so the plants will be stronger and less susceptible to damage from drought, weeds, and attack by insects and diseases. The best general plan is to water deeply and then not water again until the top inch (mm) or so of the soil dries out. Water when the garden needs it, not by the day of the week.

Another good general rule is to apply 1 inch (25 mm) of water per week. Place a coffee can halfway between the sprinkler and the outermost point the water reaches, then time how long to run a sprinkler in a given spot to deliver the right amount of water, presuming that all your neighbors aren't watering at the same time, which lowers the water pressure. Remember to position your sprinklers so that you are not wasting water by watering the street or the driveway.

To make sure that water is getting down to the roots where it is needed, complete your test by probing into the soil (8 to 12 inches or 20 to 30 cm for annuals, vegetables, lawns, and herbaceous plants, and 18 inches or 45 cm for trees and shrubs) to check its moisture. If the soil is moist to that level, you know how much water to apply and for how long.

Never water on a windy day, unless you are using drip irrigation or soaker hoses, as the wind can carry water away or cause it to evaporate before it hits the ground.

Keep track of how much it rains, either from weather reports or a rain gauge, and supplement water as necessary.

The following are the most common watering methods:

DRIP IRRIGATION

Drip irrigation is the most efficient way to water. It takes longer to water using this method, but it uses less water because it applies the water to the ground only where it is needed. Drip irrigation also prevents foliage and flowers from getting wet and consequently, may help prevent related diseases. This system uses a main tubing laid on the ground through the garden; narrow tubes, called emitters, extend from the main tubing. The ends of the emitters are placed where there is a

WALL-HUNG HOSE HANGER

PORTABLE HOSE REEL

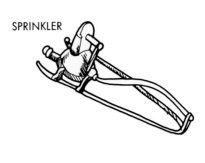

SPRINKLER

plant that needs to be watered; if there are no plants for a stretch of the main tubing, the holes can be plugged. Soaker hoses, flat hoses with tiny holes, are also laid on the ground, and work in much the same way.

A drip system can be laid on the ground, buried, or placed below the mulch. In areas with cold winters, the system should be removed in autumn if it is not buried. To prevent problems with the system, install filters at the water source, and clean the filters once a month. The holes in a drip irrigation system are very small and clog easily.

FURROWS

Large vegetable gardens are often watered by a furrow system. Furrows 6 to 12 inches (15 to 30 cm) wide are dug between the planting beds. Water is allowed to run the length of the furrow, and is absorbed by the roots. This method prevents the foliage from becoming wet, which may help prevent water-related disease.

HAND WATERING

Hand watering is a time-consuming way to water, but is necessary for watering containers, seed beds, or transplants when the entire garden does not need watering. Hand-held pistol nozzles can deliver a hard spray for washing foliage and the side of the house, or a fine mist for watering small plants. Fan nozzles give a wide, coarse spray and are useful for watering flower beds. Soaker heads deliver water with low pressure, and are good for watering seed beds and small plants as they do not make holes in the soil or disturb small plants.

HOSES

There are various ways to give plants water. The most traditional method is the use of hoses and sprinklers. Hoses come in a variety of sizes. The smallest and lightest is the 1/2-inch (12.5-mm) hose, which is easy to maneuver if you are dragging it to water container plants. However, this hose delivers water slowly, which means watering will take a longer time. The most common hose is the 5/8-inch (16-mm) hose, which delivers twice as much water as the 1/2-inch (12.5-mm) hose in the same period of time. The largest and heaviest hose is the 3/4-inch (19-mm) hose. It's hard to maneuver and store, and is used only on very large properties or with very large sprinklers.

Hoses can be made of plastic or rubber; plastic hoses are more flexible and less likely to kink. When a hose develops a hole and needs repair, purchase a repair kit from your garden center or hardware store. Make sure the kit fits the diameter of the hose you are using.

When stored, hoses should always be rolled up to prevent kinks and breakage. Hoses can be rolled up on the ground in an out-of-the-way place, or on a rounded hanger that mounts onto a wall. You can also use a hose reel; this can be wheeled around the garden, which makes rolling and storing hoses very easy.

Before storing a hose for the winter, make sure the water supply is off. Remove the nozzle, or squeeze it so that any remaining water comes out.

SPRINKLERS

Sprinklers are attached to the ends of hoses, and are either oscillating or rotating. Oscillating sprinklers are advantageous in that they throw water in a rectangular rather than a circular pattern, which causes less water waste from necessary overlapping. Sprinklers come in different sizes and cover varying square footage . Choose a sprinkler that best fits the size of your property. You also should not try to use a large sprinkler with a small hose, because you won't get the necessary water pressure to make the sprinkler work properly.

Automatic sprinkler systems are the easiest way to water a large garden. PVC pipes are laid under the ground in a trench about 8 inches (20 cm) deep; upright risers ending in sprinkler heads are placed in regular intervals along the pipe. You can hire a professional to install a system for you, or you can do it yourself. It's easier to install a system before a garden is created, but you can also install a system later on. Be sure the sprinkler heads are flush with the soil or are retractable so that they are not damaged by the lawn mower or cause people to trip over them.

It is best to set up an automatic sprinkler system with a soil moisture sensor or manual control valves, rather than with a timer, so the garden is watered only when necessary.

WATERING CONTAINER PLANTS

Plants in containers need more regular watering than they would if they were grown in the ground. This is due to the limited area around the roots, as well as the loss of water through the planting medium and sides of the container. In hot or windy spots, container plants may need watering once a day or more, depending on the size of the container. Check the medium in the container every day, and water when the top becomes dry. Use a soaker head when you water so you do not create holes in the planting medium.

WATERING EVERGREENS

To help evergreens survive the winter, it is important that the soil be moist before it freezes. If it does not rain in autumn, apply a deep watering before you drain the hoses and shut down your watering system for the winter.

WEEDS

In reality, a weed is a plant out of place. While you might want to grow dandelions in a vegetable garden for salad greens or to use the flowers for wine, you don't want dandelions in the lawn.

When weeds appear, it is often a sign of poor and compacted soil, improper soil pH, poor drainage, improper fertilization, improper watering, or insufficient light. These are signs that other corrective actions may need to be taken in addition to removing the weeds.

Weed control is essential because weeds prevent the proper growth of desirable plants. Weeds rob plants of sunlight, nutrients, and water. They are aggressive growers and usually take over the growing area from your ornamental plants. In a lawn, they can quickly replace the grass. Many insects, and many diseases, use weeds as their breeding grounds.

METHODS OF COMBATTING WEEDS

☐
EXTRACTION

There are several ways to combat weeds. If your weeds are small in number, you can either pull them up by hand, or dig them up with a hoe.

PRE- AND POST-EMERGENT HERBICIDES

Weeds are classified as broad-leaved or grassy, and different herbicides are used for each type. It is important to identify your weeds and their climatic and seasonal preferences before buying herbicides so that you buy the right product. It is important to control weeds when they are young and actively growing. If a new lawn or planting bed is being installed, eliminate all weeds before planting.

In larger areas, weeds can be chem-

WEEDS

	TYPE	TEMPERATURE
Agropyron repens Quack grass	Perennial grassy	Cool
Allium species Wild garlic and onion	Perennial grassy	Cool
Artemisia vulgaris Mugwort	Perennial broad-leaf	Any
Capsella bursa-pastoris Shepherd's purse	Annual broad-leaf	Any
Cerastium species Mouse-ear chickweed	Perennial broad-leaf	Cool
Cirsium arvense Canada thistle	Perennial broad-leaf	Any
Convolvulus arvensis Field bindweed	Perennial broad-leaf	Hot
Cyperus esculentus Nutsedge	Perennial grassy	Warm
Digitaria species Crabgrass	Annual grassy	Hot
Eleusine indica Goose grass	Annual grassy	Hot
Euphorbia supina Prostrate spurge	Annual broad-leaf	Hot
Glechoma hederacea Ground ivy, Creeping Charlie	Perennial broad-leaf	Any
Lamium amplexicaule Henbit	Annual broad-leaf	Cool
Medicago lupulina Black medic	Annual broad-leaf	Cool
Oxalis stricta Yellow wood sorrel	Perennial broad-leaf	Cool
Plantago species Plantain	Perennial broad-leaf	Cool
Poa annua Annual bluegrass	Annual or perennial grassy	Cool
Polygonum aviculare Knotweed	Annual broad-leaf	Any
Portulaca oleracea Purslane	Annual broad-leaf	Hot
Rhus radicans Poison ivy	Perennial broad-leaf	Any
Rumex Acetosella Red sorrel, Sheep sorrel	Perennial broad-leaf	Cool

WEEDS cont.

	Type	Temperature
Rumex crispus Curly dock	Perennial broad-leaf	Cool
Stellaria media Common chickweed	Annual broad-leaf	Cool
Taraxacum officinale Dandelion	Perennial broad-leaf	Cool
Trifolium repens White clover	Perennial broad-leaf	Any
Veronica species Speedwell	Perennial broad-leaf	Warm

ically treated, but with precautions. Chemicals known as pre-emergent herbicides prevent both perennial and annual weed seeds from germinating. These chemicals are applied in early to late spring, depending on the weed and its germination time. Most herbicides will do no damage to ornamental plantings, but check the label first. Many herbicides will prevent other seeds from germinating, too, and should not be used when you are seeding the lawn or a flower bed. Again, check the label or ask for information at your garden center.

Weeds that are actively growing are treated with what are known as post-emergent herbicides. These must be handled with great care so they don't damage or kill nearby garden plants. Read label instructions carefully, and never apply these chemicals on a windy day. You can treat large areas with a sprayer or a spreader (don't use the sprayer or spreader for anything else); small areas can be spot-treated.

MULCHING

Mulching helps to reduce weeds by smothering them and their seeds. The few weeds that pop up through the mulch can easily be removed.

WETTING AGENT

Wetting agent is a chemical that is added to soil or growing medium to increase its water retention and keep it uniformly moist.

WILDFLOWERS

A wildflower is a plant that will grow and flourish without the intervention of people. Wildflowers grow along roadsides, in empty fields, under the canopy of dense forests, and in deserts or marshland. Wildflowers are sometimes called "native plants," although this term is technically incorrect. While all plants are native to a particular place, many of our wildflowers today are not native to the areas in which they grow; most wildflowers have been transported to their current homes by people either intentionally or accidentally.

Gardeners recently have taken a great interest in wildflowers, and have created low-care gardens that use them. Wildflowers can be planted into numerous situations, from large sunny meadows to flower beds, borders, and small pockets in shady corners. Many wildflowers look fragile, but most can be grown with a minimum of maintenance.

SELECTING WILDFLOWERS

Wildflowers are either annuals or perennials, and choosing plants for the wildflower garden is quite similar to choosing plants for annual and perennial beds and borders. Choose annual wildflowers for temporary gardens, or if you want to change the look of your garden each year; perennial wildflowers, however, should be picked for permanent plantings. Still, most annual wildflowers freely reseed themselves, so they act as if they were perennials.

When selecting wildflowers, you will want to consider plant size, flower color, bloom time, hardiness, and climate considerations of light and moisture. Select plants that are naturally adapted to your climate to increase their chance of survival and reduce maintenance needs. Look for plants that grow in the wild in your area of the country for best success.

You can be bolder when selecting wildflowers than when selecting plants for a more formal garden. You can mix color and plants sizes more freely, and pack plants more tightly together. As with any other garden, you will want to prepare for a succession of bloom and seasonal interest throughout the year. The main goal in planting a wildflower garden is to make it look natural. Read about **Annuals** and **Perennials** for more tips on choosing plants. Many wildflowers fit well into rock gardens. See **Rock Gardens** for more information.

GROWING AND MAINTAINING WILDFLOWERS

Growing and maintaining wildflowers is in many ways the same as growing and maintaining any other annual or perennial. Plants can be purchased, and sometimes can be dug from the wild (do *not* do this if the plant is an endangered species). Seed mixtures of wildflowers are readily available, and are the easiest way to start large wildflower plantings, especially meadows. Seeds can also be collected from the wild to make your own seed mixtures. Read about sowing seeds under **Propagation.**

Caring for wildflowers is in many ways easier than caring for a more formal garden. Because you want to achieve a natural look, and because wildflowers are low-maintenance plants, you will not need to be concerned as much with pruning and deadheading. In fact, removing faded flowers will prevent reseeding, and will defeat the pur-

California poppies and pink toadflax combine to create an appealing color harmony in this beautiful meadow planting. The sunny meadow is ploughed and seeded each autumn so that the flowers will bloom in the spring.

pose of having a wildflower garden. Most wildflowers have low fertility requirements and, properly chosen, will survive with natural rainfall and rarely need additional watering, unless you are growing a woodland garden with high moisture requirements.

Soil preparation is still important, as the wildflower garden will probably be there for many years. While it may be impractical to improve the soil in a large meadow, it should be done for smaller plantings around the house. Read about **Soil.** Read also about **Planting,** as the basic principles remain unchanged.

Wildflower gardens should be weeded, especially when they are young. In time, a dense wildflower garden will choke out weedy plants. You will note in the natural progression of a wildflower garden that some plants tend to grow more aggressively than others. These can be thinned out to maintain the originally

intended balance of plants. From time to time, plants will also need dividing; read about this under **Propagation.** It is possible to propagate wildflowers by other methods than division; this is outlined in the **Wildflower Chart.**

At the end of the growing season, cut the plants back just as you would in any other flower garden. Large meadows can be mowed in late autumn to keep woody plants, undesirable weeds, and grasses from developing in the meadow. Small gardens near the house will need winter protection if the plants are growing close to their hardiness limits.

You will want to attract birds, insects, and butterflies to your wildflower garden to ensure pollination and to enhance its beauty. Be careful when using insecticides and use organic ones when needed. Read about **Birds, Insects and Insect Control,** and **Diseases and Disease Control.**

WILDFLOWERS

	PT	PH	BT	FC	L	MO	HZ	P
Abronia species Sand verbena	A,P	3″	ASu	PINK	S	D	3–10	SC,S
Aconitum species Monkshood	P	2–5′	ASu,A	BLUE	S,PSh	M	5–9	D,S
Acorus Calamus Sweet flag	P	1½′	LSp	GREEN	S,PSh	M	3–10	D
Amsonia species Bluestar	P	3–4′	LSp	BLUE	S,PSh	A	3–10	D,SC,S
Anemone canadensis Meadow anemone	P	1–3′	ASu	WHITE	S	M	3–7	D,S
Anemone quinquefolia Wood anemone	P	6–12″	MSp	WHITE	PSh	M	4–8	D,S
Aquilegia species Columbine	P	1–3′	LSp	MIX	S,PSh	A	2–8	S
Arisaema triphyllum Jack-in-the-pulpit	P	2′	LSp	GREEN	PSh	M	4–8	S
Artemisia tridentata Sagebrush	P	10′	—	—	S	D	5–10	D,SC
Aruncus dioicus Goatsbeard	P	4–6′	ESu	WHITE	PSh	M	2–8	D,S

WILDFLOWERS cont.

	PT	PH	BT	FC	L	MO	HZ	P
Asarum canadense Wild ginger	P	1'	LSp	BROWN	Sh	M	3–8	S,D
Asclepias syriaca Milkweed	P	2–6'	LSu	PINK	S	D	2–10	S,SC
Asclepias tuberosa Butterfly weed	P	2–3'	MSu	ORANGE	S	D	3–10	S,SC
Aster species Aster	P	1–6'	LSu,A	MIX	S	A	3–10	D,S
Callirhoe involucrata Poppy mallow	P	1–2'	MSu	RED	S,PSh	D	3–10	S
Caltha palustris Marsh marigold	P	1'	LSp	YELLOW	S,PSh	M	3–8	D,S
Castilleja species Indian paintbrush	P	1–2'	ESu	MIX	S	D	3–8	S,D
Chrysanthemum Leucanthemum Oxeye daisy	P	1–2'	MSu	WHITE	S	D	3–10	S,D
Salvia species Sage	P	2–5'	ASu	BLUE, RED	S	A	3–10	S,SC,D
Sanguinaria canadensis Bloodroot, Red puccoon	P	1'	MSp	WHITE	PSh,Sh	A	3–10	S,D
Silene species Campion	P	½–3'	ESu	MIX	S,PSh	A	3–10	S,D,SC
Solidago species Goldenrod	P	1–8'	LSu	GOLD	S	D	2–10	S,SC
Symplocarpus foetidus Skunk cabbage	P	2'	ESp	BROWN	PSh,Sh	M	3–9	S,D
Thalictrum species Meadow rue	P	2–8'	ESu	WHITE	S,LSh	M	2–10	S,D
Tradescantia virginiana Spiderwort	P	1–3'	ESu	BLUE	PSh	M	4–10	D
Trifolium pratense Red clover	P	½–2'	ESu	RED	S	D	3–10	S
Trillium species Wake-robin	P	1–2'	LSp	WHITE, PURPLE	PSh	M	3–10	S,D
Viola species Violet	P	½–3'	LSp	MIX	PSh,Sh	M	2–10	S,D,C

WILDFLOWERS cont.

	PT	PH	BT	FC	L	MO	HZ	P
Chrysogonum virginianum Golden star, Green and gold	P	2′	MSp	YELLOW	S,PSh	A	6–10	D,SC,S
Cichorium Intybus Chicory	P	1–3′	MSu	BLUE	S	D	3–9	S,RC
Cimicifuga racemosa Black snakeroot	P	6–8′	ESu	WHITE	S,Sh	M	3–9	S,D
Cirsium vulgare Bull thistle	P	2–4′	MSu	PURPLE	S	D	3–8	S
Claytonia species Spring beauty	P	½–1′	ESp	PINK	PSh	M	4–9	S,D
Coreopsis species Tickseed	A,P	2′	ASu	YELLOW	S	D	3–10	S,D,SC
Corydalis aurea Golden corydalis	A	6″	LSp	YELLOW	S,PSh	D	—	S
Datura inoxia Indian apple	P	2–5′	ASu	WHITE	S	D	8–10	S
Daucus Carota Carota Queen Anne's lace	P	2–3′	ESu	WHITE	S	D	3–9	S
Dodecatheon species Shooting star	P	½–1½′	LSp	LILAC	S,PSh	A	3–10	S,RC
Echinacea purpurea Purple coneflower	P	3–4′	ASu	LILAC	S	D	3-9	S,D,RC
Erigeron speciosus Oregon fleabane	P	2–3′	ASu	PINK, BLUE	S,LSh	A	3–10	S,D,SC
Erythronium americanum Trout lily	P	1′	MSp	YELLOW	PSh,Sh	A	3–9	S,D
Eschscholzia californica California poppy	A,P	1–2′	MSp	YELLOW	S	D	8–10	S
Eupatorium maculatum Joe-pye weed	P	5–7′	MSu	PURPLE	S,PSh	M	3–9	S,D
Filipendula rubra Meadowsweet, Queen-of-the-prairie	P	4–6′	ESu	WHITE	PSh	M	3–9	S,D
Gaillardia species Blanket flower	A,P	1–3′	ASu	RED, YELLOW	S	D	3–10	S,SC,D
Gentiana species Gentian	P	1–2′	ESu	BLUE	S,PSh	M	3–9	S,SC,D

WILDFLOWERS cont.

	PT	PH	BT	FC	L	MO	HZ	P
Helenium autumnale Sneezeweed	P	4–6'	LSu	YELLOW	S	A	3–10	S,D
Helianthus species Sunflower	A,P	3–10'	ASu	YELLOW	S	A–D	3–10	S,SC,D
Hedyotis purpurea *calycosa* Bluets	P	3–6"	LSp	BLUE	S	D	3–9	S,D
Lewisia species Lewisia	P	3–12"	LSp	WHITE, PINK	PSh	D	3–8	S
Liatris species Blazing star	P	2–6'	LSu	PURPLE	S	M	3–9	S,D
Linaria vulgaris Butter-and-eggs	P	1–3'	LSu	YELLOW	S	A	3–10	S
Lobelia Cardinalis Cardinal flower	P	4'	LSu	RED	PSh	M	2–10	S,SC
Lupinus subcarnosus Texas bluebonnets	A	1–2'	LSp	BLUE	S	D	—	S
Mertensia virginica Virginia bluebells	P	2'	MSp	BLUE	Sh	M	3–9	S,D
Mitchella repens Partridgeberry	P	2–4"	ESu	WHITE	PSh,Sh	M	3–10	S,SC
Monotropa uniflora Indian pipe	P	3–9"	MSu	WHITE	Sh	M	4–8	S
Oenothera species Evening primrose	P	1½–3'	ESu	YELLOW	S,PSh	A	3–10	S,D
Penstemon species Beard tongue	P	1–6'	ESu	MIX	S,LSh	A	3–10	S,SC,D
Pontederia cordata Pickerel weed	P	4'	MSu	LILAC	S	M	3–10	D
Potentilla species Cinquefoil	P	1–3'	ASu	WHITE, YELLOW	S,PSh	A–D	2–10	S,SC,D
Ranunculus species Buttercup	P	½–3'	MSp	MIX	PSh,Sh	A	3–10	S,D
Ratibida columnifera Prairie coneflower	P	4'	MSu	YELLOW	S	D	3–10	S
Rudbeckia hirta Black-eyed Susan	A	3'	ASu	YELLOW	S,LSh	D	—	S

WINTER PROTECTION

In most areas of the country, most plants will need some winter protection. Winter protection is based on a plant's hardiness, but it doesn't stop there.

Read the section on **Hardiness.** If you are growing a plant that is near its hardiness limit, winter protection is advisable in case the temperatures dip a little lower than normal. Plants grown at or below their hardiness limit should always be protected. If you have a warm microclimate, you may be able to bring a plant through a winter that it would otherwise not survive.

WINTER COVERINGS

Perennials and small shrubs die over winter not only because it is too cold, but also because the ground alternately freezes and thaws. Freezing and thawing causes plants to be heaved from the ground. Their roots break in the process, or are exposed to cold and winds, dry out, and die.

Winter Mulch

To prevent plants from injury or death, apply a layer of mulch several inches (mm) thick over the soil after the ground has frozen. Suitable materials for winter mulch are soil (only if brought in from another part of the garden), shredded oak leaves, straw, and evergreen limbs from Christmas trees.

Winter mulch should be removed gradually in the spring as the weather warms. If you use an organic mulch, it can either be completely removed or worked into the soil to improve it.

Styrofoam Covers and Wire Cages

Small shrubs and roses can be covered with purchased Styrofoam covers, or by encasing the plant in a chicken-wire cage and filling it with organic material or even shredded newspapers.

Snow Covers

The best insulation against freezing and thawing damage is a heavy snow cover. It covers plants while keeping soil temperature and moisture constant.

WINTER MULCH

SOURCES OF WINTER DAMAGE

☐
Snow

Snow can be destructive. Its weight can break or deform branches of trees and shrubs. When snow falls, brush it off branches that are sagging under its weight. Weak-wooded plants can be tied together with string if heavy snowfall is normal in your area to prevent them from being damaged.

Ice

Ice can also damage plants and should be removed if possible. When melting ice on sidewalks or driveways, do not use salt as it will damage nearby plants and the lawn; use sand instead. Plants close enough to the road to risk the damage of being splashed with salt should be protected with a snow fence or similar barrier.

Wind

Wind is another major winter culprit. In addition to breaking branches, wind takes moisture from the surface soil and from evergreen leaves. If the ground is dry or frozen, the roots can't restore moisture to the plant, and the plant can dry out and die.

Sun

Winter sun can also dehydrate a plant. The warmth of the sun causes leaves to lose water, and the plant may not be able to replace that moisture. Plants can be wrapped in burlap, or protected with evergreen boughs or snow fences. If possible, don't plant evergreens on the

ROSE BUSH COVERS

south side of the house where they are subject to sun damage.

The sun can also burn thin bark. As the water in the plant's cells freezes and thaws, cells will break and bark can split. To prevent this, especially on new trees, you can paint the bark white or wrap it in tree wrap.

LESSENING WINTER DAMAGE

Several measures can lessen winter damage. Make sure plants are well-watered in autumn before the ground freezes, particularly if sufficient rain has not fallen. Winter covers provide protection and some warm the soil. Antidesiccant sprays applied to evergreens will prevent their leaves from transpiring too much moisture. Pruning trees and shrubs so that wind can pass through them will reduce breakage from wind resistance. Windbreaks four to six times the height of the plants to be protected will also help.

If plants have been damaged, don't prune away the winter-killed stems until growth starts in spring, as premature pruning can stimulate new growth which may not survive late spring frosts.

See **Container Gardening** for methods of protecting potted plants.

XERISCAPING

Xeriscaping is a method of landscape design and maintenance for gardens with low water availability. See **Drought Resistance.**

Appendices

FROST DATES

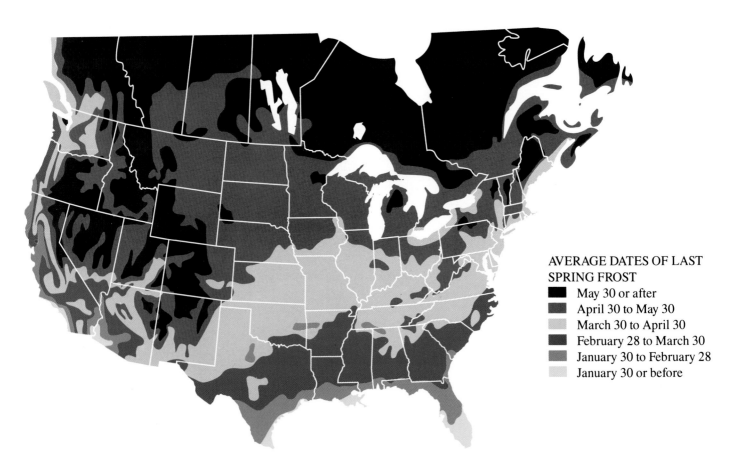

AVERAGE DATES OF LAST SPRING FROST
- May 30 or after
- April 30 to May 30
- March 30 to April 30
- February 28 to March 30
- January 30 to February 28
- January 30 or before

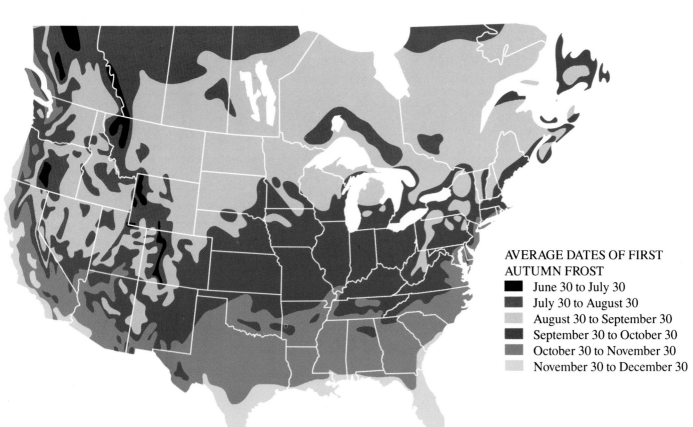

AVERAGE DATES OF FIRST AUTUMN FROST
- June 30 to July 30
- July 30 to August 30
- August 30 to September 30
- September 30 to October 30
- October 30 to November 30
- November 30 to December 30

BIBLIOGRAPHY

Art, Henry. *A Garden of Wildflowers.* Pownal, VT: Garden Way Publishing, 1986.

Better Homes and Gardens. *New Garden Book.* Des Moines, IA: 1990.

Brookes, John. *The Indoor Garden Book.* New York: Crown Publishers, 1986.

Brown, Emily. *Landscaping with Perennials.* Portland, OR: Timber Press, 1986.

Creasy, Rosalind. *The Gardener's Handbook of Edible Plants.* San Francisco, CA: Sierra Club Books, 1986.

Fell, Derek, *Annuals.* Tucson, AZ: HP Books, 1983.

Ferguson, Nicola. *Right Plant, Right Place.* New York: Summit Books, 1984.

Heriteau, Jacqueline. *The National Arboretum Book of Outstanding Garden Plants.* New York: Simon and Schuster, 1990.

Hill, Lewis and Nancy. *Successful Perennial Gardening.* Pownal, VT: Garden Way Publishing, 1988.

Hudac, Joseph. *Shrubs in the Landscape.* McGraw Hill, 1984.

MacCaskey, Michael. *Lawns and Ground Covers.* Tucson, AZ: HP Books, 1982.

Mackensie, David. *Complete Manual of Perennial Ground Covers.* Englewood Cliffs, NJ: Prentice Hall, 1989.

Martin, Laura. *The Wildflower Meadow Book.* Charlotte, NC: East Woods Press, 1986.

Paterson, Allen. *Herbs in the Garden.* London, England: J.M. Dent & Sons, 1985.

Reader's Digest. *Illustrated Guide to Gardening.* Pleasantville, NY: 1978.

Reilly, Ann. *Success with Seeds.* Greenwood, SC: Park Seed Co., 1978.

Reinhardt, Thomas. *Ornamental Grass Gardening.* Los Angeles, CA: HP Books, 1989.

Schuler, Stanley. *Gardens Are for Eating.* New York: Macmillan Publishing, 1971.

Taylor, Jane. *Fragrant Gardens.* Topsfield, MA: Salem House, 1987.

Time-Life Books. *The Time-Life Gardener's Guide,* 15 volumes, Alexandria, VA: 1988-1990.

Whiten, Faith and Geoff. *The Art of Container Gardening.* New York: E.P. Dutton, 1986.

_____. *Annuals: 1001 Gardening Questions Answered.* Pownal, VA: Garden Way Publishing, 1989.

_____. *Creative Home Landscaping.* San Francisco, CA: Ortho Books, 1987.

_____. *Taylor's Pocket Guides,* 12 volumes, Boston, MA: Houghton Mifflin Co., 1989-1990.

_____. *Taylor's Guide,* 11 volumes, Boston, MA: Houghton Mifflin Co., 1986-1990.

U.S. SOURCES

PLANTS AND TOOLS

W. ATLEE BURPEE SEED CO.
300 Park Ave.
Warminster, PA 18974

COMSTOCK, FERRE & CO.
263 Main St.
Wethersfield, CT 06109

EARL FERRIS SEED
 & NURSERY CO.
811 Fourth St., N.E.
Hampton, IA 50441

HENRY FIELD SEED
 & NURSERY CO.
Shenandoah, IA 51602

GURNEY SEED & NURSERY CO.
Yankton, SD 57079

HASTINGS
P.O. Box 11535
Atlanta, GA 30310

J.W. JUNG SEED CO.
Randolph, WI 53957

PARK SEED CO.
Cokesbury Rd.
Greenwood, SC 29647

CLYDE ROBIN SEED CO.
3670 Enterprise Ave.
Hayward, CA 94545

STOKES SEED CO.
Box 545
Buffalo, NY 14240

THOMPSON & MORGAN INC.
P.O. Box 1308
Jackson, NJ 08527

OTIS S. TWILLEY SEED CO.
P.O. Box 65
Trevose, PA 19047

PLANTS AND GENERAL

ADAMS NURSERY
P.O. Box 606
Springfield Rd.
Westfield, MA 01086

AHRENS STRAWBERRY NURSERY
R.R. 1
Huntingburg, IN 47542

BUNTING'S NURSERY
P.O. Box 270
Selbyville, DE 19975

CALIFORNIA NURSERY CO.
P.O. Box 2278
Fremont, CA 94536

CARROL GARDENS
P.O. Box 310
Westminster, MD 21157

CUMBERLAND VALLEY
 NURSERY INC.
P.O. Box 471
McMinnville, TN 37110
fruit

EMLONG NURSERY INC.
P.O. Box 236
Stevensville, MI 49127

GIRARD NURSERY
P.O. Box 428
Geneva, OH 44041
general and rhododendrons, azaleas

JOHNSON ORCHARD
 & NURSERY CO.
Rt. 5, Box 29J
Ellijay, GA 30540

KRIDER NURSERY
P.O. Box 29
Middlebury, IN 46540

LAKELAND NURSERY
Sales Dept. LKL 2662
Hanover, PA 17333

LAMB NURSERY
E. 101 Sharp Ave.
Spokane, WA 99202
general and perennials

LOUISIANA NURSERY
Rt. 7, Box 43
Opelousas, LA 70570

MELLINGER'S NURSERY
2310 W. S. Range Rd.
North Lima, OH 44452-9731

J.E. MILLER NURSERY
5060 West Lake Rd.
Canandaigua, NY 14424

NEOSHO NURSERY
940 N. College
Neosho, MO 64850

NOURSE FARMS INC.
Box 485 R.F.D.
Waitley, MA 01373
fruit

RAYNER'S
P.O. Box 1617
Salisbury, MD 21801

SAVAGE FARM NURSERY
P.O. Box 125
McMinnville, TN 37110

SPRING HILL NURSERY
6523 N. Galena Rd.
Peoria, IL 61632

SPRUCE BROOK NURSERY
Rt. 118, P.O. Box 925
Litchfield, CT 06759

STARK BROS. NURSERY
Louisiana, MO 63353
general and fruit

WAYNESBORO NURSERY
Box 987
Lyndhurst-Sherando Lake Rd.
Waynesboro, VA 22980
general and fruit

WAYSIDE GARDENS
1 Garden Lane
Hodges, SC 29695-0001

BULBS

ANTONELLI BROS.
2545 Capitola Rd.
Santa Cruz, CA 95062
tuberous begonias

FAIRYLAND BEGONIA
 & LILY GARDEN
1100 Griffith Rd.
McKinleyville, CA 95521

RUSSELL GRAHAM
4030 Eagle Crest Rd., N.W.
Salem, OR 97304
perennials

MICHIGAN BULB CO.
1950 Waldorf, N.W.
Grand Rapids, MI 49550
perennials

OREGON BULB FARMS
14071 N.E. Arndt Rd.
Aurora, OR 97002

REX BULB FARMS
Box 774
Port Townsend, WA 98368

SWAN ISLAND DAHLIAS
P.O. Box 700
Canby, OR 97013

TY TY PLANTATION
Box 159, Albany Hwy.
Ty Ty, GA 31795

VAN BOURGONDIEN
P.O. Box A
245 Farmingdale Rd.
Babylon, NY 11704

CHRYSANTHEMUMS

DOOLEY GARDENS
Rt. 1
Hutchinson, MN 55350

HUFF'S GARDENS
P.O. Box 187
Burlington, KS 66839

SUNNYSLOPES GARDENS
8638 Huntington Dr.
San Gabriel, CA 91776

DAYLILIES AND HOSTAS

HOMESTEAD DIVISION
OF SUNNYBROOK
FARM NURSERY
9448 Mayfield Rd.
Chesterland, OH 44026
hosta and miscellany

GILBERT H. WILD & SON INC.
P.O. Box 338
Sarcoxie, MO 64862
daylilies and peonies

IRISES

COMMANCHE ACRES
IRIS GARDENS
R.R. 1, Box 258
Gower, MO 64454

COOLEY'S GARDEN
P.O. Box 126
Silverton, OR 97381

SCHREINER'S GARDENS
3625 Quinaby Rd., N.E.
Salem, OR 97303

PERENNIALS

BLUESTONE PERENNIALS
7211 Middle Ridge Rd.
Madison, OH 44057

BUSSE GARDENS
Rt. 2, Box 238
635 E. Seventh St.
Cokato, MN 55321

CAPRICE FARM NURSERY
15425 S.W. Pleasant Hill Rd.
Sherwood, OR 97140

CARMAN'S NURSERY
16201 East Mozart Ave.
Los Gatos, CA 95032

CROWNSVILLE NURSERY
P.O. Box 797
Crownsville, MD 21032

ENGLERTH GARDENS
Rt. 2
22461 Twenty-second St.
Hopkins, MI 49328

GARDEN PLACE
6780 Heisley Rd.
P.O. Box 388
Mentor, OH 44061-0388

GILSON GARDENS
P.O. Box 227
Perry, OH 44081

HILLTOP HERB FARM INC.
P.O. Box 325
Romayor, TX 77368
herbs

HOLBROOK FARM & NURSERY
Rt. 2, Box 223B
Fletcher, NC 28732
native plants

MILEAGER'S GARDENS
4838 Douglas Ave.
Racine, WI 53402-2498

PRAIRIE NURSERY
P.O. Box 306
Westfield, WI 53964

PUTNEY NURSERY INC.
P.O. Box 265
Putney, VT 05346

ROCKNOLL NURSERY
9210 U.S. 50 East
Hillsboro, OH 45133

SANDY MUSH HERB NURSERY
Rt. 2, Surrett Cove Rd.
Leicester, NC 28748

SPRINGBROOK GARDENS
6776 Heisley Rd.
P.O. Box 388
Mentor, OH 44061

TAYLORS HERB GARDEN INC.
1535 Lone Oak Rd.
Vista, CA 92084
herbs

ANDRE VIETTE FARM
& NURSERY
Rt. 1, Box 16
Fisherville, VA 22939

WASHINGTON EVERGREEN
NURSERY
P.O. Box 388
Leicester, NC 28748
dwarf evergreens

WHITE FLOWER FARM
Litchfield, CT 06759

RHODODENDRONS AND AZALEAS

BOVEES NURSERY
1737 S.W. Coronado
Portland, OR 97219

STAN & DODY HALL
1280 Quince Dr.
Junction City, OR 97448

ROSLYN NURSERY
Box 69
Roslyn, NY 11576

SONOMA HORTICULTURAL
NURSERY
3970 Azalea Ave.
Sebastopol, CA 95472

TRANSPLANT NURSERY
Parkertown Rd.
Lavonia, GA 30553

WESTGATE GARDEN NURSERY
751 Westgate Dr.
Eureka, CA 95501

ROSES

FRED EDMUNDS ROSES
6235 S.W. Kahle Rd.
Wilsonville, OR 97070

JACKSON & PERKINS CO.
1 Rose Ln.
Medford, OR 97501

NOR'EAST MINIATURE ROSES
58 Hammond St.
Rowley, MA 01969

PIXIE TREASURES MINIATURE
    ROSE NURSERY
4121 Prospect Ave.
Yorba Linda, CA 92686

ROSES OF YESTERDAY & TODAY
802 Brown's Valley Rd.
Watsonville, CA 95076

THOMASVILLE NURSERY
Box 7
Thomasville, GA 31792
perennials and miscellany

MORE PLANTS AND MISCELLANY

DILATUSH NURSERY
780 Rt. 130
Robbinsville, NJ 08691
dwarf conifers

MUSSER FORESTS INC.
Rt. 119, Box 340
Indiana, PA 15701
conifers

NUCCIO'S NURSERY
P.O. Box 6160
Altadena, CA 91003
camellias and azaleas

SISKIYOU RARE PLANT NURSERY
2835 Cummings Rd.
Medford, OR 97501
rock garden/plants (hardy/dwarfs)

ELLIE & JOEL SPINGARN
P.O. Box 782
Georgetown, CT 06829
dwarf conifers; send SASE for catalog

WATER LILIES

LILYPONS
P.O. Box 10
Buckeystown, MD 21717

PARADISE WATER GARDEN
14 May St.
Whitman, MA 02382

PERRY'S WATER GARDENS
191 Leatherman Gap Rd.
Franklin, NC 28734

SLOCUM WATER GARDENS
1101 Cypress Gardens Blvd.
Winter Haven, FL 33884

WILDFLOWERS AND NATIVE PLANTS

ENDANGERED SPECIES
P.O. Box 1830
Red Hill Ave.
Tustin, CA 92681

GARDENS OF THE BLUE RIDGE
P.O. Box 10, Rt. 221
Pineola, NC 28662
native plants

GREEN HORIZONS
500 Thompson Dr.
Kerrville, TX 78028

PUTNEY NURSERY
Putney, VT 05346

TOOLS AND EQUIPMENT

BEN MEADOW CO.
P.O. Box 80549
3589 Broad St.
Chamblee, GA 30366

THE CLAPPER CO.
1121 Washington St.
West Newton, MA 02165

FLORIST PRODUCTS INC.
2242 N. Palmer Dr.
Schaumburg, IL 60195-3883

GARDENER'S EDEN
100 North Point St.
San Francisco, CA 94120-7307

GARDENER'S SUPPLY
128 Intervale Rd.
Burlington, VT 05401

KINSMAN CO.
Point Pleasant, PA 18950

A. M. LEONARD INC.
P.O. Box 816
Piqua, OH 45356

MODERN HOMESTEADER
1825 Big Horn Ave.
Cody, WY 82414

GREENHOUSES AND SUPPLIES

GOTHIC ARCH GREENHOUSES
P.O. Box 1564
Mobile, AL 36633

SANTA BARBARA GREENHOUSES
1115 Unit J, Acaso Ave.
Camerillo, CA 93010

STUPPY INC.
Greenhouse Supply Division
P.O. Box 12456
N. Kansas City, MO 64116

STURDI-BUILT MFG. CO.
11304 S.W. Boones Ferry Rd.
Portland, OR 97219

TEXAS GREENHOUSE CO.
2544 White Settlement Rd.
Ft. Worth, TX 76117

TURNER GREENHOUSES
P.O. Box 1260
Goldsboro, NC 27530

HORTICULTURE AND GARDEN ORGANIZATIONS

GENERAL INTEREST

AMERICAN HORTICULTURAL
    SOCIETY
E. Blvd. Drive
Alexandria, VA 22308

GARDEN CLUB OF AMERICA
598 Madison Ave.
New York, NY 10022

MEN'S GARDEN CLUBS OF AMERICA
5560 Merle Hay Rd.
Johnston, IA 50131

NATIONAL COUNCIL OF STATE
  GARDEN CLUBS
4401 Magnolia Ave.
St. Louis, MO 63110

NATIONAL GARDENING ASSN.
180 Flynn Ave.
Burlington, VT 05401

PLANT SOCIETIES

AMERICAN CAMELLIA SOCIETY
1 Massee Lane
Fort Valley, GA 31030

AMERICAN DAFFODIL SOCIETY
Rt. 3, 2302 Byhalia Rd.
Hernando, MS 38632

AMERICAN DAHLIA SOCIETY
159 Pine St.
New Hyde Park, NY 11040

AMERICAN FERN SOCIETY
Dept. of Botany
Univ. of Tennessee
Knoxville, TN 37996-1100

AMERICAN RHODODENDRON
  SOCIETY
P.O. Box 1380
Gloucester, VA 23061

AMERICAN ROSE SOCIETY
P.O. Box 30,000
Shreveport, LA 71130-0030

INTERNATIONAL DWARF
  FRUIT TREE ASSN.
303 Horticulture Dept.
Michigan State Univ.
East Lansing, MI 48823

NEW ENGLAND WILDFLOWER
  SOCIETY
Gardens in the Woods
Hemenway Rd.
Framingham, MA 01701

PERENNIAL PLANT ASSN.
Dept. of Horticulture
Ohio State Univ.
2001 Fyffe Court
Columbus, OH 43210
*limited to nurserymen and
professional horticulturists*

CANADIAN SOURCES

PLANT AND HORTICULTURAL SOCIETIES

ALBERTA HORTICULTURAL
  ASSOCIATION
Box 223
Lacombe, Alberta TOC 1S0

ALPINE GARDEN CLUB OF
  BRITISH COLUMBIA
566 Esquimalt Avenue
West Vancouver, British Columbia V7T 1J4

BRITISH COLUMBIA COUNCIL OF
  GARDEN CLUBS
10595 Dunlop Road
Delta, British Columbia V4C 7G2

CANADIAN BOTANICAL
  ASSOCIATION
Department of Botany
University of British Columbia
Vancouver, British Columbia V6T 2B1

CANADIAN HOBBY GREENHOUSE
  ASSOCIATION
83-270 Timberbank Boulevard
Agincourt, Ontario M1W 2M1

CANADIAN WILDFLOWER SOCIETY
35 Bauer Crescent
Unionville, Ontario L3R 4H3

FEDERATION DES SOCIETÉS
  D'HORTICULTURE ET
  D'ECOLOGIE DU QUÉBEC
1415 rue Jarry est
Montréal, Québec H2E 2Z7

GARDEN CLUBS OF ONTARIO
8 Tanager Avenue
Toronto, Ontario M4G 3R1

MANITOBA HORTICULTURAL
  ASSOCIATION
908 Norquay Boulevard
Winnipeg, Manitoba R3C 0P8

NEW BRUNSWICK
  HORTICULTURAL SOCIETY
Department of Agriculture
Horticulture Section
Box 6000
Fredericton, New Brunswick E3B 5H1

NEWFOUNDLAND
  HORTICULTURAL SOCIETY
Box 4326
St. Johns, Newfoundland A1C 6C4

NORTH AMERICAN HEATHER
  SOCIETY
1205 Copley Place
R.R. 1
Shawigan Lake, British Columbia
  V0R 2W0

NOVA SCOTIA ASSOCIATION OF
  GARDEN CLUBS
Box 550
Truro, Nova Scotia B2N 5E3

ONTARIO HORTICULTURAL
  ASSOCIATION
Ontario Ministry of Agriculture
  and Food
Rural Organizations Service Branch
Box 1030
Guelph, Ontario N1H 6N1

ONTARIO ROCK GARDEN SOCIETY
Box 146
Shelbourne, Ontario L0S 1S0

PRINCE EDWARD ISLAND RURAL
  BEAUTIFICATION SOCIETY
Box 1194
Charlottetown, Prince Edward Island
  C1A 7M8

RHODODENDRON SOCIETY OF
  CANADA
R.R. 2
St. George, Ontario N0E 1N0

ROYAL BOTANICAL GARDENS
  MEMBERS ASSOCIATION
Box 339
Hamilton, Ontario L8N 3H8

SASKATCHEWAN HORTICULTURAL
  ASSOCIATION
Box 152
Balcarres, Saskatchewan S0G 0C0

LA SOCIÉTÉ D'ANIMATION DU
  JARDIN ET DE L'INSTITUT
  BOTANIQUES
4101 rue Sherbrooke est
Montréal, Québec H1X 2B2

VANCOUVER ISLAND ROCK &
  ALPINE SOCIETY
P.O. Box 6507
Station C
Victoria, British Columbia V8P 5Z4

RETAIL NURSERIES

ALBERTA NURSERIES AND SEEDS, LTD.
Box 20
Bowden, Alberta T0M 0K0
vegetable and flower seeds, ornamental and fruit trees

ALBERTA NURSERY TRADES ASSOCIATION
10215 176th Street
Edmonton, Alberta T5S 1M1

ALPENGLOW GARDENS
13328 King George Highway
North Surrey, British Columbia V3T 2T6
rare alpines, dwarf conifers, flowering shrubs

ATLANTIC PROVINCES NURSERY TRADES ASSOCIATION
Terra Nova Landscaping
130 Bluewater Road
Bedford, Nova Scotia B4A 1G7

BEAVERLODGE NURSERY LTD.
Box 127
Beaverlodge, Alberta T0H 0C0
hardy plants suitable for northern gardens

BRITISH COLUMBIA NURSERY TRADE ASSOCIATION
Suite #101A-15290 103A Avenue
Surrey, British Columbia V3R 7A2

CANADIAN NURSERY TRADES ASSOCIATION
1293 Matheson Boulevard
Mississauga, Ontario L4W 1R1

CANADIAN SEED GROWERS ASSOCIATION
237 Argyle Avenue
Box 8455
Ottawa, Ontario K1G 3T1

JOHN CONNON NURSERIES
Waterdown, Ontario L0R 2H0
general nursery stock

WILLIAM DAM SEEDS
Highway 8
West Flamborough, Ontario L0R 2K0
untreated vegetable and flower seeds: Canadian and European varieties

DOWNHAM NURSERY, INC.
626 Victoria Street
Strathroy, Ontario N7G 3C1

H. M. EDDIE AND SONS
4100 S.W. Marine Drive
Vancouver, British Columbia V7V 1N6
roses, general nursery stock

FLOWERS CANADA
219 Silver Creek Parkway North
Unit 29
Guelph, Ontario N1H 7K4

251 Clark Street
Sherbrooke, Québec J1J 2N6

GARDENERS AND FLORISTS ASSOCIATION OF ONTARIO
540 The West Mall No. 5
Etobicoke, Ontario M9C 1G3

GREENHEDGES
650 Montée de Liesse
Montréal, Québec H4T 1N8

MANITOBA NURSERY & LANDSCAPE ASSOCIATION
104 Parkside Drive
Winnipeg, Manitoba R3J 3P8

McCONNELL NURSERIES
R.R. 1
Port Burwell, Ontario N0J 1T0

NURSERY SOD GROWERS' ASSOCIATION OF ONTARIO
Carlisle, Ontario L0R 1H0

RICHTERS
Goodwood, Ontario L0C 1A0
herb seeds, esp. basil, ginseng seed

SASKATCHEWAN NURSERY TRADES ASSOCIATION
c/o Harrison's Garden Centre
Box 460
Carnduff, Saskatchewan S0C 0S0

SHERIDAN NURSERIES
700 Evans Avenue
Etobicoke, Ontario M9C 1A1

GREENHEDGES
650 Montée de Liésse
Montréal, Québec H4T 1N8

GLENPARK
2827 Yonge Street
Toronto, Ontario M4M 2J4
perennials, roses, general nursery stock

WOODLAND NURSERIES
2151 Camilla Road
Mississauga, Ontario L5A 2K1
rhododendrons, lilacs, azaleas

LANDSCAPE DESIGN ASSOCIATIONS

ALBERTA ASSOCIATION OF LANDSCAPE ARCHITECTS
P.O. Box 3395
Station D
Edmonton, Alberta T5L 4J2

ASSOCIATION DES ARCHITECTS PAYSAGISTES DU QUÉBEC
4003 Boul DeCarie
Suite 227
Montréal, Québec H4A 3J8

ATLANTIC PROVINCES ASSOCIATION OF LANDSCAPE ARCHITECTS
362 Saunders Street
Fredericton, New Brunswick E3B 1N9

BRITISH COLUMBIA SOCIETY OF LANDSCAPE ARCHITECTS
c/o The Registrar
115-2004 Mainland Street
Vancouver, British Columbia V6B 2T5

CANADIAN SOCIETY OF LANDSCAPE ARCHITECTS
P.O. Box 3304
Station C
Ottawa, Ontario K1J 4J5

MANITOBA ASSOCIATION OF LANDSCAPE ARCHITECTS
c/o Department of Landscape Architects
Faculty of Architecture
123 Bison Building
Winnipeg, Manitoba R3T 2N2

ONTARIO ASSOCIATION OF LANDSCAPE ARCHITECTS
170 The Donway West
Suite 212
Don Mills, Ontario M3C 2G3

PUBLIC GARDENS

BUTCHARD GARDENS
Victoria, British Columbia

DOMINIUM ARBORETUM
Ottawa, Ontario

EDWARDS GARDENS
Toronto, Ontario

HUMBER ARBORETUM
Rexdale, Ontario

INDEX

INDEX OF PLANTS